Knoll

Home & Office Furniture

Nancy N. Schiffer

Schiffer Publishing Ltd

4880 Lower Valley Road, Atglen, PA 19310 USA

Title page: Paperclip table designed by Massimo and Lella Vignelli; Brno chairs designed by Ludwig Mies van der Rohe.

Italicized descriptions indicate pictured items.

Library of Congress Cataloging-in-Publication Data

Schiffer Publishing, Ltd.
Photographs Copyright © by Knoll, Inc., unless otherwise indicated
   Knoll Home & Office Furniture / Schiffer Publishing, Ltd.
      p. cm.
   ISBN 0-7643-2395-4 (hardcover)
1. Design—History—20th century. 2. Design, Industrial—History—20th century--Catalogs. I. Title.
NK1390.G36 2005
745.2'09'04075—dc22
                              2005057527

Layout by "Sue"
Type set in ZapfCalligr BT/Zurich BT

ISBN: 0-7643-2395-4
Printed in China

Published by Schiffer Publishing Ltd.
4880 Lower Valley Road
Atglen, PA 19310
Phone: (610) 593-1777; Fax: (610) 593-2002
E-mail: Info@schifferbooks.com

For the largest selection of fine reference books on this and related subjects, please visit our web site at
www.schifferbooks.com
We are always looking for people to write books on new and related subjects. If you have an idea for a book please contact us at the above address.

This book may be purchased from the publisher.
Include $3.95 for shipping.
Please try your bookstore first.
You may write for a free catalog.

In Europe, Schiffer books are distributed by
Bushwood Books
6 Marksbury Ave.
Kew Gardens
Surrey TW9 4JF England
Phone: 44 (0) 20 8392-8585; Fax: 44 (0) 20 8392-9876
E-mail: info@bushwoodbooks.co.uk
Free postage in the U.K., Europe; air mail at cost.

Contents

Chair and table designed by Warren Platner.

ACKNOWLEDGMENTS

It was not long after I began researching Knoll furniture in earnest that I realized it was all about the people. Executives, designers, draftsmen (and women), engineers, technicians, suppliers, toolers, fabricators, shippers, personnel support staff, administrators, managers, salesmen, receptionists, assistants, and housekeepers all working together for a common goal: to be the best. And that Knoll has had an uncanny share of good people. It has held to high standards throughout its history and earned the respect of competitors and three generations of talented personnel. My attempt to record their achievements is humbled by their record.

I am indebted to so many people who guided my research and offered details not found in the company files. In the New York City offices of Knoll, Inc., Carl Magnusson gave me encouragement and advice that cleared the way for progress. David Bright made the photo archives available and asked Gretchen Reiners and Chris Giampietro to assist me. At the Knoll Museum and manufacturing plant in East Greenville, Pennsylvania, Carol Connell answered my preliminary questions and toured me around the museum. She led me to Linda Kasper, Client Sales Representative, who made the research library available and later guided me to information I sought.

I am especially grateful to Bill Shea, of Shea + Latone in East Greenville, Pennsylvania, for many acts of kindness and making the museum archives available to me over many months. Together with his partner, Tom Latone, and Nellie Booth, he provided some of their lists, digital photos, and research materials that enabled the organizing and recording of the furniture to go more smoothly. His encouragement and advice at critical times helped to keep me on track.

Richard Schultz, Bob Longwell, and Jens Risom gave me their time to answer specific questions about the Knoll organization at different periods in its development. Mark Jespersen added details from his research and vital historical materials.

In my office, I am grateful to Tammy Ward for her help and organizing abilities, Doug Congdon-Martin and Ian Robertson for technical help, Jeff Snyder for editorial work, Bruce Waters for the cover design, and to Peter Schiffer for shouldering my questions, worries, and endless hours at the computer. Besides providing the initial spark that ignited the project, he fanned the flames and kept my fire of enthusiasm going throughout the book's writing stages. Around here, it's the people, too. Thank you all, heartily.

My interest in modern furniture continues, and I welcome additional information for future editions. Please contact me through the publisher. When original sources were missing, assumptions were avoided. There has been no attempt here to evaluate the furniture or judge its rarity.

Nancy Schiffer
March, 2006

The Bauhaus school for arts.

Walter Gropius

Ludwig Mies van der Rohe

Opposite: Ant chairs designed by
Arne Jacobsen.

TIMELINE

Note: *Italicized* descriptions indicate pictured items.

1919 Spring, *the Bauhaus* founded at Weimar, Germany, as a state-funded school for arts, *Walter Gropius* appointed Director

1925 Bauhaus moved to Dessau, Germany
Wassily chair 50-125 and Laccio tables 50-310 and 50-315 by Marcel Breuer; later, rights to this furniture were acquired by Knoll

1927 MR chair 247 and table by Ludwig Mies van der Rohe

1928 Hannes Meyer appointed Director of the Dessau Bauhaus
Cesca chairs 50-111, 50-115, and 50-116 by Marcel Breuer

1929 Barcelona chair 250 and stool 251 by Ludwig Mies van der Rohe
MR lounge seating 241, 242, 243 by Ludwig Mies van der Rohe
Tugendhat chair 254 by Ludwig Mies van der Rohe
Barcelona table 252 by Ludwig Mies van der Rohe

1930 *Ludwig Mies van der Rohe* appointed Director of the Dessau Bauhaus
MB Lounge Chair 50-128 by Marcel Breuer
Brno chairs 245, 245A, and 255 by Ludwig Mies van der Rohe

1932 Bauhaus moved to an abandoned telephone factory in Berlin, as a private institute
Cranbrook Academy of Art founded in Bloomfield, Michigan, Eliel Saarinen, director

1933 Berlin Bauhaus closed by Nazis, and the stars migrate to the United States
Nylon patented by DuPont

Marcel Breuer

Hardoy chairs

1936 Reclining chair 50-135 by Marcel Breuer

1937 *Hans Knoll* comes to the United States

1938 **Hans G. Knoll Furniture Company established at East 72nd Street, New York City,** to sell "modern" furniture
Hardoy chair 198 designed in Argentina by Jorge Ferrari-Hardoy, Antonio Bonet, and Juan Kurchan

Clockwise from bottom: Florence Knoll, Hans Knoll, unidentified, unidentified.

Thonet chairs

1939 *Thonet chairs* sold by Knoll Furniture Co.

1940 *Eero Saarinen and Charles Eames* awarded first prize in The Museum of Modern Art Organic Furniture competition for a molded plywood chair
First small Knoll furniture showroom established at 444 Madison Avenue, New York City

Eero Saarinen and Charles Eames

1941 Desk chair 48W by Franco Albini

July–September, Hans Knoll and Jens Risom travel together as independent freelance entrepreneurs around the U.S., especially in the West and Southwest, visiting architects and designers, with introductions from their New York friend Howard Meyers, editor and publisher of *Architectural Forum*, that promoted the cause of contemporary furniture and interiors

Jens Risom designs Knoll Furniture Company's first products, the 600 Series seating collection, from softwoods and surplus parachute webbing

Knoll purchases the first, small manufacturing facility for wooden furniture in Pennsburg, Pennsylvania

1942 Jens Risom designs the new **Knoll Furniture showroom and design studio on the top floor at 601 Madison Avenue, New York City**

Knoll furniture sold furniture to USO lounges, company lounges, and airports during WWII.

April, *the premier Knoll Furniture catalog* was handmade by Jens Risom and Hans Knoll, the photos glued on to preprinted cardboard sheets, the illustrations and cover done by Jens Risom as an independent freelance job.

1943 August, Jens Risom drafted for U. S. Army service

Ralph Rapson joins Knoll to design chairs

Florence Schust joins Knoll to design interiors and establishes **Knoll Planning Unit**

1944 Hans Knoll invited Ralph Rapson and six other designers to submit designs for the "Equipment for Living" project
Side chair N19 by George Nakashima

1945 Side chair with arms 41 by Abel Sorenson
Rocking chair 657U by Ralph Rapson
The Rapson Line advertised in an H. G. Knoll Associates advertisement in January

1946 Knoll Associates, Inc. founded
Hans Knoll and Florence Schust become business and design partners, and are married
Herbert Matter retained as director of graphics and photography
Grasshopper chair 61U by Eero Saarinen

1947 *Herbert Matter* designs Knoll's "circle K" logo
Scissors chair 92 by Pierre Jeanneret
Nesting tables 56 ABC by Ralph Rapson

Herbert Matter

Design For Today exhibition, 1944, including furniture designed by George Nakashima (N-19 chair) and Jens Risom for Knoll Furniture Co.

1948 Womb chair 70 and ottoman 74 by Eero Saarinen
Metal chair 132 by Don Knoor
Stacking chairs 130 by André Duprés
Chairs and tables by Elias Svedberg
Knoll acquires rights to Ludwig Mies van der Rohe s Barcelona Collection
Upholstered side chair 44 by Florence Knoll
Credenza 119 by Florence Knoll
Side chair 72 by Eero Saarinen

Florence and Hans Knoll

Elias Svedberg designed this furniture while he worked at Knoll from about 1947 to 1950.

an exhibition

for
modern
living

THE DETROIT INSTITUTE OF ARTS • DETROIT, MICHIGAN, U.S.A

1949 September 11 to November 20, Knoll Associates exhibits furniture at The Detroit Institute of Arts, Detroit, *"An Exhibition For Modern Living,"* Florence Knoll an advisor

1950 Tripod side table 103 by Hans Bellman
Stacking stool 75 by Florence Knoll
Stacking chair 141 by Iimari Tapiovaara
Desk lamp 8 by Clay Michie
Side chair 145 by Kurt Nordstrom

1951 Knoll opens manufacturing subsidies in France and Germany
Knoll New York Showroom moved to 575 Madison Avenue
Chairs 47, 48, 49 by Franco Albini
Stacking Table 106 by Florence Knoll

1952 Chair collection 400s by Harry Bertoia
Seating 1100 series by Don Petitt
Larger manufacturing facility bought in East Greenville, Pennsylvania

1954 Rocking stool 85 and side table 311 by Isamu Noguchi
Chair 31 by Florence Knoll
Side table 2562 by Florence Knoll

FOR MORE INFORMATION ASK KNOLL

KNOLL ASSOCIATES, INC. FURNITURE AND TEXTILES   No. 70 Chair Eero Saarinen Design

320 PARK AVENUE, NEW YORK 22

1955 **Hans Knoll dies in Havana, Cuba.** As president of Knoll Associates, Inc., his other subsidiaries were Knoll International, Inc. with divisions in Havana, Cuba; Belgium; Canada; France; Germany; Switzerland; and Sweden. In the United State, offices or showrooms were in Boston, Chicago, Dallas, Detroit, Houston, Miami, and New York. Three factories were in Pennsylvania and Washington.
Florence Knoll assumes presidency of Knoll Associates, Inc.
Parallel Bar system furniture 400s by Florence Knoll
Tables 87, 311 and 312 by Isamu Noguchi

1956 Table 301 by Hans Bellman
Tulip chair 150s and table 160s collections by Eero Saarinen

1957 Executive seating 71 by Eero Saarinen

1958 *Herbert Matter's Chimney Sweep advertisement appears, featuring Eero Sarrinen's Womb chair*
Desk 80 by Franco Albini
Square coffee table 358 and arm chair 184 by Lewis Butler
Four Seasons barstool 78 by Mies van der Rohe and Philip Johnson
Florence Knoll marries banker Harry Hood Bassett

1959 **Knoll Furniture Company sold to Art Metal, Inc. of Jamestown, New York**

1960 Sling chair 657 by Charles Pollock
Petal tables 320, 321, and 322 by Richard Schultz
SanLuca chair by Achille and Pier Castiglioni

1961 Executive Collection 2480 by Florence Knoll Bassett
Chaise Lounge 715 by Richard Schultz
Knoll New York showroom moved to 320 Park Avenue

1962 Lambda chair L-1 by Mario Zanuzo and Richard Sapper

Chaise Lounge 715 designed by Richard Schultz

Florence Knoll Bassett and Eero Saarinen, c. 1961.

1963 Desk 4106 by Richard Schultz

1964 *Florence Knoll Bassett designs* interiors for Eero Saarinen's CBS building in New York

1965 **Florence Knoll Bassett retires**
Suzanne lounge seating 55-131 by Kazuhide Takahama
Stacking chair 1601 by Don Albinson
Executive Seating 1251 by Charles Pollock
Jumbo coffee table 56T by Gae Aulenti

1966 Seating collection 1705 by Warren Platner
Seating collection 18 by Max Pearson
Outdoor Collection 1421 by Richard Schultz
Malitte seating 57-110 by Robert Matta

Suzanne lounge seating designed by Kazuhide Takahama in foreground; Bastiano sofa designed by Tobia and Afra Scarpa; Barcelona chairs and stool designed by Ludwig Mies van der Rohe; Renna hat stand designed by Bruce Tippett.

Florence Knoll Bassett and one of the chairs she designed

1967 Massimo Vignelli designs new graphics program for Knoll
Chair 1301 by William Stevens
Andre table 56-332 by Tobia and Afra Scarpa for Gavina

1968 **Knoll becomes subsidiary of Walter E. Heller International Corporation**
Knoll acquires rights to Gavina's designs of Angelo Mangiarotti's accessories

1969 **Knoll Associates becomes Knoll International**
Knoll secures distribution rights for the Hans Wegner designs 60 manufactured by Fritz Hansen, Copenhagen
Bastiano lounge seating 53-145 by Tobia and Afra Scarpa
Caori tables 54-325 by Vico Magistretti

Accessories designed by Angelo Mangiarotti

Table and chair designed by Hans Wegner for Fritz Hansen, sold by Knoll

1970 *Equity System* by Westinghouse
Morrison/Hannah multiple seating 2052 and table collection
Lunario table 52-210 by Cini Boeri
Rocking chair 1765 and ottoman 1769 by Marc Held
Knoll New York Showroom moved to 745 Fifth Avenue

1971 Lounge seating 1051 by Charles Pfister
Lounge chair 1315 by William Stephens
Lounge chair 2011 by Morrison/Hannah
Spoleto chair 50CS by Attilio Bersanelli of Ufficio Tecnico

1972 Lounge seating 1011 by Jim Eldon
Wood top table 3112 by Morrison/Hannah

1973 Executive table collection 4312 by Warren Platner
Open office furniture system 5200s by William Stephens

1974 *Seating collection 2111 by Morrison/Hannah*
Pillorama seating 61-220s by Otto Zapf

1975 Table 54-120 and lounge seating 54-101 by Gae Aulenti

1976 Executive seating 61-200s by Otto Zapf
Arm Chair 806 by Bob Defuccio

1977 **Knoll acquired by General Felt Industries**
Brigadier lounge seating 55 by Cini Boeri
Tables 3000s by Charles Pfister
Advanced chair 1180-1 by Neils Diffrient
Follow Me seating and tables 62 by Otto Zapf

1980 Table 6348 by Joe D'Urso
Executive chair 1190-7 by Neils Diffrient

1981 Desk 64 by Gwathmey/Seigel
Coffee table 6521 by Paul Haigh
Knoll New York showroom moved to 655 Madison Avenue

1982 Mega table 38TR140 by Enrico Baleri
Rocking chair 790 by Carlos Riart
Table collection 840 and 860s by Richard Meier
Stump table 701 by Lucia Mercer
Pull-up arm chair 1407 by Richard Schultz

Couch designed by Andrew Ivar
Morrison and Bruce R. Hannah

Opposite: Equity office designs

Chairs designed by Raul de Armas

1983 Exeter chair 40A by Davis Allen
Eastside 35S and Westside 37S seating and Central Park tables 34T
   by Ettore Sottsass
Heli lounge seating 63S by Otto Zapf

1984 Executive office table 3055 by Charles Pfister
Chairs 661 to 665 by Robert Venturi

1985 Handkerchief chair 49 by Vignelli Design
Pascal table 47 by Pascal Mourgue

1986 Morrison office system by Andrew Morrison
Reff wooden office system
Mandarin chair 39A and Bridge chair 36A by Sottsass Associati
Executive chair 45A by Richard Sapper

1987 Trading desk by Bruce Hannah
Professional Armchair 1A6 by Niels Diffrient

1988 Seating 57S by Robert and Trix Haussmann
Executive desk 7D16 by Gianfranco Frattini

1989 **Knoll acquires Spinneybeck leathers**
Chair 180A by Enrico Franzolini

1990 **Knoll Group formed by Westinghouse**
Side chair 37A by Joe and Linda Ricchio
Bulldog chair 7A by McCoy & Fahnstrom

Ettore Sottsass

Orchestra accessories by Hannan and Birsel

Orchestra accessories by Hannah and Birsel
Interaction tables by Rizzi and Greene
Derby desk by Gwathmey/Siegel

1991 *Chair 38A by Raul de Armas*

1992 Knoll New York showroom moved to 105 Wooster Street
Overhead storage unit by Robert Reuter
Wood chair collection 90 to 94 by Frank Gehry

Chairs designed by Frank Gehry

1993 Cactus tables 80TR and 81TR by Lawrence Laske
Surf accessories collection by Ross Lovegrove and Peart
Toledo chair 29 and tables 29TR by Jorge Pensi
Midtown, Uptown, and Downtown desks by Carl Magnusson

1994 First Knoll Design Symposium at Cranbrook Academy of Art
Soho chair 28 by Roberto Lucci and Paolo Orlandini
Paperclip tables 49TR by Vignelli Design

Paperclip table and Handkerchief chairs designed by Vignelli Design

Toledo chairs and tables designed by Jorge Pensi

Parachute chairs 6 by Dragamir Ivièeviæ
Salsa seating collection 66S by Peter Stamberg and Paul Aferiat
Propeller tables P2 by Emanuela Frattini

1995 JR chair 37AS by Joe Ricchio
Calibre desk and collection by Knoll

1997 Knoll Museum at the East Greenville, Pennsylvania, manufacturing
plant opened by Albert Pfeiffer and Carl Magnusson
Jens Risom collection reintroduced

1998 Currents system by Magnusson and Noel

Calibre desk designed by Knoll

Currents office system designed by Carl Magnusson and Noel

Seating 82A and 86L and tables 85T and 87TR by Maya Lin

1999   FOG stacking chairs 97 by Frank O. Gehry
Lounge seating S51 by Gary Lee
Lounge seating S10 by Neil Frankel
Side chair 58A by Jonathan Crinion

2000   RPM chair 8P4 by Carl Magnusson
Crinion system by Johnathan Crinion

Seating, lounge and table designed by Maya Lin

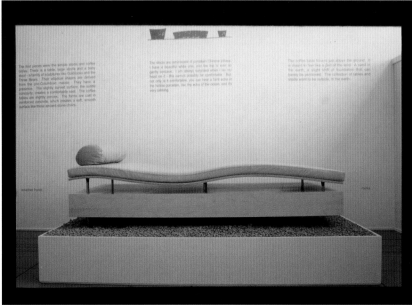

2001 *A3 office system* by Asymtote Associates, Lise-Anne Couture and Hani Rashid
Upstart office system by Robert Reuter and Charles Rozier
Visor chair 3A by Emilio Ambasz
Equity 120®

2002 *Bebop cart* by Ross Lovegrove
Life chair 55 by Formway Design
Reference executive cabinets

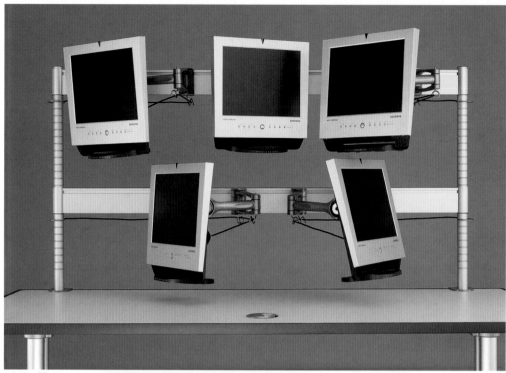

A3 office system designed by Asymtote Associates

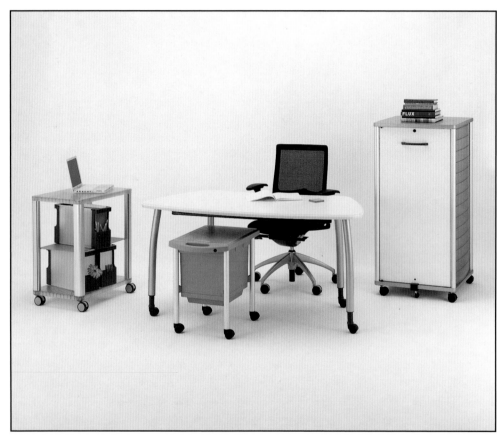

Bebop cart designed by Ross Lovegrove

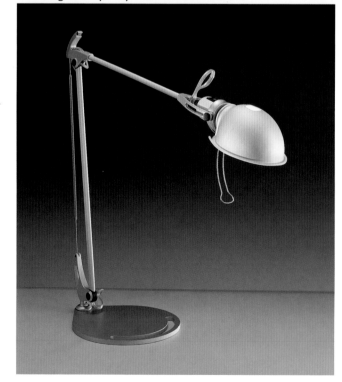

Bella desk lamp designed by Riccardo Blumer, 2005. 23" to 44" high.

2003 Krefeld collection 751 to 756 by Ludwig Mies van der Rohe
CHIP chair 23 by Antti Kotilainen
Cecilia chair 90 by Emanuella Frattini

2004 **Knoll, Inc. listed on the New York Stock Exchange**
Knoll New York moves to Chelsea showroom by Fred Schwartz
Knoll Lubin building receives LEED certification
AutoStrada office system by Robert Reuter and Charles Rozier
Divina® lounge chair 67 by Piero Lissoni
Sprite chair 27A by Ross Lovegrove
Jellyfish laptop stand by Colebrook Bosson Saunders

2005 Carl Gustav Magnusson retires as chief of Knoll's design department
Bella desk lamp designed by Riccardo Blumer
Chadwick chair 33 by Don Chadwick
Asymmetric chaise by Harry Bertoia
Copeland light by Don Copeland
Halley light by Richard Sapper
Knoll, Inc. presented with The 2005 Russel Wright Award "to honor today's leaders who carry forward one or more dimensions of Wright's legacy in design, architecture, landscape, the environment, hiking trails, and philosophy of 'easier living' and living in harmony with nature."

SEATING

HANS KNOLL FURNITURE

601 MADISON AVENUE
NEW YORK CITY. N.Y.

SIDE CHAIR AND ARM CHAIR

BIRCHWOOD FRAME

The following seating was advertised in the premier H. G. Knoll Furniture catalog of April 1942, but was not attributed to a specific designer:

801 Chair c. 1942, birch wood frame, upholstered continuous back and seat with button tufting, available as side chair or armchair.

802 Side chair c. 1942, birch wood frame, upholstered back with button tufting and separate upholstered seat.

803 Easy Chair c. 1942, birch wood frame with full upholstery and tight seat.

808 Easy Chair c. 1942, birch or maple wood frame, full upholstery with tufted back and cushioned seat.

809 Easy Chair c. 1942, birch or maple wood frame, full upholstery with pillow cushioned back and seat.

810 Side Chair c. 1942, birch or maple wood frame, three horizontal back slats and upholstered seat over u-shaped stretcher.

804 Armless Easy Chair c. 1942, birch or maple wood frame, full upholstery.

805 Easy Arm Chair c. 1942, birch or maple wood frame and arms, full upholstery.

806 Easy Chair c. 1942, birch or maple wood frame, full upholstery and cushioned back and seat.

807 Wing Chair c. 1942, birch or maple wood frame, full upholstery with button tufted back and cushioned seat.

811 Arm Chair c. 1942, birch or maple wood frame, separate upholstered back and seat over tapering legs.

816 Arm Chair c. 1942, birch or maple wood frame, upholstered back and separate upholstered seat with brass tacks.

817 Arm Chair c. 1942, birch or maple wood frame, upholstered back and separate upholstered seat over the frame, and u-shaped stretcher.

The following chairs were not in the premier Knoll catalog, but also are not attributed to a designer:

35 Arm Chair designed c. 1948, base: clear birch wood in natural finish, hardwood frame with upholstered back and seat, 29" w, 33-1/2" d, 31" h.

465 Secretarial Chair designed about 1963. Base: cast aluminum with brushed chrome finish. Seat and back upholstered. 18-1/2" w, 21" d, 30-1/2" to 37-1/2" h.

812 Side Chair c. 1942, birch or maple wood frame, rectangular framed back with caned panel with brass tacks and upholstered seat over tapering legs.

813 Side Chair c. 1942, birch or maple wood frame, rectangular woven back panel and upholstered seat.

814 Side Chair c. 1942, birch or maple wood frame, six open rectangles in the back and upholstered seat over h-shaped stretcher.

815 Side Chair c. 1942, birch or maple wood frame, four horizontal back slats and upholstered seat over an h-shaped stretcher.

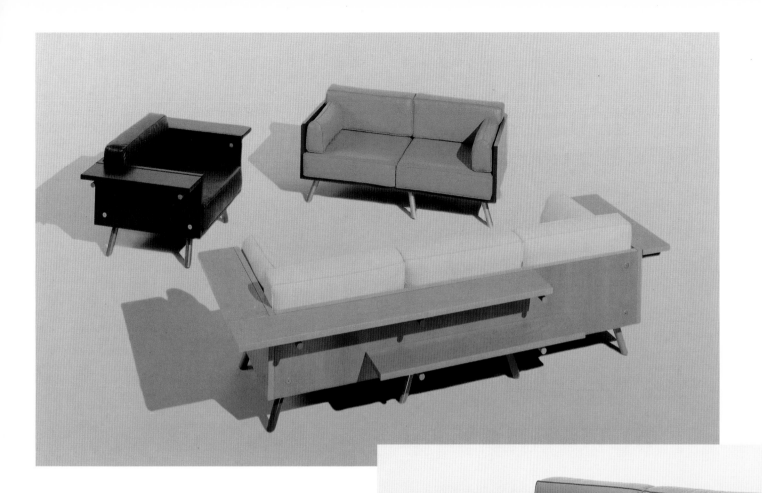

Paul Aferiat and Peter Stamberg

66S Salsa Lounge Seating designed by Paul Aferiat
and Peter Stamberg in 1994. Natural wood veneer
over 1-1/4" thick fiberboard core. Upholstery: leather
or fabric over polycore cushion, plywood and steel
frame. Available plain or with wooden side shelves,
and as single (chair), double (settee), or triple (sofa)
seats. Chair: 31" w, 30" d, 29" h. Settee: 75" w. Sofa:
88" w.

Salsa Lounge Seating designed by
Paul Aferiat and Peter Stamberg

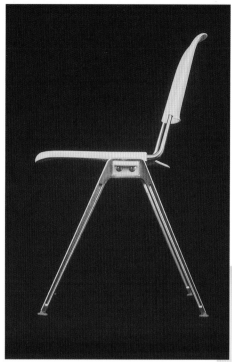

Franco Albini

47 Desk Chair designed by Franco Albini in 1941. Tubular steel base available in a variety of enamel finishes. 19" w, 23-1/4" d, 31" h.

48 Desk Chair designed by Franco Albini in 1941, manufactured 1942 to 1968. Birch, maple, or walnut wood base available in a variety of finishes. 22" w, 23-1/4" d, 31" h.

49 Lounge Chair designed by Franco Albini in 1941, manufactured 1942 to 1968 wood frame with upholstered back and seat, 25" w, 28" d, 30-1/2" h.

Don Albinson

1601 Stacking Chair designed by Don Albinson in 1965, manufactured 1965-1974. Base: cast aluminum frame, bright burnished finish. Shell: molded plastic with textured surface, available in a variety of colors. Ganging device: plastic. Glides: nylon swivel. 21" w, 21" d, 32" h.

1600-1 Dolly. For use with 1601, 1603, and 1601G.

1600-2 Dolly. For use with 1602

1600-3 Tablet Arm

1600-4 Bookrack

1602 Double Stacking Chair Unit. Same as 1601, but 41" w.

1603 Triple Stacking Chair Unit. Same as 1601, but 60-1/4" w.

Davis Allen

40A Exeter Arm Chair designed by Davis Allen in 1983. Laminated maple arms and back, with solid maple seat frame, spindles, and legs in lacquered coating and waxed finish. Plywood seat basket with foam on elastic platform. 22" w, 22-1/2" d, 36" h.

40C Exeter Armless Chair. Same as 40A, but without arms, 21-1/2" d.

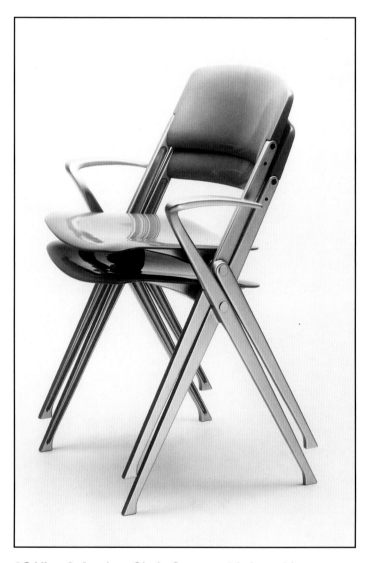

Amat-3

31C Twist Bar-height Barstool *designed by Amat-3* in 2003, manufactured 2005. Constructed of polished, anodized aluminum with an unpadded seat cover. 21" w, 21" d, 30-1/2" h.

31C2 Twist Counter-height Barstool. Same as 31C, but 26" h.

Emilio Ambasz

3A Visor® Arm Chair designed by Emilio Ambasz, manufactured in 2003.

3C Visor® Armless Chair. Same as 3A, but without arms.

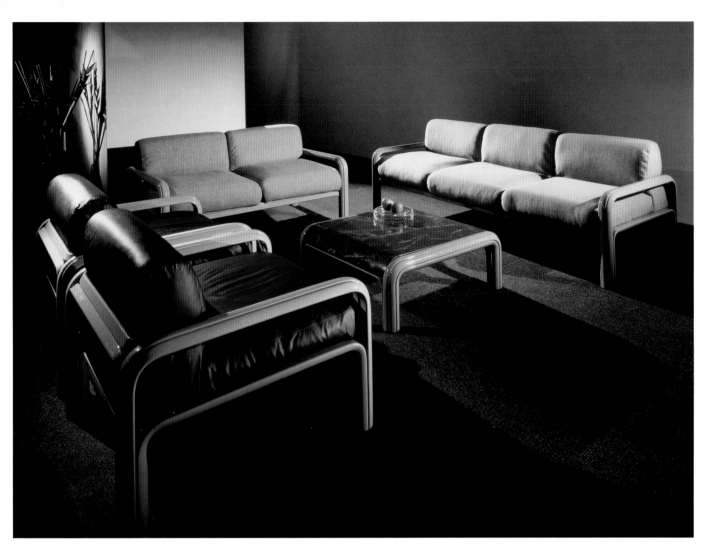

Gae Aulenti

54-101 Armless Chair designed by Gae Aulenti in 1975, manufactured 1979-1996. Frame: extruded aluminum, fused finish. Seat and back: foam bonded to curved laminated plywood. 20-1/2″ w, 20-3/4″ d, 31-3/4″ h.

54-102 Arm Chair. Same as 54-101, but with arms, 22-3/4″ w.

54-103 Lounge Chair designed by Gae Aulenti in 1975. Frame: extruded aluminum, fused finish. Seat and back: foam bonded to curved, laminated plywood. 27-1/2″ w, 27-1/2″ d, 30-3/4″ h.

54-111 Lounge Chair designed by Gae Aulenti in 1975. Frame: extruded aluminum, fused finish. Upholstery: separate cushions of foam with convoluted foam wrap over rubber and steel suspensions. 32-3/4″ w, 33-1/4″ d, 28-3/4″ h.

54-112 Settee. Same as 54-111, but 64-1/4″ w.

54-113 Sofa. Same as 54-111, but 87-1/2″ w

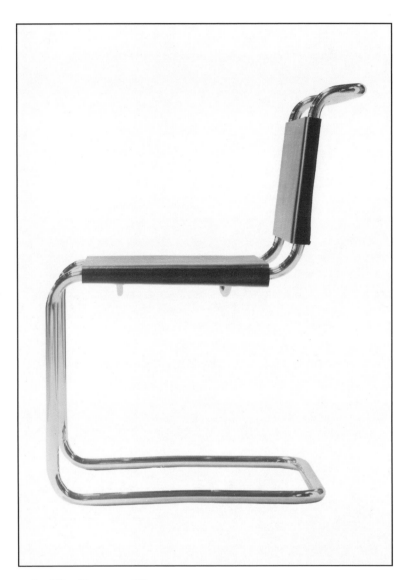

Attilio Bersanelli

50CS Spoleto Chair designed by Attilio Bersanelli of Ufficio Tecnico in 1971, manufactured 1988. Frame: tubular steel in polished chrome finish. Upholstery: Saddle leather or canvas slings with nylon laces. 18-1/2" w, 23-1/2" d, 31-1/2" h.

Seating designed by Harry Bertoia

Opposite: Side chairs designed by Harry Bertoia,
Paperclip table designed by Vignelli Design

Harry Bertoia

400 Slat Bench designed by Harry Bertoia in 1952.
Base: steel rod, black epoxy finish. Top: ash wood
slats, available in a variety of finishes and in 66", 72",
and 82" widths, 17-1/4" d, 15-1/4" h.

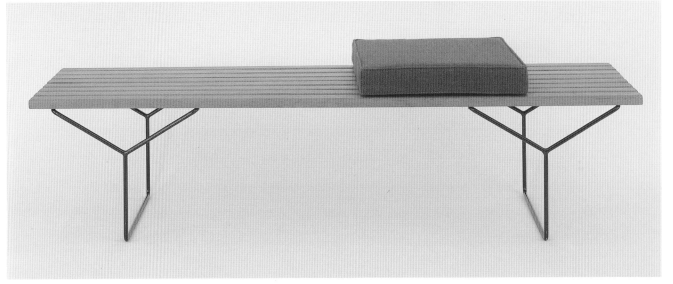

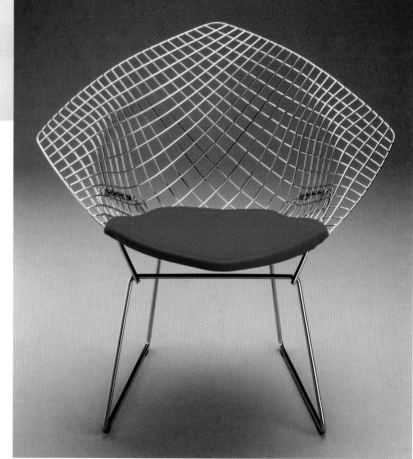

420 Side Chair designed by Harry Bertoia in 1952, manufactured from 1955. Seat and back: welded steel wire in a variety of finishes. Base: welded steel rod in a variety of finishes. Upholstery: foam rubber seat pad or fully upholstered foam rubber detachable seat cover. Also available with fully upholstered foam rubber seat and back covers. 21″ w, 22-1/2″ d, 30″ h.

421 Small Diamond Chair designed by Harry Bertoia in 1952. Seat and back: welded steel wire in a variety of finishes. Base: welded steel rod in a variety of finishes. Upholstery optional: fully upholstered foam rubber, detachable cover. Also available with fully upholstered foam rubber seat pad. 33-3/4″ w, 28″ d, 30-1/2″ h.

422 Large Diamond Chair designed by Harry Bertoia in 1952. Seat and back: welded steel wire in a variety of finishes. Base: welded steel rod in a variety of finishes. Optional upholstery: fully upholstered foam rubber, detachable cover. Fully upholstered from 1988. 45″ w, 32″ d, 28-1/4″ h.

423 High Backed "Bird" Chair designed by Harry Bertoia in 1952. Base and basket: welded steel wire in a variety of finishes and colors. Upholstery: fully upholstered foam rubber, detachable cover. 38-1/2" h, 34-1/2" d, 39-1/4" h

424 Ottoman designed by Harry Bertoia in 1952. Same as 423. 24" w, 17-1/4" d, 14-3/4" h.

425 Child's Chair designed by Harry Bertoia in 1952, manufactured 1955-1984. Seat and back: welded steel wire in a variety of finishes. Base: welded steel rod in a variety of finishes. Upholstery: fully upholstered foam rubber seat pad. 15-3/4" w, 16-1/4" d, 24" h.

426 Small Child's Chair. Same as 425, but smaller dimensions. 13-1/4" w, 13-1/2" d, 20" h.

427 Side Chair designed by Harry Bertoia in 1952, manufactured 1952-1968. Seat and back: plastic available in a variety of colors. Base: steel rods available in a variety of finishes. 20-1/2" w, 22" d, 30-1/2" h.

428 Barstool designed by Harry Bertoia in 1952, manufactured 1964-1973 and 1984-1996. Base: nickel plated or black finish. Plastic shell available in a variety of colors un-upholstered or upholstered on inside only. 21-3/4" w, 22" d, 39-1/2" h.

Asymmetric Chaise designed by Harry Bertoia in 1952, manufactured 2005. 33" w, 53" d, 40" h.

Cini Boeri

55SH1 Brigadier High Back Lounge Chair designed by Cini Boeri in 1977, manufactured 1988. Frame: hardwood panels with high gloss polyester finish and inner seat frame of steel with springs. Upholstered seat and back cushions. 50-1/3" w, 41" d, 33-1/2" h.

55SH2 Brigadier High Back Settee. Same as 55SH1, but 70" w.

55SH3 Brigadier High Back Sofa. Same as 55SH1, but 89-3/4" w.

55SL1 Brigadier Low Back Lounge. Same as 55SH1, but low back 21-3/4" h.

55SL2 Brigadier Low Back Settee. Same as 55SL1, but 70" w.

55SL3 Brigadier Low Back Sofa. Same as 55SL1, but 89-3/4" w.

Opposite: Seating by Marcel Breuer

Marcel Breuer

50-111 Cesca Side Chair designed by Marcel Breuer in 1928, manufactured from 1970. Frame: tubular steel, polished chrome finish. Seat and back: machine woven or hand-woven cane with solid wood frame in a variety of finishes. 18-1/4" w, 25-5/8" d, 31-1/2" h.

50-115 Cesca Arm Chair designed by Marcel Breuer in 1928, manufactured from 1970. Frame: tubular steel, polished chrome finish. Seat and back: machine woven or hand-woven cane with solid wood in a variety of finishes. Arms: solid wood in a variety of finishes. 23-5/8" w, 23-5/8" d, 31-1/2" h.

50-116 Cesca Arm Chair designed by Marcel Breuer in 1928, manufactured from 1970. Frame: tubular steel, polished chrome finish. Seat and back: solid wood frame in a variety of finishes. Upholstery: foam rubber over bent plywood, inset in seat and back frame.
23-5/8" w, 23-5/8" d, 31-1/2" h.

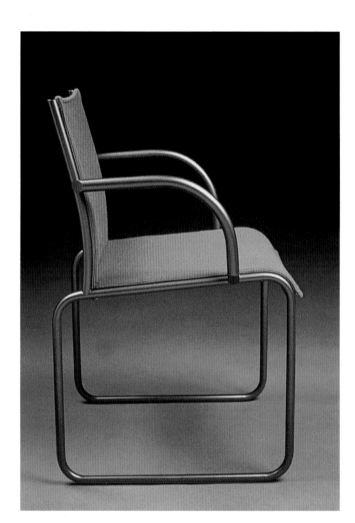

50-120 Spolto Chair designed by Marcel Breuer, manufactured from 1970. Frame: tubular steel, polished chrome finish. Upholstery: double faced cowhide or reinforced canvas. 18-1/4" w, 25-3/8" d, 30" h.

50-125 Wassily Lounge Chair designed by Marcel Breuer in 1925, manufactured 1968-1988. Base: tubular steel, polished chrome finish. Seat, back, and arms: double faced cowhide or reinforced canvas. 30-3/4" w, 27" d, 28-1/2" h. Breuer originally called this chair the "steel club chair," and Bauhaus pamphlets refer to it as the "abstract" chair. It came to be known as the Wassily chair because of its original use in the Bauhaus studio of artist Wassily Kandinsky.

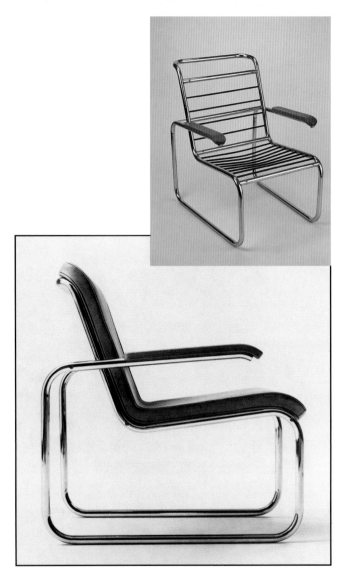

50-128 MB Lounge Chair designed by Marcel Breuer in 1930, manufactured 1976-1978. Frame: tubular steel in a variety of finishes. Upholstery: separate leather-covered cushion of foam over rubber and steel suspension. Arms with wooden surface painted black. Evolved from Breuer's initial designs with steel tubing and cantilevered seating, the MB chair has a frame made from a single, continuous piece of bent tubing, beginning with one arm and winding along the outline of the chair to the end of the other arm. The MB Lounge chair is one of the more complex and successful of Breuer's cantilevered chair designs. 25" w, 29-3/4" d, 42" h.

50-135 Reclining Chair designed by Marcel Breuer in 1936, manufactured in 1970. Frame: laminated beech wood available in a variety of finishes. Upholstery: leather over foam rubber over plywood. Designed during Breuer's brief time in the United Kingdom with Walter Gropius at Isokon. 26" w, 51" d, 22-1/8" to 31-3/4" h. *Photo courtesy SOLLO:RAGO Modern Auctions, Lambertville, N.J.*

Lewis Butler

183 Lounge Chair designed by Lewis Butler in 1958. Wood frame with cushioned back and seat. 24" w, 28-1/2" d, 30" h.

184 Arm Chair. Same as 183, but 27" d, 33" h.

645 Lounge Chair designed by Lewis Butler about 1943. Wood frame with upholstered back and seat. 26" w, 28-1/2" d, 29-1/4" h.

49

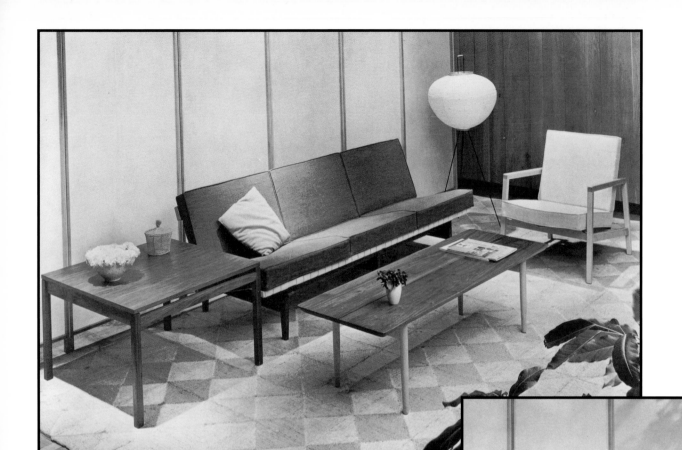

Lounge chairs and Webbed sofa designed by Lewis Butler

655 *Lounge Chair* designed by Lewis Butler c. 1957, maple frame in natural finish with upholstered walnut plywood back and seat with foam rubber and zippered fabric covers. 26-1/8" w, 29" d, 29-1/2" h.

676 *Webbed Sofa* designed by Lewis Butler in 1955, manufactured 1955-1961. Maple and walnut base with natural webbing and upholstered foam cushions. 80" w, 30" d, 28-1/4" h

Vincent Cafiero

180 *Arm Chair* designed by Vincent Cafiero in 1972, manufactured from 1973. Legs: square tubular steel in a variety of finishes. Also available with revolving base. Upholstery: restrained by stitched pattern and shallow tufting over foam rubber. Also available with solid wood legs in a variety of finishes. 25-1/2" w, 27" d, 33" h.

181 High Back Swivel Arm Chair. Same as 180, but with spring suspension and steel cap base, available in a variety of finishes. 40" to 42-5/8" h.

182 Arm Chair. Same as 180, but 24" w, 28" d, 31" h.

183 Lounge Chair. Same as 180, but 24" w, 28" d, 30" h.

184 Lounge Chair. Same as 180, but 30" w, 31" d, 33" h.

185 Lounge Chair designed by Vincent Cafiero. Base: stainless steel cap over steel armature, available in a variety of finishes. Upholstery: foam rubber and polyester attached cushions with welted pattern and tufting. Castors: hard rubber or plastic. 30" w, 31" d, 33" h.

186 Ottoman designed by Vincent Cafiero. Same as 185 with platform instead of spring suspension and jute webbing. 22" square, 17" h.

187 Swivel Arm Chair Same as 185, but 27-1/4" w, 27-3/4" d, 36-1/2" to 38-1/2" h.

Achille and Pier Castiglioni

Sanluca Reclining Chair designed by brothers Achille and Pier Castiglioni, for Gavina (acquired by Knoll in 1968)

Don Chadwick

33 Chadwick Chair designed in 2003 by Don Chadwick, manufactured 2005. Frame and seat:

integrally-colored glass-filled nylon, with a variety of fabric colors. Adjustable arms or armless, swivel and tilt options, pneumatic seat height. 26-1/2" h, 26-1/2" d, 37-1/2 to 42" h.

54

Pepe Cortes

30C Jamaica Bar-height Barstool designed by Pepe Cortes in 1993, manufactured 1994. Base: chrome plated steel with plastic glides. Seat and frame: cast aluminum with 360-degree swivel. 19" w, 19" d, 30-1/2" h.

30C2 Jamaica Counter-height Barstool. Same as 30C, but 17-1/2" w, 17-1/2" d, 28-1/4" h.

30C3 Jamaica Low Barstool. Same as 30C, but on casters, 19" w, 19" d, 17-3/4" h.

Jonathan Crinion

58A Crinion Arm Chair with Upholstered Seat
designed by Jonathan Crinion in 1999, manufactured 2000. Clear maple or stained beech hardwood frame with upholstered seat pad and plywood back panel. 23-1/4", 9-1/2" d, 30-3/4" h.

58A-W Crinion Arm Chair with Wood Seat. Same as 58A, but with maple or beech plywood seat.

58C Crinion Armless Chair with Upholstered Seat. Same as 58A, but without arms, 20-1/2" w.

58C-W Crinion Armless Chair with Wood Seat. Same as 58A, but without arms and with maple or beech plywood seat, 20-1/2" w.

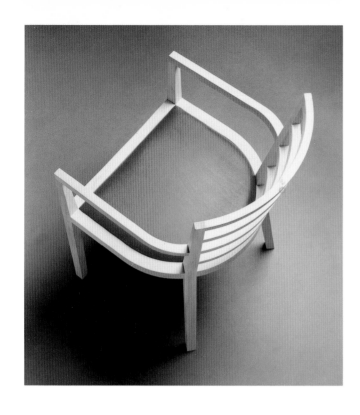

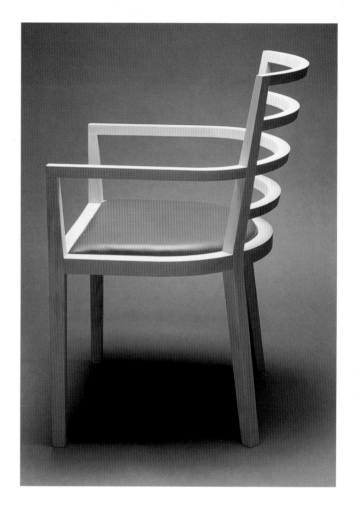

Raul de Armas

38A Arm Chair designed by Raul de Armas in 1991, manufactured 1992. Frame: maple in clear or stained finish. Seat: elastic woven suspension with polyurethane foam insert. 21-1/4" w, 22-1/2" d, 33-1/2" h.

38C Armless Chair. Same as 38A, but without arms.

41A Vertical Arm Chair designed by Raul de Armas in 2000, manufactured 2001. Frame: clear maple or beech with waxed finish. Seat: woven suspension with polyurethane foam and leather or fabric upholstery. 21-1/4" w, 22-1/2" d, 33-1/2" h.

41A-U Vertical Arm Chair. Same as 41A, but back upholstered.

41C Vertical Armless Chair. Same as 41A, but without arms.

41C-U Vertical Armless Chair. Same as 41A, but without arms and back upholstered.

Robert DeFuccio

806 Arm Chair designed by Robert DeFuccio in 1976. Frame: thin laminations of wood veneer, available in a variety of finishes. Upholstery: molded foam bonded to formed plywood. Glides: nylon. 22" w, 22" d, 32" h.

Niels Diffrient

1A6 Professional Armchair designed by Niels Diffrient, manufactured 1987. Base: 5-star cast aluminum. Seat and back: steel with epoxy gray finish. Urethane armrests on curved steel supports. Cushioned back and seat. 26" w, 22-7/8" d, 36" to 41-1/2" h.

1C6 Professional Chair. Same as 1A6, but without arms.

1A7 Upper Management Low Back Armchair designed by Niels Diffrient, manufactured 1987. Base: 5-star cast aluminum with epoxy finish. Swivel and tilt mechanisms. 24-3/8" w, 24-7/8" d, 32-1/4" to 35" h.

1A8 Upper Management High Back Armchair. Same as 1A7, but high back. 26-3/4" deep, 36-1/4 to 39" h.

1A31 Sled-based Armchair designed by Niels
Diffrient c. 1978. Tubular steel frame with textured
epoxy finish. Seamless-stretch upholstery on polyurethane foam, on steel shell with polyester finish.
26″ w, 24″ d, 31″ h.

1C31 Sled-based Chair. Same as 1A31, but without
arms.

1180-1 Basic Task Chair designed in 1977 by Niels
Diffrient. Separate seat and back shells: 16-gauge
stamped steel, textured finish. Arms: tubular steel,
textured finish, plastisol armrests. Base: five-star die-
cast aluminum with plastisol skin. Upholstery:
seamless fabric bonded to polyurethane foam
cushion. Castors: Kevi or Bassick twin-wheels.

1180-2 Advanced Operational Armchair. Same as
1180-1, but with arms.

1180-3 Multiple Seating Base, manufactured 1983. Three-position base, with and without arms.

1180-4 Multiple Seating Base, manufactured 1983. Four-position base, with and without arms.

1180-4 Multiple Seating. Same as 1180-1, but with continuous back and seat shell, and several mounted together on base of steel tube welded to two steel tube legs, and with table of plastic laminate with vinyl edge molding, 100″ w.

1180-5 Multiple Seating Base, manufactured 1983. Five-position base, with and without arms.

1180-7 Basic Management Chair. Same as 1180-1, but with continuous back and seat shell, and screw-post height adjustment. Available with arms.

1180-8 Advanced Management Chair. Same as 1180-1, but with swivel and tilt mechanism. Available with arms.

1190-7 Executive Low-back Chair designed by Niels Diffrient in 1980. Frame: molded plywood back with welded steel frame. Arms: tubular steel, textured finish; urethane foam armrests. Base: five-star die-cast aluminum in either powder-coated or polished chrome finishes. Upholstery: selection of leathers and fabrics over molded foam and polymer seat. Castors: Kevi twin wheels.

1190-17 Executive H-back Chair. Same as 1190-7, but with h back, 40" h.

André Duprés

130 Stacking Chairs designed by André Duprés in 1948, manufactured 1953-1966. Chrome-finished tubular metal frame with crisscrossing rope back and seat. 19-1/2" w, 21" d, 32" h.

Joseph D'Urso

1060 Sofa designed by Joseph D'Urso in 1981, manufactured from 1982. Square frame, curved seat cushions, and pillows available in any combination of fabric and leather. 96" w, 48" d, 24" h.

1061 Large Sofa. Same as 1060, but with rounded corner and 132" w, 132"d.

1062 Large Sofa. Same as 1061, but with square corner.

Jim Eldon

1011 Chair designed by Jim Eldon in 1972. Legs: solid wood available in two finishes. Upholstery: reversible seat and back, foam rubber cushions.

1012 Settee. Same as 1011, but with two seats.

1013 Sofa. Same as 1011, but with three seats.

1031 Bench designed by Jim Eldon. Base: solid wood available in a variety of finishes. Upholstery: foam rubber over plywood platform. 26″ w.

1032 Bench. Same as 1031, but 50″ w.

1033 Bench. Same as 1031, but 74″ w.

Dale Fahnstrom

7A1 Bulldog Management Arm Chair designed by Dale Fahnstrom and Michael McCoy in 1989, manufactured 1990. Base: 5-star, textured and colored nylon. Back and seat: textured and colored polypropylene with foam and textile covering; with various tilt and swivel mechanisms. Armrests textured and colored polyester with thermoplastic arm pads. 25-1/2" w, 20-3/4" d,   31-1/4" to 35-3/4" h.

7C1 Bulldog Management Armless Chair. Same as 7A1, but without arms, 21" w.

7A2 Bulldog Task Arm Chair. Same as 7A1, but 23-1/2" w, 20-1/2" d, 31" to 35" h.

7C2 Bulldog Task Armless Chair. Same as 7A2, but without arms, 20" w.

7A3 Bulldog Executive Arm Chair. Same as 7A1, but lower back, 25-1/2" w, 20-1/2" d, 37-3/8" to 41-7/8" h.

7C3 Bulldog Executive Armless Chair. Same as 7C3, but without arms, 21" w.

7A4 Bulldog Operational Arm Chair. Same as 7A1, but 23-1/2" w, 21-1/4" d, 33" to 37-1/2" h.

7C4 Bulldog Operational Armless Chair. Same as 7A4, but without arms, 20" w.

7A5 Bulldog High Back Task Arm Chair. Same as 7A1, but 23-1/2" w, 20-1/2" d, 37-1/4" to 47-3/4" h.

7C5 Bulldog High Back Task Armless Chair. Same as 7A5, but without arms, 20" w.

7A6 Bulldog Professional Arm Chair. Same as 7A1, but 24-1/4" w, 21-3/4" d, 31-1/2" to 36-1/4" h.

7C6 Bulldog Professional Armless Chair. Same as 7A6, but without arms, 21" w.

7A6SL Bulldog Side Arm Chair designed by Dale Fahnstrom and Michael McCoy in 1989, manufactured 1990. Frame: 16-gauge steel tube with powder coat paint or chrome finish. Back and seat: urethane foam with textile upholstery. 25-1/4" w, 23" d, 32" h.

7C6SL Bulldog Side Armless Chair. Same as 7A6SL but without arms, 21" w.

7A7 Bulldog High Back Professional Arm Chair. Same as 7A1, but 24-1/4" w, 21-3/4" d, 37-1/4" to 42" h.

7C7 Bulldog High Back Professional Armless Chair. Same as 7A7, but without arms, 21" w.

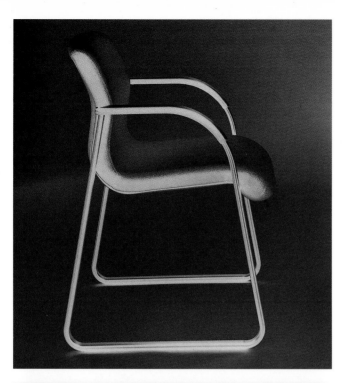

Bulldog side arm chair

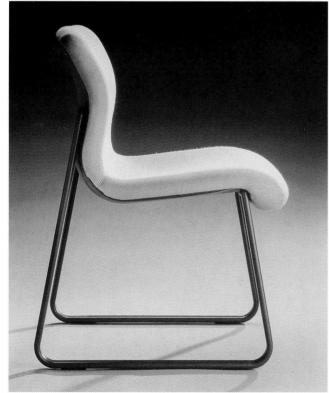

Bulldog side armless chair

Jorge Ferrari-Hardoy, Antonia Bonet, and Juan Kurchan

198 Hardoy Chair designed by Jorge Ferrari-Hardoy, Antonio Bonet, and Juan Kurchan in 1938, manufactured by Knoll 1947-1951. Leather or fabric sling seat on iron rod frame. 31" w, 27-1/2" d, 34-1/4" h. Also called "Butterfly" or "AA" chair, the BKF, the African chair, the Argentinian, and the sling chair. In 1940 it was introduced at the major interior design exhibition in Buenos Aires, and 1941 the chair was awarded the Acquisition Prize by the Museum of Modern Art in New York.

Formway Design

55 Life® Chair designed by Formway Design, manufactured in 2003

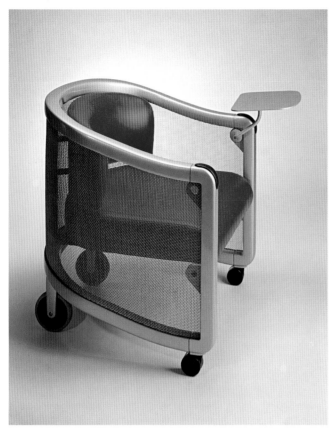

Neil Frankel

S10LMC Frankel Lounge Chair designed by Neil Frankel in 1999, manufactured 2000. Molded aluminum frame with powder coated finish, stainless steel wire mesh panels, and castors. Wire shelf and left or right tablet arms available. 28" w, 26-1/2" d, 29" h.

Enrico Franzolini

180A Unupholstered Arm Chair designed by Enrico Franzolini in 1989, manufactured 1991. Frame: steam-bent beech wood with stained finish. Arms with stainless steel supports. Back and seat: continuous laminated beech wood. 22" w, 19-1/4" d, 30-3/4" h.

180C Unupholstered Armless Chair. Same as 180A, but without arms, 16-1/2" w.

Upholstered Arm Chair. Same as 180A, but with fabric upholstery.

Emanuela Frattini

90A Cecilia Arm Chair designed by Emanuela Frattini in 2003, manufactured 2004. Frame: maple or beech hardwood. Seat: elastic belt suspension with foam and fabric or leather upholstery. 22-1/2" w, 19" d, 31-1/2" h.

90C Cecilia Armless Chair. Same as 90A, but without arms.

Frank Gehry

91A Hat Trick Arm Chair designed by Frank Gehry in 1989, manufactured 1992. White maple veneer strips, 2" wide by 1/24" thick, laminated to 5 or 7-ply thickness. Back flexes. Foam cushion envelopes the seat like a shower hat. 23-3/8" w, 22-1/4" d, 33-1/2" h.

Chairs and table designed by Frank Gehry

Previous page:
91C Hat Trick Armless Chair. Same as 91A, but without arms, 20" w.

92 High Sticking High Back Chair designed by Frank Gehry in 1989, manufactured 1992. White maple veneer strips, 2" wide by 1/32" thick, laminated to 5 or 7-ply thickness. Back flexes. Foam cushion snap-locks underneath the seat. 20-1/8" w, 23-7/8" d, 43-3/8" h.

93A Cross Check Arm Chair designed by Frank Gehry in 1989. Hard white maple laminated wood in 6 to 8-ply thickness with a natural finish. Back flexes. Fish-shaped foam cushion snap-locks underneath seat. 28-1/2" w, 24-7/8" d, 33-5/8" h.

93C High Back Stacking Chair designed by Frank Gehry in 1989. White maple frame of 5 to 7-ply thickness in a variety of finishes and cushions of high resilience. 20-1/8" w, 23-7/8" d, 43-3/8" h.

94 Power Play Club Chair designed by Frank Gehry in 1989, manufactured 1992. White maple veneer strips, 2" wide by 1/32" thick, laminated to 6, 7, or 8-ply thickness. Back flexes. Square foam cushion snap-locks underneath seat. 31-3/8" w, 30-1/8" d, 32-7/8" h.

94 Off Side Ottoman designed by Frank Gehry in 1989, manufactured 1992. White maple veneer strips, 2" wide by 1/32" thick, laminated to 6, 7, or 8-ply thickness. Back flexes. Square foam cushion snap-locks underneath seat. 23-3/8" square, 8-1/8" to 13-7/8" h.

97A FOG® Stacking Chair designed by Frank Gehry in 1999, manufactured 2000. Base: 1" diameter tubular polished stainless steel legs and arm supports, with aluminum arm pads and nylon glides. 25" w, 24" d, 31-3/4" h.

97C FOG® Stacking Armless Chair. Same as 97A, but without arms, 21" w.

Robert and Trix Haussmann

57S1 Freestanding Club Chair designed by Robert and Trix Haussmann in 1988, manufactured 1990. Hardwood frame with steel supports. All exposed areas upholstered in fabric or leather. Mirrored glass sides and back available. 31-7/8" w, 33-7/8" d, 29-1/8" h.

57S2 Freestanding Settee. Same as 57S1, but 54-3/4" w.

57S3 Freestanding Sofa. Same as 57S1, but 77-1/8"w.

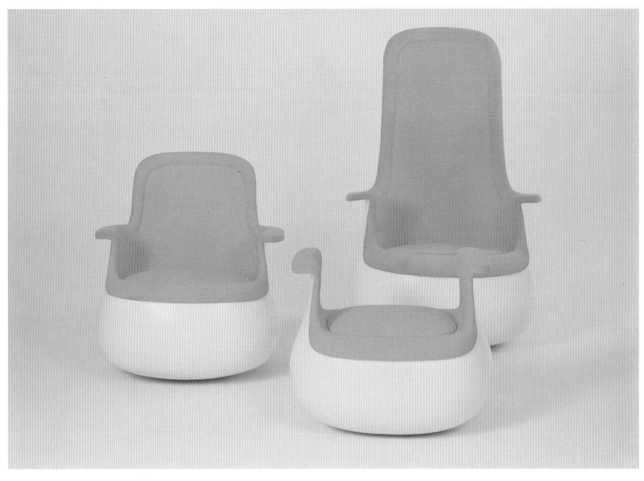

Marc Held

1765 Chair designed by Marc Held in 1970, manufactured 1972-1974. Shell: molded polyester and fiberglass with a lacquer finish. Upholstery: inside of shell upholstered with a foam rubber cushion in fabric, vinyl, or leather. 27-1/2" w, 28" h. Marc Held conceived the idea of an easy chair that could both swivel and rock in 1965. The chair was intended to relieve the muscular strain of motionlessness, based on the assumption that movement is less tiring than being still. The collection included three pieces - a h-back chair, a lounge chair, and an ottoman.

1769 Ottoman. Same as 1765, but 25-1/2" w, 22-1/2" d, 22" h.

1775 High Back Chair. Same as 1765, but 30" w, 30" d, 45-1/2" h.

Alfred Homann

FHB10 Ensemble Stacking Unupholstered Armless Chair designed by Alfred Homann for Fritz Hansen in 1992, manufactured 1999. Base: steel tubing with mirror or satin chrome finish. Shell: composite with textured surface. 22-3/4" w, 21-1/2" d, 33-1/2" h.

FHM10 Ensemble Stacking Upholstered Armless Chair. Same as FHB10, but upholstered inside shell with molded urethane foam, thicker in center, and glued fabric.

FHB11 Ensemble Stacking Unupholstered Arm Chair. Same as FHB10, but with steel arms, with mirror or satin chrome finish.

FHM11 Ensemble Stacking Upholstered Arm Chair. Same as FHB10, but with upholstered inside shell and with steel arms, with mirror or satin chrome finish.

Dragomir Ivièeviæ

6A4 Parachute Two-piece Arm Chair designed by Dragomir Ivièeviæ in 1993, manufactured 1994. 5-star base on casters and arm rests of colored, textured, glass-reinforced nylon. Separate plastic shell back and seat with foam and fabric upholstery. Swivel and height mechanism, and optional tilt adjustment. Arm pads are adjustable. 26-3/4" w, 22" d, 32-1/2" to 40" h.

6C4 Parachute Two-piece Armless Chair. Same as 6A4, but without arms.

6A8 Parachute One-piece Arm Chair. Same as 6A4, but continuous back and seat construction and maximum 37" h.

6C8 Parachute One-piece Armless Chair. Same as 6A8, but without arms.

6A8 Parachute Side Arm Chair. Same as 6A8 One-piece Arm Chair, but frame of steel tube with epoxy powder-coat paint finish in a variety of colors, 22" w, 23-1/2" d, 32-1/2" h.

6C8 Parachute Side Armless Chair. Same as 6A8 Side Arm Chair, but without arms, 21" w.

Arne Jacobsen

FH3101 Ant Stacking Armless Chair designed by Arne Jacobsen in 1952, manufactured 1999. Base: 1/2" tubular steel legs with mirror or satin chrome finish. Shell: plywood of 9 layers of sliced veneer and 2 sandwiched layers of textile. Can stack unupholstered armless chairs 15 high. 19" w, 19" d, 30-1/4" h.

FH3107 Seven Stacking Unupholstered Armless Chair designed by Arne Jacobsen in 1955, manufactured 1999. Base: 1/2" tubular steel legs with mirror or satin chrome finish. Shell: plywood of 9 layers of sliced veneer and 2 sandwiched layers of textile. Can stack unupholstered armless chairs 15 high. 19-3/4" w, 20-1/2" d, 30-3/4" h.

FH3107K Seven Stacking Upholstered Armless Chair. Same as FH3107, but upholstered inside shell over 1/2" thick urethane foam. Can stack upholstered armless chairs 10 high.

FH3107U Seven Stacking Upholstered Armless Chair. Same as FH3107, but fully upholstered shell over 1/2" thick urethane foam.

FH3117 Seven Swivel Unupholstered Armless Chair designed by Arne Jacobsen in 1955, manufactured 2000. Base: 5-star tubular steel legs with swivel and height adjustment on casters. Shell: plywood made of 9 layers of sliced veneer and 2 sandwiched layers of textile in natural veneer finish. 19-3/4" w, 20-1/2" d, 30-3/4" to 33-3/4" h.

FH3117K Seven Swivel Armless Chair. Same as FH3117, but upholstered inside shell.

FH3117U Seven Swivel Armless Chair. Same as FH3117, but fully upholstered shell.

FH3127 Egg Stool designed by Arne Jacobsen in 1958, manufactured 2000. Base: satin chromed steel column with tilt and swivel mechanism and 4-star aluminum legs with black glides. Shell: reinforced polyurethane and fire-retardant foam with glued-on fabric or leather upholstery. 22-1/4" w, 16" d, 16-1/4" h.

FH3207 Seven Stacking Unupholstered Arm Chair designed by Arne Jacobsen in 1955, manufactured 1999. Base: 1/2" tubular steel legs with mirror or satin chrome finish. Shell and arms: plywood of 9 layers of sliced veneer and 2 sandwiched layers of textile. Can stack arm chairs 4 high. 23-1/2" w, 20-1/2" d, 30-3/4" h.

FH3207K Seven Stacking Upholstered Arm Chair. Same as FH3207, but upholstered inside shell and arms over 1/2" thick urethane foam.

FH3207U Seven Stacking Upholstered Arm Chair. Same as FH3207, but fully upholstered shell over 1/2" thick urethane foam.

FH3217 Seven Swivel Unupholstered Arm Chair designed by Arne Jacobsen in 1955,

manufactured 2000. Base: 5-star tubular steel legs on casters with swivel and height adjustment. Shell: plywood of 9 layers of sliced veneer and 2 sandwiched layers of textile in veneer, lazur, or lacquer finish. 23-1/2" w, 20-1/2" d, 30-3/4" to 33-3/4" h.

FH3217K Seven Swivel Arm Chair. Same as FH3217, but upholstered inside shell and with wood arms.

FH3217U Seven Swivel Arm Chair. Same as FH3217, but fully upholstered shell.

FH3316 Egg Lounge Chair designed by Arne Jacobsen in 1958, manufactured 2000. Base: satin

chromed steel column with tilt and swivel mechanism and 4-star aluminum legs with black glides. Shell: reinforced polyurethane and fire-retardant foam with glued-on fabric or leather upholstery. 33-3/4" w, 31" to 37-1/2" d, 42" h.

FH3320 Swan Lounge Arm Chair designed by Arne Jacobsen in 1958, manufactured 2000. Base: satin chromed steel column with tilt and swivel mechanism and 4-star aluminum legs with black glides. Shell: reinforced polyurethane and fire-retardant foam with glued-on fabric or leather upholstery. 29-1/4" w, 26-3/4" d, 29-1/4" h.

Pierre Jeanneret

92 Scissors Chair designed by Pierre Jeanneret c. 1947, manufactured 1950-1966. Birch or maple frame in a variety of finishes, with cloth and elastic webbing and upholstered cushion back and seat. 22" w, 31" d, 29" h.

Henry Kann

46 Barstool designed by Henry Kann in 1947, manufactured 1947-1949. Birch or maple wood frame with leather webbing and solid brass foot rest/stretcher. 16" w, 19-1/2" d, 42" h.

Poul Kjaerholm

FHPK22 Armless Lounge Chair designed by Poul Kjaerholm in 1954, manufactured 2000. Matte polished stainless steel frame with leather upholstery or untreated wicker seat and back. 24-3/4" w, 24-3/4" d, 28" h.

FHPK24 Adjustable Armless Wicker Lounge Chair
designed by Poul Kjaerholm in 1965, manufactured
2000. Stainless steel adjustable frame with hand-
woven untreated wicker seat and back and leather
headrest. 26-1/2" w, 61" d, 34-1/4" h.

FHPK33 Round Sitting Stool designed by Poul
Kjaerholm in 1959, manufactured 2000. Matte stainless steel legs with ring-shaped laminated wood seat
shell for cushion attachment. 21" diameter, 13-1/2" h.

FHPK91 Folding Stool designed by Poul Kjaerholm in
1961, manufactured 2000. Matte polished stainless
steel legs with leather or canvas sling. 23-1/2" w, 17-
3/4" d, 14-1/2" h.

*FHPK20 Armless High Cantilevered Leather Lounge
Chair* designed by Poul Kjaerholm in 1967, manufactured 2000. Matte polished stainless steel frame with
leather upholstery and headrest. 31-1/2" w, 30" d, 35"
h.

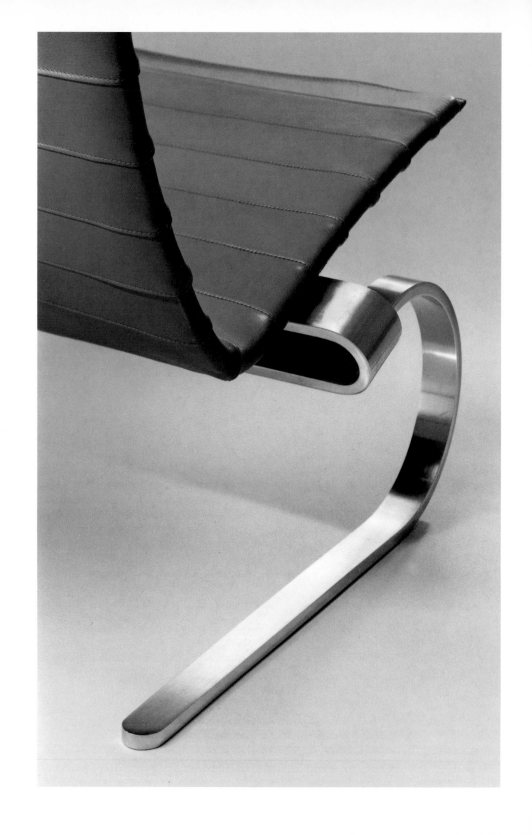

FHPK20 Armless Low Cantilevered Wicker Lounge Chair. Same as FHPK20 Leather Chair, but hand-woven untreated wicker seat and back, 26-3/4" d, 28-3/4" h.

Florence Knoll

25 Arm Chair designed by Florence Knoll c. 1948, with wood frame and upholstered cushion back and seat. Base: four wooden legs. 30″ w, 32″ d, 30″ h.

26 Sofa same as 25, but with three seats, 90″ w.

27 Settee same as 25, but with two seats, 60″ w.

31 Chair designed by Florence Knoll in 1954, manufactured 1954-1968. Tubular steel base with black finish, or brushed or polished chrome. Upholstered back and seat cushions. 24" w, 27" d, 29" h.

32 Settee. Same as 31, but 48" w.

33 Sofa. Same as 31, but 72" w.

43 Arm Chair designed by Florence Knoll c. 1946, with swivel base.

44 Upholstered Side Chair designed by Florence Knoll in 1948. Birch legs with natural, standard walnut or ebony finish and fully upholstered in cloth or leather. Also available with swivel base. 26" w, 26" d, 31-1/2" h.

45 Upholstered Settee designed by Florence Knoll in 1948. Same as 44, but 48" w, 26" d, 31-1/2" h.

51 Parallel Bar System Lounge Chair designed by Florence Knoll in 1955. Frame: wood or steel, parallel bar legs in a variety of finishes. Upholstery: attached foam rubber cushions with stitched pattern and shallow tufting. This chair without arms, also available with arms as number 55. 24" w, 31" d, 30" h.

52 Parallel Bar System Settee. Same as 51 without arms, but with two back and seat cushions, 56" w.

53 Parallel Bar System Sofa. Same as 51 without arms, but with three back and seat cushions, and 84" w.

55 Parallel Bar System Arm Chair designed by Florence Knoll in 1955. Steel parallel bar base with brushed chrome and black finish, and available in other finishes. 29" w, 31" d, 30" h.

56 Parallel Bar System Settee. Same as 55, but with
two back and seat cushions, 56" w.

57 Parallel Bar System Sofa. Same as 55, but with
three back and seat cushions, 89" w.

Opposite:
65 Lounge Chair designed by Florence Knoll c. 1954.
Base square tubular and solid steel in a variety of
finishes, and can have arms. Upholstery: foam
rubber attached cushions with rectangular welted
pattern. 28" w, 30" d, 31-1/2" h.

65 Lounge Chair designed by Florence Knoll c. 1954.
Base square tubular and solid steel in a variety of
finishes, and can have arms. Upholstery: foam
rubber attached cushions with rectangular welted
pattern. 28" w, 30" d, 31-1/2" h.

66 Settee. Same as 65 but seats two and can have arms, 56″ w.

75 Stacking Stool designed by Florence Knoll in 1950, manufactured 1950-1970. Birch top with bent iron rod legs. Later available with laminated black, white, or maple top. 13" d, 18" h.

67 Sofa. Same as 65, but seats three and can have arms, 84" w.

83 Arm Chair designed by Florence Knoll
c. 1954. Base: wood legs or cast aluminum
swivel. Seat and back with continuous arms
upholstered. 26-1/2″ w, 26″ d, 33-1/2″ h.

84 Arm Chair designed by Florence Knoll
c. 1954, base: wooden legs or cast aluminum
swivel action base on hard rubber castors,
upholstered back, arm, and seat. 26-3/4″ w, 26″
d, 33″ h.

95 Arm Chair designed by Florence Knoll
c. 1954. Base: tubular steel in black oxide finish,
hardwood frame with upholstered coil springs,
laced hair, and foam rubber back, seat, and
arms. 29-3/4″ w, 31″ d, 29-3/4″ h.

96 Sofa same as 95, but 80-1/4″ w.

97 Settee same as 95, but 50-3/4″ w.

330 T-angle Bench designed by Florence Knoll c.
1956. Wood or plastic veneer top on T-angle steel legs
with black epoxy finish. 40-1/8″ w, 20″ d, 15-1/2″ h.

331 Bench. Same as 330, but 60-1/4″ w.

332 Bench. Same as 330, but with center legs and
80-3/8″ w.

333 Bench. Same as 330, but white epoxy finish.

334 Bench. Same as 331, but white epoxy finish.

335 Bench. Same as 332, but white epoxy finish.

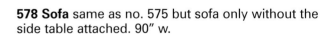

578 Sofa same as no. 575 but sofa only without the side table attached. 90″ w.

1205 Lounge Chair designed by Florence Knoll c. 1960. Base: solid wood, available in a variety of finishes. Upholstery: fabric over polyester and foam core, separate seat and back cushions, 32″ w, 31-1/2″ d, 30″ h.

576 Sofa same as no. 575 but base with attached magazine rack unit.

577 Sofa same as no. 575 but base with attached table of open case and glass top.

575 Sofa designed by Florence Knoll c. 1954. Base: with table or two drawers attached to one side. Sofa, 90″ w, 30″ h. Table attached, 30″ w.

1206 Settee. Same as 1205, but 62" w.

1207 Sofa. Same as 1205, but 90" w.

1209 Ottoman. Same as 1205, but 26" square, 17" h.

2530-3 Bench designed by Florence Knoll. Base: square tubular steel in a variety of finishes. Upholstery: foam rubber attached cushions. 36″ w, 18″ d, 17″ h; also available 60″ w, 38″ d.

2530-6 Bench. Same as 2530-3, but 72″ w.

2530-9 Bench. Same as 2530-3, but 108″ w.

2530-12 Bench. Same as 2530-3, but 144″ w.

95

2551 Solid Bar Lounge Chair without Arms designed by Florence Knoll c. 1954. Show frame: square solid steel in a variety of finishes. Upholstery: attached foam rubber cushions with stitched pattern and shallow tufting. 30" w, 31" d, 29" h.

2552 Settee. Same as 2551 but 56" w.

2553 Sofa. Same as 2551, but 84" w.

2555 Arm Chair. Same as 2551, but with arms.

2556 Settee with Arms. Same as 2555 but 56″ w.

2557 Sofa with Arms. Same as 2555 but 84″ w.

Donald R. Knorr

132 Metal Chair designed by Donald R. Knorr in 1948, manufactured 1950-1952. Round steel legs with yellow or black sheet metal back and seat. Also available upholstered with rubber seat cushion. First Prize winner for 1949 Museum of Modern Art Low-cost Design Competition. 20" w, 19.5" d, 29" h.

Donald Knorr developed this chair with the encouragement of his mentor, Eero Saarinen, at Cranbrook Academy. Knorr decided to enter it in the Museum of Modern Art competition for low-cost furniture in 1950, and was named co-winner of the first prize in the seating category. The chair was called "one of the most ingenious structural schemes seen in modern furniture." The claim was derived from the use of a simple flat sheet of material being formed into a sculptural seat. The seat was also fitted with a pad for comfort that also covered the bottom seam. Knoll took over production, but found that wartime restrictions on materials during the Korean conflict eventually put this chair out of production.

Antti Kotilainen

23A CHIP Arm Chair designed by Antti Kotilainen in 2002, manufactured 2003. Steel frame, arms, and legs in powder coated or chrome plated finish. Seat and back: melamine covered molded birch. 21-1/2" w, 19-3/4" d, 31" h.

23AK CHIP Arm Chair. Same as 23A, but with plywood seat pad in fabric upholstery.

23C CHIP Armless Stacking Chair with seat pad. Same as 23A, but without arms, 20" w. CHIP armless chairs can stack 12 chairs high on the floor and 20 chairs high in a dolly (23DOLLY).

23CK CHIP Armless Stacking Chair. Same as 23A, but without arms and with seat pad.

23CH-C CHIP Barstool. Same as 23C, but in chrome finish, with leg stretchers, and without back, 19-1/2" w, 17-1/2" d, 33-3/4" h.

Gary Lee

S51L Lee Lounge Chair designed by Gary Lee in 1999, manufactured 2000. Plywood frame with foam on seat, inside surrounds, top, and front rails; fully upholstered in fabric or leather. Legs: anodized aluminum in satin finish. Leather trim optional. 32" w, 21" d, 28" h.

S52L Lee Settee. Same as S51L, but 56" w.

S53L Lee Sofa. Same as S51L, but 78" w.

Maya Lin

82A-L-I 30-degree® Asymmetrical Arm Chair. Designed by Maya Lin in 1998, manufactured 1999. Maple seat frame and arms, plywood back with upholstery inside back. 4 arm supports and legs of stainless steel tubes with black plastic glides. The back is rotated 30 degrees to the left and rests on 3 back supports, upholstery inside back.

82A-L-U 30-degree® Asymmetrical Arm Chair. Same as 82A-L-I, but fully upholstered back.

82A-M-I 0-degree® Symmetrical Arm Chair designed by Maya Lin in 1998, manufactured 1999. Maple seat frame and arms, plywood back with upholstery inside back. 4 arm supports and legs of stainless steel tubes with black plastic glides. 24" w, 20" d, 33" h.

82A-M-U 0-degree® Symmetrical Arm Chair. Same as 82A-M-I, but fully upholstered back.

82A-R-I 30-degree® Asymmetrical Arm Chair. Same as 82A-L-I, but the back is rotated 30 degrees to the right and rests on 3 back supports, upholstery inside back.

82A-R-U 30-degree® Asymmetrical Arm Chair. Same as 82A-R-I, but fully upholstered back.

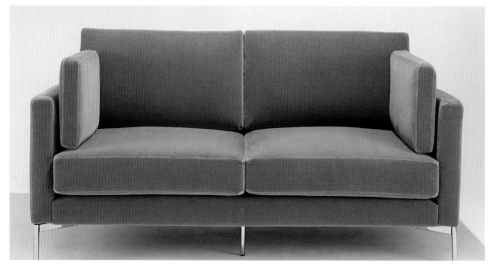

Piero Lissoni

86L Longitude® Chaise Longue designed by Maya Lin in 1998, manufactured 1999. Base: maple in clear or stained finish, with curved maple plywood top and 4 stainless steel legs with black plastic glides. Pad: single 2-1/2" thick foam with fabric or leather cover. Bolster: 4" by 6" oval foam core with Dacron wrap and fabric or leather upholstery. 74" w, 30" d, 17" h.

67 Divina® Standard Lounge Chair designed by Piero Lissoni in 2001, manufactured 2002. Frame: wood and exposed tubular steel legs with polished chrome finish on polyurethane glides. Seat and back cushions of polyurethane. Frame and cushions upholstered in leather or fabric. 35-1/2" w, 35-1/2" d, 32" h.

67S Divina® Petite Lounge Chair. Same as 67 Divina® Chair, but 28-1/4" w, 29-!/4" d, 31-1/2" h.

68 Divina® Settee. Same as 67 Divina® Chair, but 64-3/4" w, 35-1/2" d, 32" h.

69 Divina® Sofa. Same as 67 Divina® Chair, but 90" w, 35-1/2" d, 32" h.

Josep Lluscà

26A Street Stacking Chair designed by Josep Lluscà in 2002, manufactured 2003. Frame: polished anodized aluminum tube with spiral inserts. Back and seat: stamped anodized aluminum. 22" w, 22-3/8" d, 31-7/8" h. Can be stacked 6 chairs high.

Ross Lovegrove

27A Sprite Arm Chair designed by Ross Lovegrove in 2004, manufactured 2005. Base: 5/8" tubular steel with mirror chrome finish. Continuous back and seat of 6-layer molded maple plywood, in the same or a combination of veneer and/or painted finish. Armpads: black polyurethane or molded plywood. 22" w, 22" d, 32" h.

27C Sprite Armless Chair. Same as 27A, but without arms.

Roberto Lucci and Paolo Orlandini

28A SoHo Task Arm Chair designed by Roberto Lucci and Paolo Orlandini in 1994, manufactured 1996. Base: colored, textured, glass-reinforced nylon 5-star design on casters, with tilt and height adjustments. Continuous seat and back, with optional separate upholstered cushions. 24" w, 22" d, 30" to 35" h.

28C SoHo Task Armless Chair. Same as 28A, but without arms, 22" w.

Vico Magistretti

46A Cirene Unupholstered Stacking Arm Chair
designed by Vico Magistretti in 1999, manufactured
2001. Frame: chrome-plated tubular steel. Back and
seat shell: molded plywood in natural wood veneer
or lacquer or melamine finish in a variety of colors.
Black polypropylene molded arm pads. 22-5/8" w,
20-1/2" d, 29-1/2" h. Cirene unupholstered chairs
stack 10 high.

46A-U Cirene Upholstered Arm Chair. Same as 46A,
but upholstered in leather or fabric. Upholstered
Cirene chairs do not stack.

46C Cirene Unupholstered Stacking Armless Chair.
Same as 46A, but without arms, 21" w, 21-1/4" d.

46C-U Cirene Upholstered Armless Chair. Same as
46C, but upholstered in leather or fabric.

59A-N Silver Arm Chair designed by Vico Magistretti
in 1999, manufactured 2001. Legs and arms: extruded aluminum with satin finish. Seat and back: die
cast aluminum frame with inset of black, white, and
gray polypropylene. Silver chairs in satin chrome do
not stack. 24" w, 20" d, 31-1/2" h.

59A-S Silver Stacking Arm Chair. Same as 59A-N,
but in polished chrome finish, can stack 6 high.

59C-N Silver Armless Chair. Same as 59A-N, but
without arms.

59C-S Silver Stacking Armless Chair. Same as 59A-
S, but without arms.

***FHVM1 Vico Stacking Un-upholstered Conference
Arm Chair*** designed by Vico Magistretti for Fritz
Hansen in 1994, manufactured 1999. Base: oval steel
tubing with satin chrome finish. Seat, backrest, and
arms of molded veneer. Can stack 5 chairs high.
25-1/4" w, 22" d, 30-3/4" h.

**FHVM2 Vico Stacking Conference Arm Chair with
Seat Cushion**. Same as FHVM1, but seat cushions of
rubber coconut fiber filling and glued upholstery
attached with Velcro tape.

FHVM3 Vico Stacking Conference Arm Chair with Seat and Back Cushions. Same as FHVM2, but with back and seat cushions (shown with table FHVM66).

FHVM101 VicoDuo Un-upholstered Stacking Arm Chair without Arm Pads designed by Vico Magistretti for Fritz Hansen in 1997, manufactured 1999. Legs and arms: 3/4" steel tubing with gray powder-coat or satin chrome finish. Continuous back and seat shell is 10 layers of laminated veneer with 2 textile layers in veneer or lazur finish. Can stack 6 chairs high. 22-1/2" w, 20-3/4" d, 29-1/2" h.

FHVM102 VicoDuo Upholstered Stacking Arm Chair without Arm Pads. Same as FHVM101, but with slip cover.

FHVM111 VicoDuo Un-upholstered Stacking Arm Chair with Arm Pads. Same as FHVN101, but with injection molded, gray, arm pads.

FHVM112 VicoDuo Upholstered Stacking Arm Chair with Arm Pads. Same as FHVM111, but with slip cover.

FHVM201 VicoSolo Armless Un-upholstered Stacking Chair designed by Vico Magistretti in 1999, manufactured 2000. Frame: steel with powder-coat or satin chrome finish. Seat: laminated wood veneer in a variety of colors and coatings. Back rest: flexible gray plastic welded around back rail. Can stack 16 chairs high. 18" w, 19-3/4" d, 28-3/4" h.

FHVM202 VicoSolo Armless Stacking Chair. Same as FHVM201, but with detachable seat cover.

104

Carl Magnusson

8P4 RPM® Chair designed by Carl Magnusson, manufactured in 2002. Chrome-plated base with swivel and height adjustment, supporting colored polypropylene and fiberglass shell and black polypropylene molded arm pads. 19" w, 25" d, 33-1/2" to 38-1/4"h.

Marco Maran

87A Gigi® Stacking Arm Chair designed by Marco Maran in 2000, manufactured 2001. Legs and arms: steel with chrome plated finish. Seat and back: continuous colored polypropylene in a variety of colors. 19-3/4″ w, 20″ d, 34-1/4″ h.

87C Gigi® Stacking Armless Chair. Same as 87A, but without arms.

87C-K-N Gigi® Non-stacking Armless Chair with Seat Pad. Same as 87A, but without arms and with permanent seat pad.

87C-K-S Gigi® Stacking Armless Chair with Seat Pad. Same as 87A, but without arms and with permanent seat pad.

87CH Gigi® Bar-height Barstool. Same as 87AS, but on 4 straight legs with stretchers. Seat 19-3/4″ w, 20″ d, 29-1/2″ h.

87CM Gigi® Counter-height Barstool. Same as 87CH, but seat 24″ h.

87CS Gigi® Swivel Armless Chair. Same as 87AS, but without arms.

Roberto Sebastian Matta

57-110 *Malitte Lounge* designed by Roberto Sebastian Matta in 1966, manufactured 1968-1976. Foam polyurethane blocks upholstered in special fabric, available in a variety of colors. This design was innovative and functional, well suited for the minimalist interiors popular in the late 1960s. 63" w, 25" d, 63" h.

Richard Meier

810 Arm Chair designed by Richard Meier in 1982, manufactured 1983-1988. Laminated maple veneer and maple frame with hand-rubbed finish and mortise and tenon construction. Richard Meier's personal mark is printed on each piece. 21" w, 20" d, 27-1/2" h.

820 Low Stool designed by Richard Meier in 1982, manufactured 1983-1988. Laminated maple veneer and maple frame with hand-rubbed finish and mortise and tenon construction. Richard Meier's personal mark is printed on each piece. 17-5/8" diameter, 15-1/4" h.

822 High Stool. Same as 820, but 15-3/8" diameter, 27-1/2" h.

830 Chaise. Same as 820, but available in natural, black, or white finish and channel-tufted cushion and pillow. 72" w, 27-1/2" d, 25-1/8" h.

108

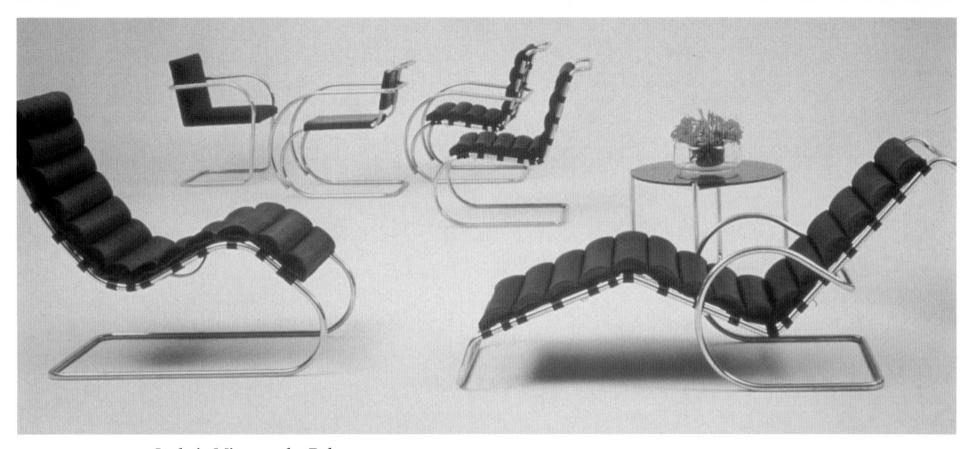

Ludwig Mies van der Rohe

78 Four Seasons Barstool designed in 1958 by Ludwig Mies van der Rohe and Philip Johnson, manufactured 1958-1968. Seat 13-1/8" w, legs 14-1/2" w, 15" d, 30" h. Designed for the Four Seasons Hotel in New York.

241 MR Chaise Lounge designed by Ludwig Mies van der Rohe in 1929. Frame: tubular stainless steel, polished finish. Seat and back: pleated foam upholstery, saddle leather straps. 23-5/8" w, 47-1/4" d, 37-1/2" h.

242 MR Adjustable Chaise Lounge designed by Ludwig Mies van der Rohe in 1929. Frame: tubular stainless steel, polished finish. Seat and back: pleated foam upholstery, saddle leather straps. 26" w, 70-1/4" d, 30-1/2" to 35-1/4" h.

243 MR Stool. Same as 241, but seat only, 23-1/2" w, 22-1/2" d, 17" h.

247 MR Armless Lounge Chair designed by Ludwig Mies van der Rohe in 1929, manufactured 1979-1996. Frame: tubular stainless steel, polished finish. Seat and back: rattan or pleated foam upholstery with saddle leather straps. Same as 248, but without arms. 23-1/2" w, 34-3/4" d, 33" h. The MR lounge chairs were designed for the Weissenhof housing project, which became the "fullest communal realization" of the International Style. Mies was a participant and the director of the project. His design of a cantilevered chair postdated both Marcel Breuer and Mart Stam of Holland, who both are credited with the invention of the cantilevered tubular chair.

248 MR Lounge Chair with Arms designed by Ludwig Mies van der Rohe in 1929, manufactured 1979-1996. Frame: tubular stainless steel, polished finish. Seat and back: rattan or pleated foam upholstery with saddle leather straps. See also 247. 25-1/2" w, 36-1/4" d, 33" h.

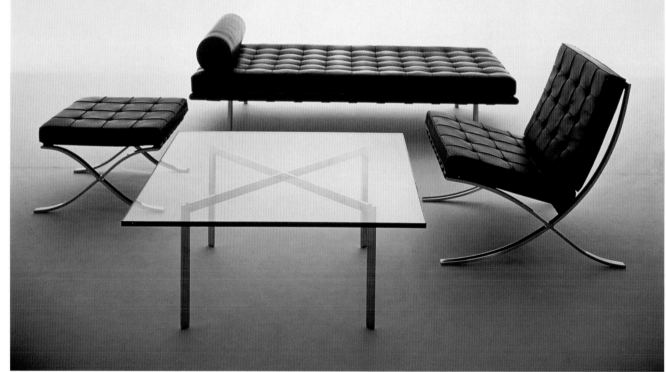

245 Brno Tugendhat Arm Chair, Tubular Frame
designed by Ludwig Mies van der Rohe in 1930.
Frame: tubular stainless steel, polished finish. Hardwood frame with thin seat and back upholstered.
23-3/4" w, 22-1/2" d, 31-1/2" h.

245A Brno Tugendhat Arm Chair, Tubular Frame.
Same as 245, but with thick upholstery: hardwood
frame with foam rubber over spring suspension seat
and black leather covering. 22" w, 23-1/4" d, 32-1/2" h.

258 Barcelona Couch designed by Ludwig Mies van
der Rohe in 1931, manufactured from 1970. Frame:
tubular stainless steel. Platform: wood frame, in a
variety of finishes, with saddle leather straps over
webbing. Upholstery: foam rubber mattress with
polyester padding, covered in top grain leather.
Bolster: foam rubber detachable straps. 1977 Museum of Modern Art Award, New York, USA. 78" w,
39" d, 15-1/2" h.

250 Barcelona Chair designed by Ludwig Mies van
der Rohe in 1927, manufactured 1957. Frame:
stainless steel, polished finish. Upholstery: saddle
leather straps with foam rubber cushions covered in
top grain leather, constructed from individual welted
panels with button tufting. 29-1/2" w, 28" d, 29-1/2" h.

251 Barcelona Stool designed by Ludwig Mies van
der Rohe in 1927, manufactured from 1957. Frame:
stainless steel, polished finish. Upholstery: saddle
leather straps with foam rubber cushions covered in
top grain leather, constructed from individual welted
panels with button tufting. 23" w, 21-1/2" d, 14" h.

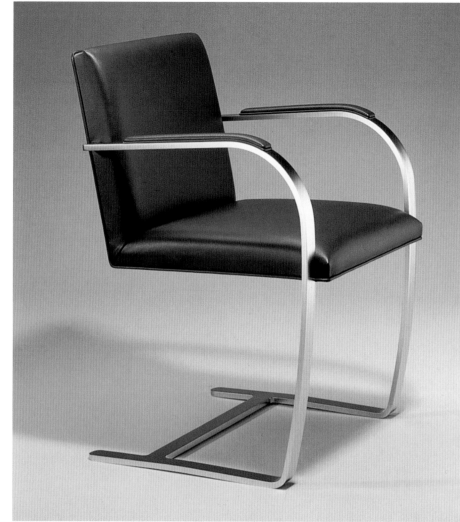

251 Barcelona Barstool designed by Ludwig Mies van der Rohe in 1958, manufactured in 1958 specifically for Philip Johnson, architect's, Four Seasons Hotel restaurant bar, in New York City. It was never mass-produced. Frame: stainless steel, polished or chrome finish. Upholstery: saddle leather straps with foam rubber cushions covered in top grain leather, constructed from individual welted panels with button tufting. 26 pounds weight, 14-1/2" w, 15" d, 30" h.

253 Small Barcelona Stool designed by Ludwig Mies van der Rohe in 1927, manufactured from 1954. Frame: stainless steel. Upholstery: saddle leather sling. 22-1/2" w, 21-1/2" d, 11-3/4" h.

254 Tugendhat Chair designed by Ludwig Mies van der Rohe in 1929, manufactured 1965-1976. Frame: stainless steel, polished finish. Upholstery: saddle leather straps with foam rubber cushions covered in top grain leather. 29-3/4" w, 27-1/4" d, 32-3/4" h. Knoll acquired the rights to manufacture this chair and 254A from the designer Ludwig Mies van der Rohe, and subsequently from the Museum of Modern Art in 1948.

254A Tugendhat Arm Chair designed by Ludwig Mies van der Rohe in 1929, manufactured 1965-1976. Frame: stainless steel, polished finish. Upholstery: saddle leather straps with foam rubber cushions covered in top grain leather. This chair was designed for the living room of a house built for Greta and Fritz Tugendhat in Brno, Czechoslovakia. 29-3/4" w, 27-1/4" d, 32-3/4" h.

255 Brno Arm Chair, Flat Frame designed by Ludwig Mies van der Rohe in 1930. Frame: flat stainless steel, polished finish. Upholstery: hardwood frame with foam rubber over spring suspension seat and rubber webbed back, can have arm pads. 23" w, 23" d, 31-1/2" h.

256 MR Armless Dining Chair designed by Ludwig Mies van der Rohe in 1927, manufactured from 1970. Frame: tubular stainless steel, polished finish. Seat and back: saddle leather with rawhide lacing. 19-1/2" w, 27-1/4" d, 31" h.

256A MR Dining Arm Chair designed by Ludwig Mies van der Rohe in 1927. Frame: tubular stainless steel, polished finish. Seat and back: saddle leather with nylon lacing. Same as 256, but with arms, 21" w, 32-1/2" d.

57 MR Lounge Chair designed by Ludwig Mies van der Rohe. Same as 256, but 23" w, 34" d, 30-1/4" h.

261 Lounge Chair designed by Ludwig Mies van der Rohe, manufactured from 1973. Base: wood veneer in a variety of finishes. Upholstery: polyester fiber rill over polyurethane core with separate seat and back cushions. 34-1/2" w, 34" d, 28" h.

262 Settee. Same as 261, but 62-1/2" w.

263 Sofa. Same as 261, but 90-1/2" w.

751 Krefeld Lounge Chair designed by Ludwig Mies van der Rohe in 1930, manufactured 2003. Hardwood and plywood frame with coil spring suspension and ash legs with stained finish. Upholstered side panels and seat and back foam cushions. 32" w, 27" d, 30" h.

752 Krefeld Settee. Same as 751, but 57" w.

753 Krefeld Sofa. Same as 751, but 82" w.

754 Krefeld Ottoman. Same as 751, but 26" w, 10-1/2" d, 17" h.

755 Krefeld Medium Bench Same as 754, but 51" w.

756 Krefeld Large Bench. Same as 754, but 76" w.

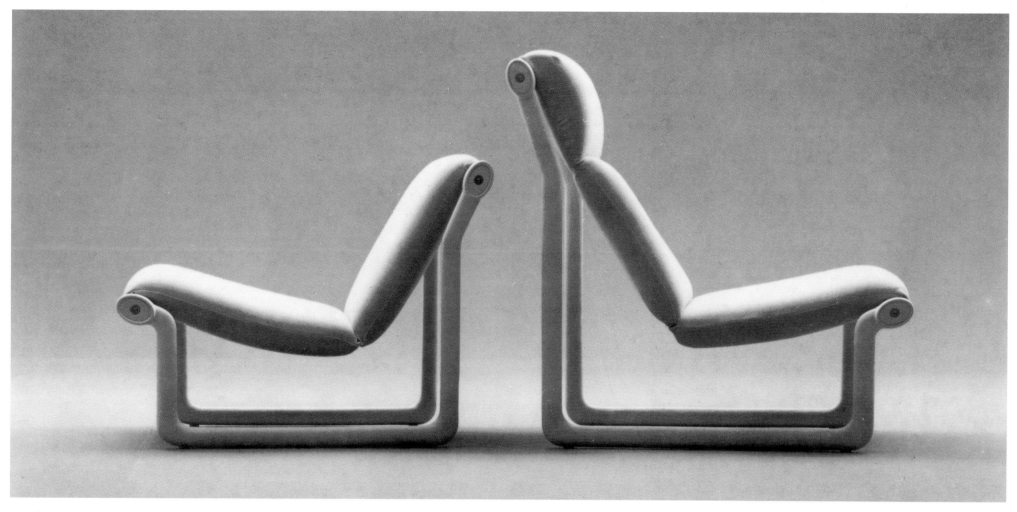

Andrew Morrison and Bruce Hannah

23A1 Low Back Office Chair designed by Andrew Ivar Morrison and Bruce R. Hannah in 1974. Frame: cast aluminum with swivel and tilt mechanism and 5-star base. Upholstered seat and back cushions. Button detail in back. 24-3/4" w, 24-1/2" d, 36" to 40" h.

23A3 High Back Office Chair. Same as 13A1, but welt detail in back.

2001 High Back Chair designed by Andrew Ivar Morrison and Bruce R. Hannah. Frame: cast aluminum in a variety of finishes. Stretchers: extruded aluminum in a variety of finishes. Glides: molded plastic. Upholstery: molded polyurethane foam reinforced with fiberglass vinyl, 28-1/4" w, 37-1/2" d, 35" h.

2002 High Back Settee. Same as 2001, but 55" w.

2003 High Back Sofa. Same as 2001, but 82" w.

2004 High Back Four-seater. Same as 2001, but 109" w.

2011 Lounge Chair designed by Andrew Ivar Morrison and Bruce R. Hannah in 1971, manufactured 1972-77. Frame: cast aluminum in a variety of finishes. Stretchers: extruded aluminum in a variety of finishes. Upholstery: molded foam rubber reinforced with fiberglass vinyl. Glides: molded plastic, 28-1/2" w, 34" d, 26" h.

2012 Lounge Settee. Same as 2011, but 55" w.

2013 Lounge Sofa. Same as 2011, but 82" w.

2014 Lounge Four Seater. Same as 2011, but 109" w.

2021 Contract Chair designed by Andrew Ivar Morrison and Bruce R. Hanna in 1971, manufactured 1972-1977. Frame: cast aluminum in a variety of finishes. Stretchers: extruded aluminum in a variety of finishes. Upholstery: molded foam rubber reinforced with fiber glass vinyl. Glides: molded plastic, 28-1/4" w, 30" d, 28" h.

2022 Contract Settee. Same as 2021, but 55" w.

2023 Contract Sofa. Same as 2021, but 81" w.

2024 Contract Four Seater. Same as 2021, but 109" w.

2031 Bench designed by Andrew Ivar Morrison and Bruce R. Hannah. Frame: cast aluminum in a variety of finishes. Stretcher: extruded aluminum in a variety of finishes. Upholstery: molded foam rubber reinforced with fiberglass vinyl. Glides: molded plastic, 28-1/4" w, 25-1/2" d, 17" h.

2032 Bench. Same as 2031, but 55" w.

2033 Bench. Same as 2031, but 82" w.

2034 Bench. Same as 2031, but 109" w.

114

2043 Sofa with Arms. Same as 2041, but 69-1/2" w.

2044 Multiple Seating. Same as 2041, but 93-1/4" w.

2046 Multiple Seating. Same as 2041, but 137-1/4" w.

2041 Arm Chair designed by Andrew Ivar Morrison and Bruce R. Hannah. Frame: cast aluminum in a variety of finishes. Stretchers: extruded aluminum in a variety of finishes. Glides: molded plastic. Upholstery: molded polyurethane foam reinforced with fiber glass vinyl, 25-1/2" w, 30-1/4" d, 28" h.

2042 Settee with Arms. Same as 2041, but 47-1/2" w.

2052 Multiple Settee designed by Andrew Ivar Morrison and Bruce R. Hannah on 1970. Frame: cast aluminum in a variety of finishes. Stretchers: extruded aluminum in a variety of finishes. Glides: molded plastic. Upholstery: molded polyurethane foam reinforced with fiber glass vinyl; some models have an integral table. 49-1/4" w.

2053 Multiple Sofa. Same as 2052, but 73" w. May have an integral table.

2954 Multiple Seating. Same as 2052, but 96-3/4" w. May have an integral table.

115

2055 Multiple Seating. Same as 2052, but 120-1/2" w. May have an integral table.

2056 Multiple Seating Same as 2052, but 144-1/4" w. May have an integral table.

2071 Bench designed by Andrew Ivar Morrison and Bruce R. Hannah in 1971, manufactured 1972-1974. Frame: cast aluminum in a variety of finishes. Upholstery: polyurethane foam. 33" w, 26" d, 17-1/4" h.

2072 Bench. Same as 2071, but 59" w.

2073 Bench Same as 2071, but 84" square.

2080 Bolster. 39" w, 16" d, 3-1/2" h.

2081 Bench. Same as 2071, but 39" square.

2082 Bench. Same as 2081, but 59" w.

2111 Reversible Pad Chair designed by Andrew Ivar Morrison and Bruce R. Hannah in 1973. Frame: cast aluminum in a variety of finishes. Stretchers: extruded aluminum in a variety of finishes. Upholstery: molded foam rubber cushions over fiber glass vinyl sling. Glides: molded plastic, 28-1/2" w, 34" d, 26" h.

2112 Reversible Pad Settee. Same as 2111, but 55" w.

2113 Reversible Pad Sofa. Same as 2111, but 82" w.

2121 Reversible Pad Chair. Same as 2111, but 28-1/4" w, 30" d, 28" h.

2122 Reversible Pad Settee. Same as 2121, but 55" w.

2123 Reversible Pad Sofa. Same as 2121, but 82" w.

2180 Bolster for 2183 couch, polyurethane foam with upholstery, 39" w, 16" d, 3-1/2" h.

2183 Couch designed by Andrew Ivar Morrison and Bruce R. Hannah. Frame: cast aluminum in a variety of finishes. Upholstery: polyurethane foam. 84" w, 39" d, 17-1/4" h.

2221 Molded Shell Chair designed by Andrew Ivar Morrison and Bruce R. Hannah. Frame: cast aluminum in a variety of finishes. Stretchers: extruded aluminum in a variety of finishes. Glides: molded plastic. Upholstery: molded plastic shell; some in this series with an integral table. 28-1/8" w.

2222 Molded Shell Settee. Same as 2221, 55" w.

2223 Molded Shell Sofa. Same as 2221, 82" w.

2241 Molded Shell Arm Chair. Same as 2221, 25-1/8" w.

2242 Molded Shell Settee With Arms. Same as 2221, 47-1/2" w. Also available in multiple seating configurations.

2252 Molded Shell Multiple Settee. Same as 2221, 49-1/4" w.

2253 Molded Shell Multiple Sofa. Same as 2221, 73" w.

2301 Secretarial Chair designed by Andrew Ivar Morrison and Bruce R. Hannah in 1970, manufactured from 1973. Base: cast aluminum in a variety of finishes. Frame: cast aluminum in a variety of finishes. Castors: plastic or hard rubber. Upholstery: separate back and seat foam cushions attached to frame with molded plastic buttons. 24" w, 24-1/2" d, 32" h.

2305 Arm Chair designed by Andrew Ivar Morrison and Bruce R. Hannah. Same as 2301.

2308 Swivel Arm Chair. Same as 2301, but with swivel and tilt mechanism. 24" w, 24-1/2" d, 31-1/4" h.

2309 Stool. Same as 2301. Glides: nylon.

2310 Stool. Same as 2301. Castors: plastic or hard rubber.

2311 Secretarial Chair. Same as 2301, but with inverted upholstery fasteners.

2315 Arm Chair. Same as 2301, but with continuous back and seat foam cushion and upholstery. Glides: nylon.

2318 Swivel Arm Chair. Same as 2301, but with continuous back and seat foam cushion and upholstery and swivel and tilt mechanism.

2325 Arm Chair. Same as 2315, but slightly wider and higher.

2328 Swivel Arm Chair. Same as 2318, but slightly wider and higher.

2338 Swivel Arm Chair. Same as 2308, but upholstery: foam cushions attached to frame with either button or cord. Castors: plastic.

2348 Swivel Arm Chair. Same as 2308, but upholstered in leather.

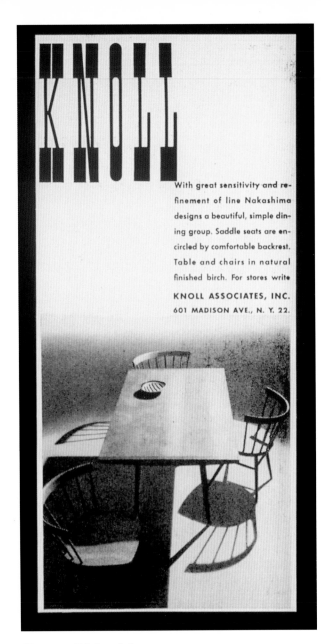

George Nakashima

N-19 Side Chair designed by George Nakashima c. 1944, manufactured 1947-1955. Birch, walnut, cherry, or ebony in natural finish with mortise and tenon joints. 24" w, 20" d, 28" h. This is the first chair produced by George Nakashima for Knoll. Before 1947 the seat was flat, after 1947 the seat was contoured.

N-20 Arm Chair designed by George Nakashima c. 1947. Birch, walnut, cherry, or ebony in natural finish with mortise and tenon joints. 20" w, 21" d, 27.5" h.

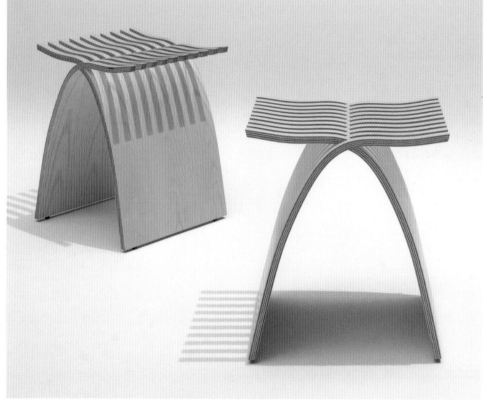

Isamu Noguchi

85 Rocking Stool designed by Isamu Noguchi in 1954, manufactured 1955-1960. Solid teak or walnut round top and base with chrome plated wire. 14" diameter, 10.5" h. From this design, the no. 311 dining table and no. 87 child's table evolved.

86 Rocking Stool, same as no. 85 but 16-3/4" h.

87 Child's Table, same as no. 85 but black or white plastic laminate top on black iron base and black steel wire column. Manufactured 1955-1964. 23-7/8" diameter, 20" h.

Stool with Interlocking Seat designed by Isamu Noguchi

119

The Pearson Chairs

Max Pearson

18A1 Pearson Arm Chair designed by Max Pearson in 1966. Base: 5-star cast aluminum in black epoxy finish with polished stainless steel top caps, on castors. Frame: plastic shell back and seat. Swivel and optional tilt mechanism. Upholstered with polyurethane foam and leather or fabric. 27-1/4" w, 25-1/4" d, 35" to
38-1/4" h.

18A2 Pearson Executive Arm Chair. Same as 18A1, but 29-1/2" w, 27-1/2" d, 35-3/4" to 39" h.

18C1 Pearson Chair. Same as 18A1, but without arm supports, 25-1/4" w, 23-1/4" d, 33" to 36-1/4" h.

Kurt Nordstrom

145 Side Chair designed by Kurt Nordstrom c. 1950, manufactured 1957-1960. Tubular steel frame with black finish and wood tips on legs. Plywood teak molded back and seat with natural finish. 18.75" w, 19.25" d, 30" h.

146 Side Chair designed c. 1951, bentwood beech frame with caned seat and back and foam upholstered cushions, 17" w, 21" d, 33" h.

147 Arm Chair. Same as 146, but 19-1/2" w.

Odelberg-Olson Design

60 Swivel Chair designed by Odelberg-Olson Design of Stockholm, Sweden, c. 1948, back rest and seat of shaped plywood, 4-way action adjustable, on four raking metal legs.

41 Secretarial Chair designed by Max Pearson in 1961. Back support: stainless steel cap over black epoxy finish cast aluminum. Base: stainless steel cap over steel armature. Upholstery: foam rubber seat and back, available in a choice of Knoll fabrics. Castors: plastic carpet castors.

43 Drafting Stool designed by Max Pearson. Back support: stainless steel cap over cast aluminum. Base: stainless steel cap over steel armature. Available in a variety of finishes. Upholstery: foam rubber over plywood seat and molded plastic back. Castors: hard rubber or plastic.

46. Secretarial Chair designed by Max Pearson in 1961. Back support: cast aluminum. V-swivel base: stainless steel cap over steel armature, available in a variety of finishes. Upholstery: foam rubber seat and back. Casters: hard rubber or plastic. 18-1/2" w, 18-1/2" d, 35" h.

1801 Side Chair designed by Max Pearson in 1968. Base: polished stainless steel cap over black steel armature, available in a variety of finishes. Upholstery: foam rubber over molded plastic shells. Rotates but does not tilt. Glides: nylon. 22" w, 23" d, 32-1/2" to 34-1/8" h.

1802 Side Chair. Same as 1801, but rests on hard rubber or plastic castors.

1804 Swivel Arm Chair. Same as 1802, but with swivel mechanism.

1805 Small Arm Chair designed by Max Pearson in 1968. Base: stainless steel cap over steel armature, available in a variety of finishes. Rotates but does not tilt. Upholstery: foam rubber over molded plastic shells. Glides: nylon. 26" w, 24-1/2" d, 34" h.

1806 Small Arm Chair. Same as 1805, but on castors.

1808 Small Swivel Arm Chair. Same as 1805, but with swivel and tilt mechanism and hard rubber or plastic castors.

1815 Large Arm Chair. Same as 1805. Rotates but does not tilt. 28" w, 26-1/2" d, 35-3/8" h.

1816 Large Arm Chair. Same as 1815, but on castors.

1818 Large Swivel Arm Chair. Same as 1815, but with swivel and tilt mechanism. 38" h.

Opposite page:
Jorge Pensi

29 Toledo Arm Chair designed by Jorge Pensi.

Jorge Pensi

29 Toledo Arm Chair designed by Jorge Pensi in 1988, manufactured 1990. Arms and legs of anodized polished tubular aluminum with cast aluminum seat and back. They can be stacked up to 8 chairs high. 21-3/5" w, 21-1/4" d, 30" h.

Donald Petitt

1105 Side Arm Chair designed by Donald Petitt in 1973. Frame: continuous, curved laminations of wood veneer, available in a variety of finishes. Upholstery: foam rubber bonded to formed metal seat and back. Glides: nylon. 22-1/2" w, 24" d, 32" h.

1115 Arm Chair. Same as 1105, but base: laminated cast aluminum armature, available in a variety of finishes. Base rotates but does not tilt. 24" w, 25-1/2" d, 31-3/4" h.

1118 Swivel Arm Chair. Same as 1105. Base: adjustable swivel and tilt mechanism. 32-3/4" to 35-1/4" h.

124

Charles Pfister

1050 Pull-up Chair designed by Charles Pfister in 1984. Variable density polyurethane foam seat with 2-way elastic suspension and leather covering. Back with 2-way elastic belt suspension and polyester fabric. 23-1/2" w, 23" d, 31" h.

1051 Lounge Chair designed by Charles Pfister in 1971, manufactured from 1983. Base: tubular steel, polished chrome finish. Upholstery: hardwood frame with sag-less webbing in back and zigzag springs in seat; reversible seat and back cushions filled with foam core and waterfowl feathers or foam core and polyester fiber wrap. 33" w, 33" d, 26" h.

1052 Settee. Same as 1051, but 60" w.

1053 Sofa. Same as 1051, but 87" w.

1059 Ottoman. Same as 1051, but 27-3/4" square, 17" h.

Warren Platner

1705 Easy Chair designed by Warren Platner c. 1966, manufactured 1966-1996. Base and basket: steel rods, available in a variety of finishes. Upholstery: molded foam rubber over fiberglass. Cushion: polyester over foam core with zippered cover and Velcro fastening. Glides: clear plastic extrusion ring. 40-3/4" w, 36-1/2" d, 39" h.

1709 Ottoman manufactured 1966-1996. Same as 1705, but 24-1/2" diameter, 15" h.

1715 Lounge Chair. Same as 1705, but 30-1/2" h.

1716 Sofa. Same as 1705, but 68" w.

1719 Stool. Same as 1705, but 15-1/2" diameter, 19" h.

1725 Arm Chair manufactured 1966-1996. Same as 1705, but open back with rods and 26-1/2" w.

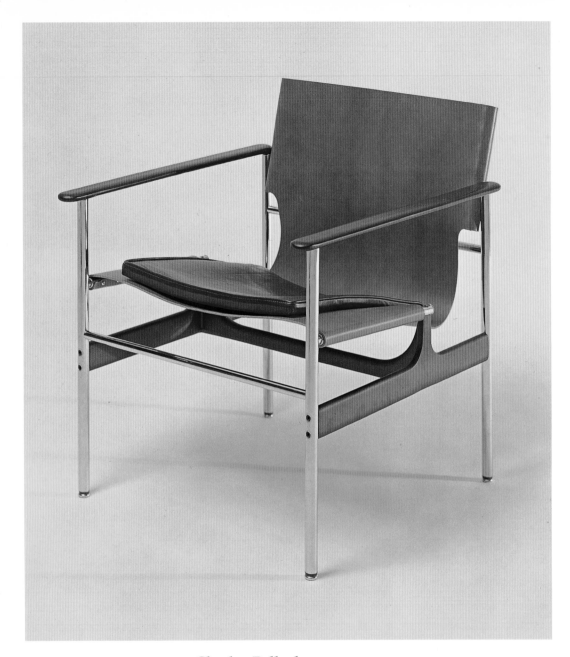

Charles Pollock

657 Sling Arm Chair designed by Charles Pollock in 1960, manufactured 1964-1979. Legs: tubular steel with a variety of finishes. Arms and stretchers: cast aluminum, available in a variety of finishes. Upholstery: saddle leather sling with foam rubber, separate cushion covered in leather. 25" w, 26" d, 27-3/4" h.

1255 Arm Chair. Same as 1251, but with solid black plastic arms. Optional fixed jury base available.

1258 Swivel Arm Chair. Same as 1251, but with arms and swivel and tilt mechanism. Available with various finishes.

1251 Side Chair designed by Charles Pollock in 1965. Base: stainless steel cap over steel armature, available in a variety of finishes. Upholstery: polyurethane and polyester over plastic shell with aluminum frame in a variety of finishes. Castors: hard rubber or plastic. 23-1/2" w, 27" d, 31" h.

1252 Side Chair. Same as 1251, but with swivel mechanism.

1254 Armless Swivel Chair. Same as 1251, but with swivel and tilt mechanism.

Ralph Rapson

657A Rocking Chair designed by Ralph Rapson in 1944 as part of the "Equipment for Living" project. Birch frame with webbed fabric or upholstered seat and back. 28-1/2" w, 24" d, 32" h. Hans Knoll selected this rocker as part of a series produced immediately after the departure from Knoll of Jens Risom in 1943.

658 Sectional Sofa designed by Ralph Rapson in 1945. Birch frame with two upholstered back and seat cushion. Available without arms, or with right or left arm. Dimensions unknown.

Jorgen Rasmussen

1901 Side Chair with Glides designed by Jorgen Rasmussen in 1973, manufactured from 1973. Base and back support: cast aluminum, satin finish. Glides: nylon. Seat and back: molded plastic in a variety of colors or with attached foam rubber cushions covered in stretch fabrics. 24-3/8" w, 24-3/8" d, 20-1/2" h.

1904 Side Chair with Castors. Same as 1901, with twin-wheel castors.

1905 Arm Chair with Glides. Same as 1901, with arms, 22-1/16" h.

1908 Arm Chair with Glides. Same as 1905, with glides, 22-1/16" h.

1909 Stool. Same as 1904 without back. 24-3/8" diameter, 18" to 22" high.

1913 Drafting Stool. Same as 1904, but taller base. 26" to 29" high.

1916 Drafting Stool with Foot Ring. Same as 1913, but with foot ring.

Knoll
Carlos Riart Chair

Carlos Riart

790 Riart Rocking Chair designed by Carlos Riart in 1982, manufactured 1982-1988. Molded ebony frame with horizontal cross members of purple heart, mother-of-pearl inlay in arms, upholstered seat. 24-1/2" w, 42-1/2" d, 39-1/4" h. Designed to commemorate the 50th anniversary of Mies van der Rohe's Barcelona pavilion at the 1925 World's Fair. Carlos Riart's personal mark is engraved on each chair.

Joseph and Linda Ricchio

37A Arm Chair designed by Joseph and Linda Ricchio in 1990, manufactured 1991. Frame: White beech wood with stained finish. Seat: wood or upholstered; or optional seat, back, and side upholstery. 21-5/8" w, 23" d, 32" h.

37A-U Arm Chair*. Same as 37A, but fully upholstered seat and back.

37A-UP Arm Chair*. Same as 37A, but with fully upholstered seat, back, and side panels.

37C Armless Chair designed by Joseph and Linda Ricchio. Same as 37A, but without arms.

37C-U Armless Chair, Same as 37A, but without arms and fully upholstered seat and back.

37AS JR® Arm Chair designed by Joseph Ricchio in 1995, manufactured 1996. Maple frame with dowel and mortise construction in clear or stained finish. Cushioned seat. 23-1/2" w, 21-5/8" d, 32-1/8" h.

37CS JR® Armless Chair designed by Joseph Ricchio. Same as 37AS, but without arms, 20-1/4" w.

48A Joe® Arm Chair designed by Joe Ricchio, manufactured 2005. Maple or beech hardwood frame with foam seat in leather or fabric upholstery. 24" w, 22" d, 32" h.

37CH High Barstool. Same as 37A, but without arms and with upholstered seat, 18-1/2" w, 21" d, 40" h.

37CM Medium Barstool. Same as 37CH, but 34" h.

Jens Risom

Child's High Chair designed by Jens Risom or Abel Sorensen c. 1941. Spruce wood with canvas webbing. 14" w, 26" d, 32" h.

620 Easy Chair designed by Jens Risom, c. 1942, cherry wood, on recessed wooden base. Also available as a sofa, 78" long, and as a love seat, 56" long. *Photo: From the 1942 Premier Knoll catalog.*

621 Easy Chair designed by Jens Risom, c. 1942, cherry wood, upholstered with seat cushion, frame base 7" h. Also available as a sofa, 78" long, and as a loveseat, 56" long. *Photo: From the 1942 Premier Knoll catalog. Design: Jens Risom, independent designer, 1941-1946.*

622 Arm Chair designed by Jens Risom, c. 1942, cherry wood with leather lacing and optional seat cushion. *Photo: From the 1942 Premier Knoll catalog. Design: Jens Risom, independent designer, 1941-1946.*

623 Side Chair designed by Jens Risom, c. 1942, cherry wood with leather lacing and optional seat cushion. *Photo: From the 1942 Premier Knoll catalog. Design: Jens Risom, independent designer, 1941-1946.*

645 Lounge Arm Chair designed by Jens Risom in 1941, manufactured 1941-1960. Spruce or birch wood frame with tan leather webbed or separate upholstered seat and back. 26" w, 28-1/2" d, 29 1/4" h, upholstered 33" h.

650 Arm Chair designed by Jens Risom, in 1941. Birch or maple frame in natural finish with mortise and tenon joints, separate webbed or tufted upholstered seat and back. 24" w, 28" d, 33" h.

652 Settee. Same as 650, but with two seats.

654 Lounge Chair, with and without arms designed by Jens Risom in 1941, patented 1945, manufactured 1941-1960. Spruce frame in natural finish with full or separate upholstered back and seat. 20" w, 28" d, 30" h. Surplus parachute straps were used on the earliest examples due to wartime material shortages materials. Later ones, c. 1957, can be upholstered.

137

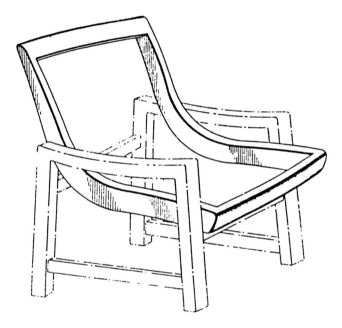

INVENTOR.

JENS RISOM

BY *[signature]*

ATTORNEY

UNITED STATES PATENT OFFICE

141,703

DESIGN FOR A CHAIR FRAME OR THE LIKE

Jens Risom, New York, N. Y., assignor to H. G. Knoll, Associates, New York, N. Y., a New York company

Application December 11, 1943, Serial No. 111,991

Term of patent 7 years

(Cl. D15—1)

To all whom it may concern:

Be it known that I, Jens Risom, a subject of King of Denmark, residing at New York, in the county and State of New York, have invented a new, original, and ornamental Design for a Chair Frame or the like, of which the following is a specification, reference being made to the accompanying drawing, forming a part thereof.

The figure is a perspective view of a chair frame or the like, showing my new design.

The dominant feature of my design resides in the portion shown in full lines.

I claim:

The ornamental design for a chair frame or the like, substantially as shown and described.

JENS RISOM.

21 Upholstered Chair designed by Jens Risom ca. 1941, manufactured 1942 to 1968. Birch wood frame with attached foam cushions and upholstery. 23-3/4" w, 30-1/2" d, 30-3/4" h.

22 Settee similar to no. 21 but with two seats, 49-1/2" w.

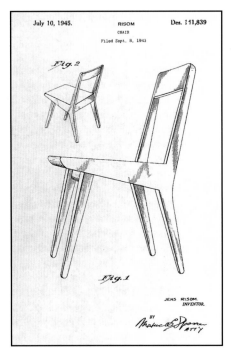

23 Sofa similar to no. 21 but with three seats, 73-1/2" w.

666 Side Chair designed by Jens Risom in 1941, the first Knoll-manufactured chair, manufactured 1942 to 1958. Birch or maple wood back and frame, with wood or webbing back and seat; and later fabric or Naugahyde upholstery over plywood seat. 17" w, 21" d, 30-3/4" h.

667 Stool designed by Jens Risom in 1941, manufactured 1941 to 1958. Spruce wood with natural finish and cotton webbing. 15" w, 16" d, 17" h.

Eero Saarinen

46 Secretarial Chair designed by Eero Saarinen in 1953. Base: swivel action stainless steel cap over steel armature. Seat and back: foam rubber with upholstery. 18-1/2" w, 18-1/2" d, 30" to 36-1/4" h.

61 Grasshopper Arm Chair designed by Eero Saarinen in 1946, manufactured 1946-1965. Birch or maple laminated base available in a variety of finishes, with fully upholstered back and seat. 23" w, 31" d, 29" h, upholstered 26-1/2" w, 34" d, 35-1/4" h. This is the first design he produced for Knoll.

62 Grasshopper Ottoman designed by Eero Saarinen in 1946. Birch or maple laminated base in a variety of finishes, with upholstery. 23-1/2" w, 17-3/4" d, 16" h.

68 Arm Chair designed by Eero Saarinen in 1948. Legs: bent wood, or tubular steel, or swivel base, available in a variety of finishes. Upholstery: foam rubber over plastic shell and plywood platform. Glides: stainless steel and nylon. 26" w, 24-1/2" d, 33-1/2" h.

141

69 Side Chair designed by Eero Saarinen in 1948. Legs: tubular steel or swivel base, available in a variety of finishes. Upholstery: foam rubber over plastic shell and plywood platform. Glides: stainless steel and nylon.

70 Womb Easy Chair designed by Eero Saarinen in 1946. Base: steel rod, available in a variety of finishes. Frame and upholstery: foam rubber over molded reinforced plastic shell; loose cushions of polyester fiber with polyurethane foam core. Glides: stainless steel and nylon swivel. 40" w, 33-1/2" d, 36-1/2" h.

142

71 Arm Chair designed by Eero Saarinen in 1957.
Legs: wood or tubular steel. Base: stainless steel cap
over steel armature, available in a variety of finishes.
Upholstery: foam rubber over plastic or fiberglass
and plywood platform. Castors: hard rubber or
plastic. Available with a variety of bases and finishes.
26″ w, 24″ d, 34″ h.

72 Side Chair designed by Eero Saarinen in 1948, manufactured 1948-1976. Frame: molded reinforced plastic back shell, contour plywood seat form. Legs: wood or tubular steel. Base: stainless steel top cap over steel armature; also available with tubular steel, polished chrome finish. Back: plastic or upholstered over varied density foam. Castors: hard rubber carpet castors. Also made in metal, manufactured 1948-1972. 22" w, 21" d, 32" h. The first chairs designed for the office in the Knoll line.

73 Two-seat Womb Settee. Same as no. 70, but 62" w.

74 Ottoman. Same as 70, but with foam rubber over molded plywood seat. 26" w, 20" d, 15-1/4" h.

76 Secretarial Chair designed by Eero Saarinen c. 1950. Frame: die cast aluminum swivel base and back support with adjustable tilting mechanism. Hard rubber castors. 18" w, 18-1/2" d, 28-3/4" to 35-3/4" h.

77 Drafting Stool. Same as 76 but with foot ring, 20" d, 35-1/2" to 40-1/2" h.

150 Tulip Arm Chair designed by Eero Saarinen in 1956, manufactured 1956-1996. Base: fixed or revolving, cast aluminum, fused plastic finish. Available in a variety of colors. Plastic shell upholstered on inside only. Shell color matches finish on base. 26" w, 23-1/2" d, 32" h.

144

151 Tulip Armless Side Chair designed by Eero Saarinen in 1956, manufactured 1956-present. Base: fixed or revolving cast aluminum, fused plastic finish. Available in a variety of colors. Plastic shell upholstered on inside only. Shell color matches finish on base. 19-1/2" w, 22" d, 32" h.

152 Stool designed by Eero Saarinen. Base: cast aluminum, fused plastic finish. Available in a variety of colors. Revolving seat. Upholstery: latex foam rubber. 15" diameter, 16" h.

153 Stool. Same as 152, but 17-5/8" h. Height raised in 1990 to 18-1/2" h.

145

Richard Sapper

45A Executive Chair with Arms designed by Richard Sapper, manufactured 1987. Frame: concealed metal with inner nylon mesh bracing and sliding lumbar support. Fabric or leather upholstery. Base: 5-star cast aluminum with black finish. Arms: black urethane cushion on steel inserts. 26" w, 28-3/4" d, 38-1/2" to 41-1/4" h.

146

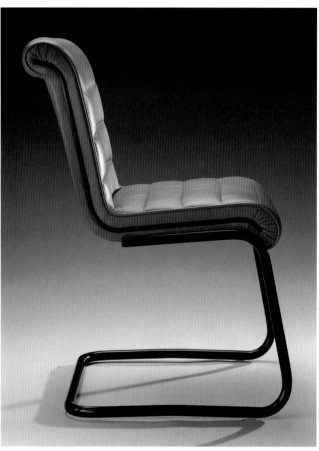

45A Sled Base Chair with Arms designed by Richard Sapper, manufactured 1987. Base: cantilevered design of 1" diameter steel tube in black finish. 24-3/4" w, 27-1/2" d, 34-3/4" h.

45C Executive Chair without Arms. Same as 45A Executive Chair, but without arms.

45C Sled Base Chair without Arms. Same as 45A Sled Base Chair, but without arms.

L-1 Lambda Chair designed by Richard Sapper and Marco Zanusso in 1962.

Tobia Scarpa

53-125 Grande Pigreco Arm Chair designed by Tobia
Scarpa, manufactured from 1970. Frame: solid wood,
lacquer finish. Upholstery: foam rubber over plywood. 23" w, 17-1/2" d, 27" h.

53-145 Bastiano Lounge Chair designed by Tobia
and Afra Scarpa in 1969. Frame: solid wood, lacquer
finish. Upholstery: separate cushions of down and
foam rubber over rubber and steel suspension.
35-3/4" w, 30-3/4" d, 27-1/2" h.

53-146 Bastiano Settee. Same as 53-145, but
59-3/4" w.

53-147 Bastiano Sofa. Same as 53-145, but 83-1/2" w.

53-148 Bastiano Sofa. Same as 53-145, but 109" w.

Richard Schultz

147 Arm Chair designed by Richard Schultz in 1982, manufactured 1982-1984.

148 Side Chair designed by Richard Schultz in 1960. Base: aluminum, fused plastic finish, available in a variety of colors or polished chrome finish. Plastic shell upholstered on inside only; shell color matches plastic finish on base. 20" w, 22-1/2" d, 32 " h.

149 Stacking Side Chair designed by Richard Schultz in 1960. Base: aluminum, polished chrome finish, available in a variety of colors in fused plastic finish. Fully upholstered seat and back unit. Also with asymmetrical base for non-stacking version. 20" w, 22-1/2" d, 32" h.

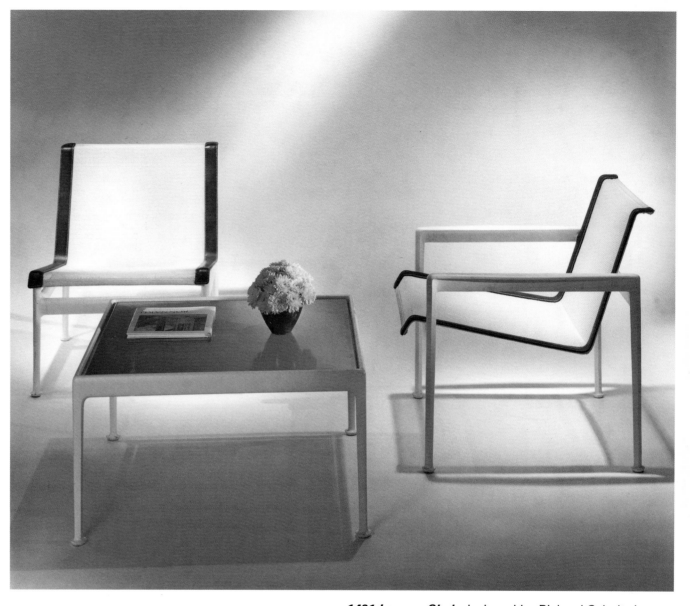

703 Convertible Sofa/Bed designed by Richard Schultz about 1961. Base: steel with black epoxy finish. Back and seat upholstered. 76" w, 31-3/4" d, 28-1/2" h.

704 Convertible Arm Sofa. Same as 703 but with upholstered arms and 82" w.

715 Chaise Lounge designed by Richard Schultz in 1961, manufactured 1964-1970. Steel wire basket, white fused plastic finish, with or without two wheels. Cushions available in a variety of colors. 76-1/2" w, 29" d, 14-1/2" h. Selected by the Museum of Modern Art in New York for their permanent design collection in 1963.

1407 Pull-up Arm Chair designed by Richard Schultz in 1982, manufactured 1982-84. Frame: 3/4" diameter tubular steel painted or polished chrome finish. Arms, 1" diameter tubular steel. Upholstery: fabric, vinyl, or leather over polyester mesh and foam, 21-3/4" w, 20-1/4" d, 32" h. Optional slides: fixed plastic.

1408 Side Chair. Same as 1407, but without arms and 19-3/4" d.

1421 Lounge Chair designed by Richard Schultz in 1965. Frame: cast and extruded aluminum available in a variety of finishes. Sling: woven Dacron mesh with vinyl straps available in a variety of colors. Glides: plastic. 23" w, 28-1/4" d, 26-1/2" h.

1425 Lounge Chair with Arms. Same as 1421, but with arms and 26" w.

1441 Dining Chair. Same as 1421, but 20" w, 24-1/4" d, 29" h.

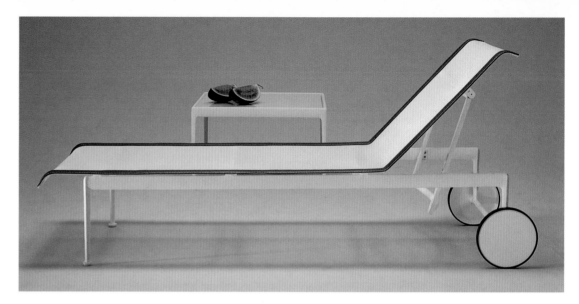

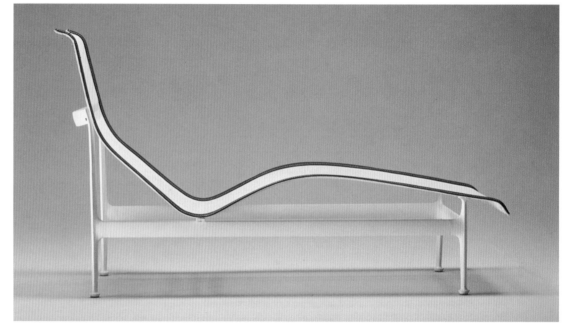

1445 Dining Chair with Arms. Same as 1421, but with arms and 24-1/4" d, 29" h.

1462 Settee designed by Richard Schultz. Frame: steel base in a variety of finishes. Stretchers: steel. Upholstery: foam over molded plastic shell. 57" w, 34-1/2" d, 30" h.

1463 Sofa. Same as 1462, but 85-1/2" w.

7441 Contour Chaise Lounge designed by Richard Schultz in 1967. Frame: cast and extruded aluminum, available in a variety of finishes. Sling: woven Dacron mesh with vinyl straps, available in a variety of colors. 24-1/2" w, 58" d, 33-3/4" h.

7442 Chaise Lounge. Same as 7441, but with adjustable back and plastic wheels with rubber ring. 25-1/2" w, 76" d, 14-1/2" to 35-1/2" h.

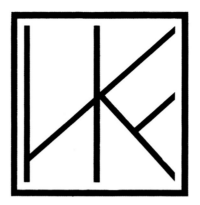

Ernest Schwadron

200 Loveseat designed by Ernest Schwadron c. 1942, upholstered, 38" w. *Photo: From the 1942 Premier Knoll catalog.*

200 Fireside Chair same as no. 200, but 23" w.

201 Chair designed c. 1951. Legs: clear birch in natural finish, hardwood frame with upholstered tight seat, 28-1/2" w, 30" d, 34" h.

202 Easy Chair designed by Ernest Schwadron c. 1942, upholstered with loose seat cushion and tight back. *Photo: From the 1942 Premier Knoll catalog.*

203 Easy Chair designed by Ernest Schwadron c. 1942, upholstered with loose seat cushion and loose back. *Photo: From the 1942 Premier Knoll catalog.*

204 Sofa Chair designed by Ernest Schwadron c. 1942, upholstered with three loose seat cushions, 66" long. Photo: *From the 1942 Premier Knoll Catalog.*

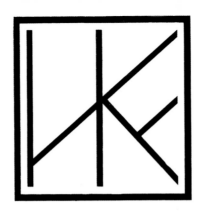

210 Easy Chair designed by Ernest Schwadron
c. 1942, with loose cushion in back and seat. *Photo:
From the 1942 Premier Knoll catalog.*

211 Sofa designed by Ernest Schwadron, similar to
no. 210 easy chair but 72" long.

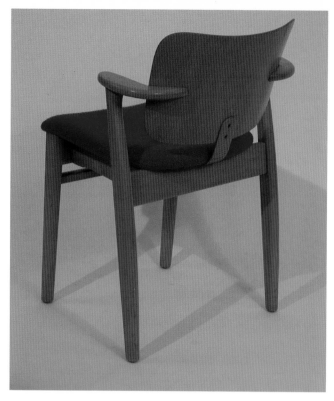

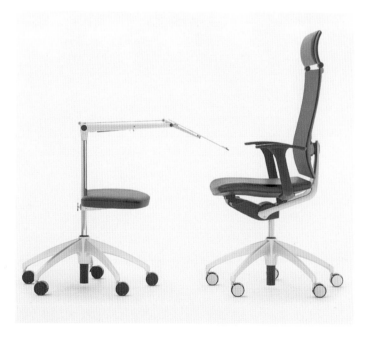

40 Side Chair designed by Abel Sorenson in 1945. Wood frame with wood back and seat. 23-1/2" w, 20" d, 24" h.

Mathias Seiler

S901 Open Up® Chair designed by Mathias Seiler for Sedus Design Group, manufactured in 2003.

Abel Sorenson

703 Armchair designed by Abel Sorensen about 1945, manufactured 1945-1946. Maple wood frame with vinyl webbing, 19" w, 23" d, 33" h.

41 Side Chair with Arms designed by Abel Sorenson in 1945. Wood frame with upholstered back and seat or with canvas webbing. 23-1/2" w, 20" d, 24" h; upholstered 33" h.

Ettore Sottsass

35S1 Eastside Lounge Chair designed by Ettore Sottsass in 1983, manufactured 1984-1987. Steel frame with springs; arm, seat, back, and head cushions of foam covered in leather or fabric. 32" w, 31" d, 34" h.

35S2 Eastside Two-seat Sofa. Same as 35S1, but 54" w.

35S3 Eastside Three-seat Sofa. Same as 35S1, but 75" w.

37 Eastside Sofa. Same as 35S1, but 78" w.

36A Bridge Arm Chair designed by Sottsass Associati in 1986, manufactured 1988. Stained beach frame and legs with molded arms, upholstered seat and back cushions set into wood frame and elastic belts. 19-3/4" w, 21-3/4" d, 32-3/4" h. Different dimensions in 1990: 23-1/2" w, 23-1/4" d, 30" h.

36C Bridge Armless Chair. Same as 36A, but without arms.

37S1 Westside Lounge Chair designed by Ettore Sotsass in 1983, manufactured 1987. Steel frame with springs; arm, seat, and back foam cushions covered in one, two, or three colors of the same "Tone" fabric. Legs of heavy gauge steel with ivory or ebony finish. 35" w, 31" d, 31" h.

37S2 Westside Two-seat Sofa. Same as 37S1, but 62" w.

37S2 Westside Three-seat Sofa. Same as 37S1, but 85" w.

38 Settee. Same as 35, but 54" w.

39A Mandarin Arm Chair designed by Sottsass Associati in 1986, manufactured 1987. Frame: tubular steel and detachable legs painted black. Seat and back: elastic belt seat suspension and polyurethane foam with upholstery. Arms: one piece bent rattan or painted tubular steel. 26" w, 24-3/8" d, 32-1/2" h.

39C Mandarin Armless Chair. Same as 39A, but without arms, 18" w.

William Stephens

360 Chair

700 Series Office Chair

158

1301 Side Chair designed by William Stephens in 1967, manufactured 1968-1988. Frame: thin laminations of laminated oak wood veneer with caned or upholstered seat and back, available in a variety of finishes as well as variations. Shell: molded plastic. Upholstery: foam rubber over plastic shell with fabric. Glides: nylon. 19" w, 22-1/2" d, 32" h.

1304-1 Armless Swivel. Same as 1301, but base of cast aluminum, available in a variety of finishes and with swivel and tilt mechanism. Castors: hard rubber or plastic.

1304-2 Armless Swivel. Same as 1301, but base has solid wood cap, in a variety of finishes, over cast aluminum.

1305 Pull-up Arm Chair. Same as 1301, but with arms. 22-1/4" w, 22" d, 32" h.

1308-1 Swivel Arm Chair. Same as 1301, but cast aluminum base.

1308-2 Swivel Arm Chair. Same as 1301, but base with solid wood cap.

1301 Side Chair designed by William Stephens with variation caned seat and back.

5001 Task Swivel Chair designed by William Stephens ca. 1980, manufactured 1982-1984. Seat and back: plywood insert with molded foam cushion. Back support: cast aluminum, painted finish. Base: 5-star steel armature with painted steel top caps, 10" diameter. Upholstery: selection of leather or fabrics over molded foam cushion. Castors: Kevi twin-wheels. 30-1/2" w, 22" d, 37-1/2" h.

5003 Operational Swivel Chair. Same as 5001, but with arms, 23" w.

5007 Management Chair. Same as 5001, but with upholstered arms, 28" w, 26" d, 31" h.

5017 Executive Chair. Manufactured 1982-1985. Same as 5007, but 29-1/2" w, 27" d, 37-1/2" h.

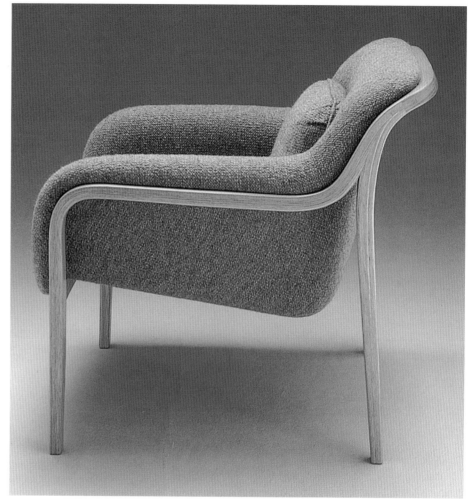

1315 Lounge Chair designed by William Stephens in 1971. Frame: thin laminations of wood veneer, available in a variety of finishes. Shell: molded plastic. Upholstery: foam rubber over plastic shell and covered with leather or fabric, 30″ w, 30-1/2″ d, 29″ h.

161

Kazuhide Takahama

55-131 Suzanne Lounge Chair designed by Kazuhide Takahama in 1965. Frame: tubular steel, polished chrome finish. Upholstery: separate foam polyurethane cushions. 29-7/8" w, 34-5/8" d, 26-3/4" h.

55-133 Suzanne Settee. Same as 55-131, but 59-7/8" w.

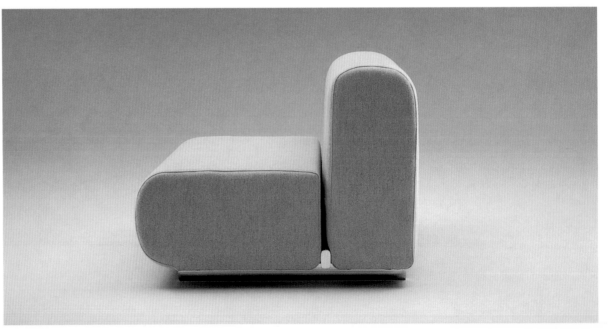

162

55-141 Suzanne Double Lounge Chair. Same as 55-131, but two chairs with common back. 58-5/8" d.

55-143 Suzanne Sofa. Same as 55-131, but 97-5/8" w.

55-151 Raymond Lounge Chair designed by Kazuhide Takahama in 1969, manufactured from 1970. Base and back support: white, fiber glass reinforced plastic. Upholstery: separate foam polyurethane cushions. 29-1/2" w, 31-1/8" d, 24-3/4" h.

55-161 Marcel Lounge Chair designed by Kazuhide Takahama in 1969, manufactured from 1970. Frame: aluminum bar, satin finish. Upholstery: separate foam polyurethane cushions. 31-1/2" w, 34-5/8" d, 25-1/2" h.

55-163 Marcel Sofa. Same as 55-161. 97-5/8" w, 34-5/8" d, 25-1/2" h.

55-169 Marcel Ottoman. Same as 55-161. 31-1/2" w, 24" d, 13;3/4" h.

55-171 Marcel Double Lounge Chair. Same as 55-161. 97-5/8" w, 34-5/8" d, 25-1/2" h.

Iimari Tapiovaara

140 Stacking Arm Chair designed by Iimari Tapiovaara in 1947, manufactured 1951-1957. Clear birch and molded plywood with clear, walnut, or ebony finish. Wood back and seat. 22" w, 21" d, 30" h.

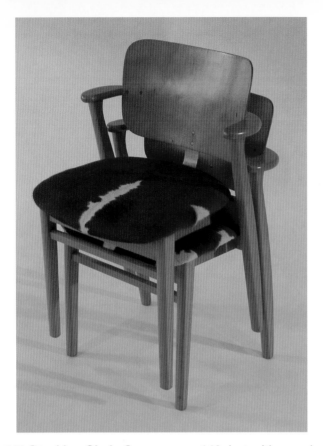

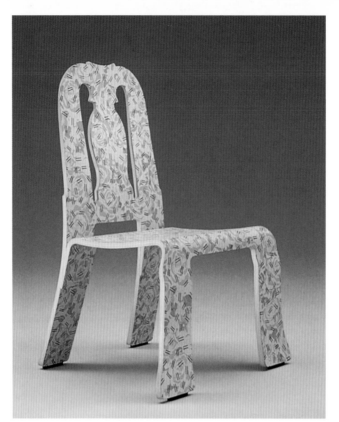

141 Stacking Chair. Same as no. 140, but with wood back and upholstered seat.

142 Stacking Chair. Same as no. 140, but with upholstered back and seat.

Robert Venturi

661 Queen Anne Chair designed by Robert Venturi in 1984, manufactured 1984 to 1988. Bent wood lamination and laminated veneer with a walnut finish. This is an interesting and playful design interpretation of 18th century furniture. 26-1/4" w, 23-1/2" d, 38-1/2" h.

662 Chippendale Chair designed by Robert Venturi in 1984.

663. Empire Chair designed by Robert Venturi in 1984, manufactured 1984-1988. Molded laser-cut plywood with plastic laminate face and natural wood edges, painted with stencil decoration, fixed nylon glides. 23-1/4" w, 23-3/4" d, 32-1/2" h.

664 Sheraton Chair designed by Robert Venturi in 1984, manufactured 1984-1988. Molded laser-cut plywood with plastic laminate face and natural wood edges, painted with stencil decoration, fixed nylon glides. 23-1/4" w, 23-3/4" d, 33-1/4" h.

665 Art Deco Chair designed by Robert Venturi in 1984, manufactured 1984-1988. Molded laser-cut plywood with plastic laminate face and natural wood edges, painted with stencil decoration, fixed nylon glides. 23-1/4" w, 23-3/4" d, 31-1/2" h.

680 Sofa designed by Robert Venturi in 1984, manufactured 1987. Frame: Wooden deck with fiberglass and spring cushion support. Reversible seat cushions of foam and polyester batting. 87" w, 43-1/2" d, 33-3/4" h.

Vignelli Designs

49A Rattan Handkerchief Stacking Arm Chair
designed by Vignelli Designs in 1995, manufactured
1996. Base: 5/16" steel wire in polished chrome
finish. Back and seat: metal frame with natural rattan
hand-woven shell. Arm rests: solid ash in clear finish.
Chairs stack 6 high. 26" w, 22-1/2" d, 29-1/2" h.

49C Rattan Handkerchief Stacking Armless Chair.
Same as 49A, but without arms, 23" w.

*4901 Handkerchief Stacking Unupholstered Armless
Chair* designed by Vignelli Associates in 1985,
manufactured 1990. Base: 5/16" steel wire with
powder paint or chrome finish. Back and seat:
colored and molded fiberglass. Unupholstered chairs
stack 25 chairs high. 23" w, 22-1/2" d, 29" h.

4901U Handkerchief Upholstered Armless Chair.
Same as 4901, but with woven rattan or upholstered
shell. Upholstered chairs do not stack.

**4902 Handkerchief Stacking Unupholstered Arm
Chair.** Same as 4901, but with arms, 26" w.

4902U Handkerchief Upholstered Arm Chair. Same
as 4901U, but with upholstered shell, 26" w.

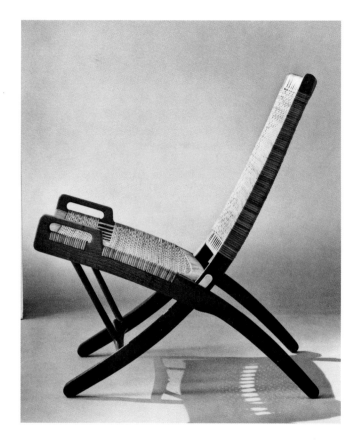

Opposite: Chairs designed by Hans Wegner

Hans Wegner

60-101 Folding Chair designed by Hans Wegner, manufactured in 1970. Frame: solid oak, wax finish, folding with notch for storing on hook. Seat and back: woven cane. 24-1/2″ w, 29-1/4″ d, 30-1/2″ h.

60-105 Lounge Chair designed by Hans Wegner, manufactured from 1970. Frame: slatted ash, lacquer finish with bentwood frame and solid ash legs, oil finish. Seat: woven cord. 30″ w, 29″ d, 41″ h.

60-109 Stool designed by Hans Wegner, manufactured in 1970. Frame: solid wood, available in a variety of finishes. Seat: woven cord or cane. 26″ w, 15″ d, 17″ h.

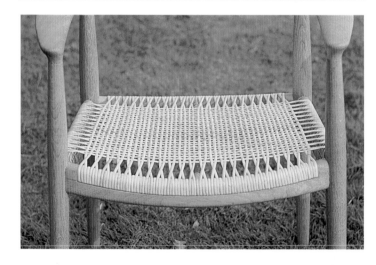

60-115 Small Arm Chair designed by Hans Wegner, manufactured in 1970. Frame: solid wood, available in a variety of finishes. Upholstery: foam rubber over plywood. 23-1/4" w, 22-1/4" d, 33-1/2" h.

60-121 Armless Side Chair designed by Hans Wegner, manufactured in 1970. Frame: solid wood, available in a variety of finishes. Upholstery: foam rubber over plywood. 21" w, 22" d, 32-1/2" h.

60-125 Arm Chair designed by Hans Wegner, manufactured in 1970. Frame: solid wood, available in a variety of finishes. Upholstery: foam rubber over plywood. 26-1/4" w, 23" d, 35-1/2" h.

60-135 Lounge Chair designed by Hans Wegner, manufactured in 1970. Frame: solid wood, available in a variety of finishes. Upholstery: foam rubber over plywood. 27-1/2" w, 27-1/2" d, 33-1/4" h.

60-145 Arm Chair designed by Hans Wegner, manufactured in 1970. Frame: solid wood, available in a variety of finishes. Upholstery: foam rubber over plywood. 24" w, 22-1/2" d, 31-1/2" h.

60-155 Arm Chair designed by Hans Wegner c. 1960, manufactured 1970 -1978. Frame: solid wood, available in a variety of finishes. Upholstery: woven cane. 24-1/2" w, 20-1/2" d, 30" h.

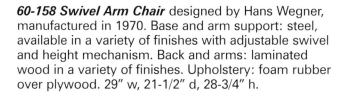

60-158 Swivel Arm Chair designed by Hans Wegner, manufactured in 1970. Base and arm support: steel, available in a variety of finishes with adjustable swivel and height mechanism. Back and arms: laminated wood in a variety of finishes. Upholstery: foam rubber over plywood. 29" w, 21-1/2" d, 28-3/4" h.

60-171 Side Chair designed by Hans Wegner, manufactured in 1970. Frame: solid wood, available in a variety of finishes. Upholstery: woven cane or upholstery. 23" w, 17-3/4" d, 29" h.

60-175 Side chair designed by Hans Wegner, manufactured in 1970. Frame: solid wood, available in a variety of finishes. Upholstery: foam rubber over plywood. 28-1/2" w, 17-1/2" d, 28-3/4" h.

60-185 Stacking Side Chair designed by Hans Wegner, manufactured in 1970. Frame: tubular steel, available in a variety of finishes. Back: solid wood with rosewood detail; in a variety of finishes. Upholstery: foam rubber over plywood. 24-3/4" w, 17-1/2" d, 26-3/4" h.

60-191 Valet Chair designed by Hans Wegner, manufactured in 1970. Frame: solid wood, available in a variety of finishes. Seat: solid wood with brass hinge, available in a variety of finishes. 20" w, 19-1/2" d, 37" h.

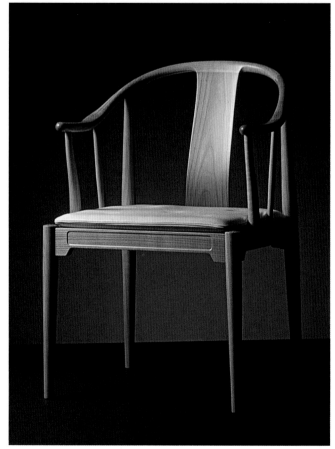

FH4283 China Arm Chair designed by Hans Wegner
for Fritz Hansen in 1944, manufactured 1999. Matte
lacquered cherry or mahogany frame with loose,
reversible seat cushion in leather and decorative
upholstery buttons. 21-1/2" w, 21-1/2" d, 32-1/4" h.

Otto Zapf

61-203 Low-back Swivel Arm Chair designed by
Otto Zapf in 1974. Base: polished stainless steel top
cap over steel armature; 4- and 5-star bases available
on glides or with swivel and tilt mechanism. Upholstery: foam covered plywood forms. Castors: Kevi
twin wheels. 31″ w, 32-1/2″ d, 35-1/2″ h.

61-204 High Back Swivel Arm Chair designed by
Otto Zapf in 1974. Base: polished stainless steel top
cap over steel armature; 4- and 5-star bases available. Upholstery: foam covered plywood forms.
Castors: Kevi twin wheels. 30″ w, 28-1/8″ d, 41″ to
45″ h.

61-205 Low Back Arm Chair. Same as 61-203, but without swivel or tilt, on glides, and with steel frame. 31″ w, 32-1/2″ d, 32-1/2″ h.

61-206 Low Back Swivel Arm Chair. Same as 61-205, but with swivel mechanism, 32-1/2″ to 35-1/4″ h.

61-208 Low Back Swivel and Tilt Arm Chair. Same as 61-205, but with swivel and tilt mechanism.

61-209 Ottoman. Same as 61-205, but 29″ w, 24″ d, 19″ h.

61-215 High Back Arm Chair. Same as 61-205, but 41-1/2″ h.

61-216 High Back Swivel Arm Chair. Same as 61-206, but 41-1/2″ to 44-1/4″ h.

61-218 High Back Swivel and Tilt Arm Chair. Same as 61-208, but 41-1/2″ to 44-1/4″ h.

61-219 High Back Lounge Chair. Same as 61-215, but tilting, 39-1/2″ to 42-1/4″ h.

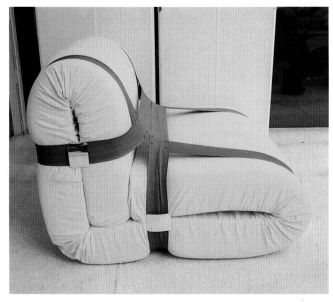

61-221 Pollorama Pollo designed by Otto Zapf in 1974, manufactured 1974. Reversible pillow of polyurethane core with polydacron fill and upholstered in leather or fabric in a variety of colors. 24-1/5" square, 12" h. The Pollorama system of seating can be used individually or in any combination.

61-222 Pollorama Pollo. Same as 61-221, but 24-1/5" square, 2" h.

61-233 Pollorama Pollo. Same as 61-221, but 24-1/5" w, 36-3/5" d, 2" h.

61-255 Pollorama Pollo. Same as 61-221, but 24-1/5" w, 59" d, 2" h.

61-266 Pollorama Pollo. Same as 61-233, but 24-1/5" w. 73-4/5" d, 2" h.

61-301 Pollorama Chair designed by Otto Zapf in 1974, manufactured 1974. Separate foam cushions upholstered in fabrics and secured by leather or canvas straps, 2-1/2" wide, in various colors. 24-1/5" w, 36-3/5" d, 24" h.

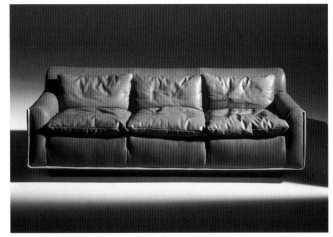

61-302 Pollorama Chair. Same as 61-301, but 36-3/5" square.

61-303 Pollorama Sofa. Same as 61-301, but 73-4/5" w, 36-3/5" d.

61-304 Pollorama Corner Unit, Right. Same as 61-301, but including back pillow on the right, 36-3/5" square.

61-305 Pollorama Corner Unit, Left. Same as 61-301, but including back pillow on the left, 36-3/5" square.

61-306 Pollorama Chaise Lounge. Same as 61-301, but 73-4/5" w, 36-3/5" d.

61-321 Pollorama Pollo. Same as 61-221, but 36-3/5" w.

61-331 Pollorama Pollo. Same as 61-221, but 36-3/5" square.

61-333 Pollorama Pollo. Same as 61-233, but 36-3/5" square, 2" h.

61-355 Pollorama Pillo, designed by Otto Zapf in 1974, manufactured 1974. Reversible pillow of polyurethane core with polydacron fill and upholstered either in the same cover both sides or in combinations, in leather or fabric in a variety of colors. 36-3/5" w, 59" d, 2" h. Can be used with a round bolster, 19-3/5" w (R-2) or 32-3/5" (R-3) w, 7-4/5" diameter.

61-361 Pollorama Pollo. Same as 61-221, but 36-3/5" w, 73-4/5" d.

61-366 Pollorama Pillo. Same as 61-255, but 36-3/5" w, 73-4/5" d, 2" h.

63S1 Heli Lounge Chair designed by Otto Zapf in 1983, manufactured 1985 to 1990. Steel frame with springs. Arm, seat, and back: cushions of Dacron, polyurethane, or down in leather or fabric upholstery. 1984 Design Center Stuttgart Award, West Germany. 36" w, 33" d, 29" h.

63S2 Heli Two-seat Sofa. Same as 63S1, but 60" w.

63S3 Heli Three-seat Sofa. Same as 63S1, but 82" w.

Opposite: Heli Lounge Chairs designed by Otto Zapf.

BEDS

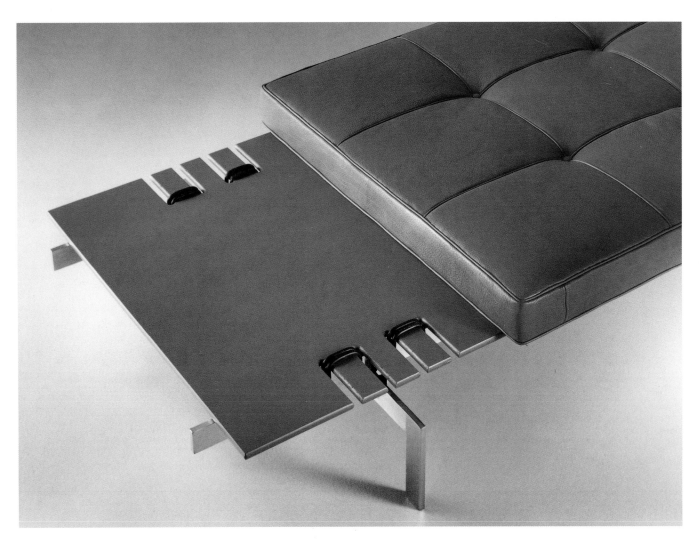

Poul Kjaerholm

FHPK80 Day Bed designed by Poul Kjaerholm for Fritz Hansen in 1957, manufactured 2000. Matte polished stainless steel legs supporting a painted plywood panel for a loose leather-covered mattress. 74-3/4" w, 31-1/2" d, 11-3/4" h.

Florence Knoll

332 T-angle Bed and/or Bench designed by Florence Knoll c. 1957.

701 Convertible Sofa Bed designed by Florence Knoll with Charles Niedringhaus c. 1950. 83-1/2" w, 30" to 37" d, 31" h.

703 Convertible Sofa Bed designed by Florence Knoll c. 1950.

708 Bed designed by Florence Knoll c. 1954. Wooden headboard and platform on four tubular metal legs. 76" w, 35" d, 28" h.

722 Double Bed designed by Florence Knoll c. 1961.

739 Single Bed designed by Florence Knoll c. 1960.

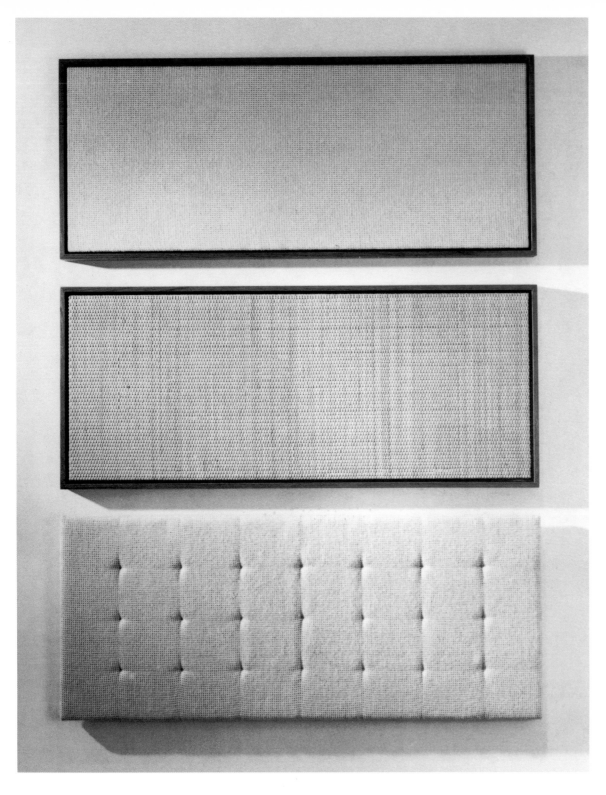

740 Headboard series designed by Florence Knoll c. 1960.

755 Headboard series designed by Florence Knoll c. 1960.

781 Headboard series designed by Florence Knoll c. 1960.

2530 Bed designed by Florence Knoll c. 1957.

Andrew Ivar Morrison and Bruce Hannah

2083 Couch or Daybed designed by Andrew Ivar Morrison and Bruce Hannah. Same as chair 2081, manufactured 1972-1974, 84″ w.

2093 Bed. Same as chair 2081, but 84″ w, 78″ d

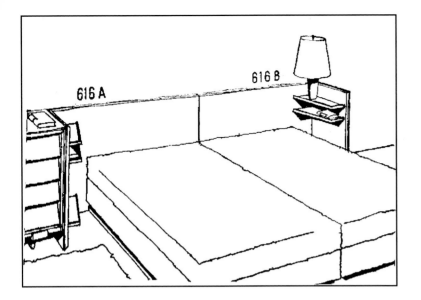

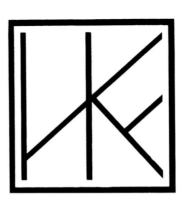

Jens Risom

616A Headboard designed by Jens Risom c. 1942, cherry wood, shelving on left side, 48" w, 16" d, 32-1/2" h. *Photo: From the 1942 Premier Knoll catalog. Design: Jens Risom, independent designer, 1941-1946.*

616B Headboard designed by Jens Risom c. 1942, cherry wood, shelving on right side, 48" w, 16" d, 32-1/2" h. *Photo: From the 1942 Premier Knoll catalog. Design: Jens Risom, independent designer, 1941-1946.*

617 Studio Couch with cabinet designed by Jens Risom c. 1942, cherry wood, with space for bed clothes and attached upholstered back panel, open as bed 39" d, closed as couch 24" d. *Photo: From the 1942 Premier Knoll catalog. Design: Jens Risom, independent designer, 1941-1946.*

Richard Schultz

704 Convertible Sofa Bed with Arms designed by
Richard Schultz c. 1957.

721 Single Bed designed by Richard Schultz c. 1957, or/with Florence Knoll c. 1961, with caned headboard. Bed: 77" long, 38" w, 15-1/2" h; headboard: 29-5/16" h.

Richard Stein

700 Convertible Sofa Bed designed by Richard Stein. Product Design Associates c. 1948, with tufted upholstered back cushion and cushion seat, base of wood frame and four legs. 76" w, 34" d, 27" h. *Photo courtesy SOLLO:RAGO Modern Auctions, Lambertville, NJ.*

TABLES

Sergio Asti

89-370 Park Avenue Table designed by Sergio Asti
in 1973. Base: aluminum laminate with chrome
finish. Top: Black or white plastic laminate, 55" w,
55" d, 28" h.

89-371 Park Avenue Table. Same as 89-370, but 110"
deep.

Gae Aulenti

54-120 Coffee Table designed by Gae Aulenti in 1975. Frame: extruded aluminum, fused finish. Top: rounded on two sides, 44" w, 44" d, 12-3/4" h. Available in a variety of finishes.

54-121 Coffee Table. Same as 54-120, but 33-3/4" w, 33-3/4" d, 12-3/4" h.

54-123 Coffee Table. Same as 54-120, but 63-3/4" w, 33-3/4" d, 12-3/4" h.

54-124 Coffee Table. Same as 54-120, but 82-3/4" w, 57-1/8" d, 12-3/4" h.

54-125 Dining Table. Same as 54-120, but 33-3/4" w, 33-3/4" d, 28-3/4" h.

54-127 Dining Table. Same as 54-125, but 62-3/4" w.

54-128 Dining Table. Same as 54-125, but 82-3/4" w.

54-129 Dining Table. Same as 54-125, but 44" w and 44" d.

56T Jumbo Coffee Table designed by Gae Aulenti in 1965. Base and top: white, black, or red marble columns and slab. 44-1/2" square, 15" h.

56-500 Coffee Table designed by Gae Aulenti in 1973. Base and top: marble with polished finish. 44-3/4" w, 44-3/4" d, 14-1/2" h.

Enrico Baleri

38TR140 Mega Round Table designed by Enrico Baleri in 1982, manufactured 1986. Base: Beta granite from Sardinia triangular legs in rough finish. Top: Beta granite with polished surface and natural border and beveled edge. 55-1/4" diameter, 28-3/4" h. Mega tables won the Design Center Stuttgart Award in West Germany in 1983.

38TR150 Mega Square Table. Same as 38TR140, but 59" square.

38TR200 Mega Rectangular Table. Same as 38TR140, but 100" w, 78" d.

38TR300 Mega Rectangular Table. Same as 38TR140, but 110" w, 118" d.

Hans Bellman

103 Small Tripod Side Table, designed by Hans Bellman in 1950, manufactured 1953-1960. Birch or maple round top on folding and breakdown legs. Also available with white or walnut-finish plastic top. 24" diameter, 20" h.

114 Large Tripod Table, designed by Hans Bellman in 1950, manufactured 1953-1960. Birch or maple round top on folding, breakdown legs. Also available with white or walnut-finish plastic top. 36" diameter, 22" h.

301 Extension Table designed by Hans Bellman c. 1956 with rectangular wooden top on four tapering wooden legs. 60" to 78" w, 34" d, 28-1/2" h.

302 Dining Table designed by Hans Bellman ca. 1950. Round wooden top on three raking, v-shaped, wooden legs. 48" diameter, 28" h.

Cini Boeri

52-099 Two-section End Table designed by Cini Boeri in 1973, manufactured from 1973. Telescoping unit of polystyrene in a variety of colors. 30-1/2" to 59" w, 36" d, 21-1/4" h.

52-100 Three-section End Table. Same as 52-099, but 39-1/3" to 113-1/3" w.

52-200 Oval Lunario Table designed by Cini Boeri in 1973. Base: steel, polished chrome finish. Top: 1/2" tempered glass or plastic laminate, 59" w, 44" d, 11" h.

52-201 Oval Lunario Table. Same as 52-200, but 15-3/4" h.

52-202 Oval Lunario Table. Same as 52-200, but with inset chromed steel cap in top, 27-1/2" h.

52-210 Round Lunario Table designed by Cini Boeri in 1970, manufactured 1973-1982. Polished chromed steel base with concealed counter weights and 1/2-inch tempered glass top, 59" diameter, 11" h.

52-211 Round Lunario Table. Same as 52-210, but 15-3/4" h.

52-212 Round Lunario Table. Same as 52-210, but 27-1/2" h.

189

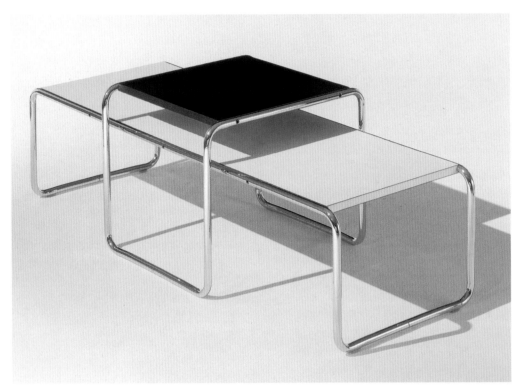

Marcel Breuer

50-310 Laccio Side Table designed by Marcel Breuer in 1925. Base: tubular steel, polished chrome finish. Top: plastic laminate. 21-5/8" w, 18-7/8" d, 17-3/4" h.

50-315 Laccio Side Table. Same as 50-310, but 53-1/2" w, 13-3/8" h.

Lewis Butler

352 Conference Table designed by Lewis Butler about 1950, manufactured 1957-1970. Walnut plywood top with laminated maple stretcher and walnut legs. 54" diameter, 25-1/2" h.

353 Dining Table. Same as 352, but 28" h.

355 End Table designed by Lewis Butler in 1950, manufactured 1957-1970. Walnut plywood top and walnut straight legs. 30" square, 19" h.

356 End Table. Similar to 355, but with optional plastic laminate top and walnut base. 27" square.

358 Rectangular Coffee Table designed by Lewis
Butler in 1950, manufactured 1957-1970. Walnut base
available in a variety of finishes, and plastic top of
two white and two black sections. 38-1/8″ w, 34-1/8″
d, 16″ h.

359 Coffee Table designed by Lewis Butler in 1950.
Base: solid walnut, available in a variety of finishes.
Top: white plastic, available in a variety of materials.
54″ w, 24″ d, 16″ h.

360 Plank Coffee Table designed by Lewis Butler in 1950. Two wood planks resting on turned wooden legs with bracing. 60" w, 20-1/4" d, 16" h.

361 End Table. Same as 359, but 26-1/2" square, 17" h.

1590 Round Conference Table designed by Lewis Butler in 1961. Base: steel, brushed chrome finish, other finishes available; also available with wood base in a variety of finishes. Top: walnut, available in a variety of finishes, or white plastic laminate, or white Italian marble with grey vein. 54" diameter, 28-1/2" h.

1591 Round Conference Table. Same as 1590, but 25-1/5" h.

1592 Round Conference Table. Same as 1590, but walnut top only, 72" diameter.

1593 Round Conference Table. Same as 1590, but walnut top only, 96" diameter.

3590 Round Conference Table designed by Lewis Butler about 1950. Top: walnut veneer with beveled edge, or white plastic laminate with lacquered edge, or white Italian marble with gray vein. Base: walnut legs with stretchers. 54" diameter, 28-1/2" h.

3591 Round Conference Table. Same as 3590, but 25-1/2" h.

3592 Round Conference Table. Same as 3590, but 72" diameter.

3593 Round Conference Table. Same as 3590, but top in 2 sections, 96" diameter.

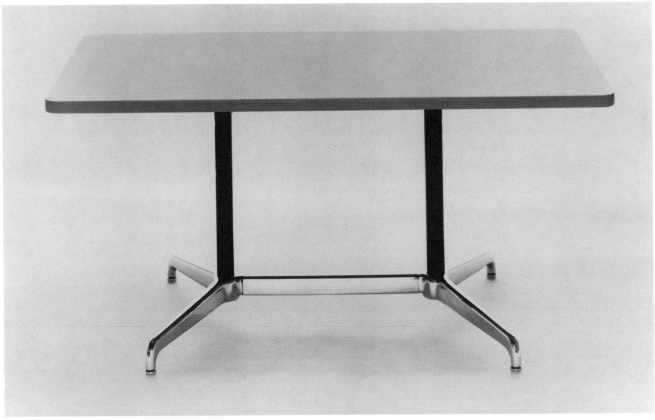

Andreas Christen

3610 Square Table designed by Andreas Christen in 1972. Top: plastic laminate with matching edge. Posts: steel, black finish. Base: cast aluminum, bright burnished finish. Glides: metal and nylon, adjustable. Available with 30", 36", and 42" square tops, and in 15-1/2", 25-1/2", and 28-1/2" heights.

3617 Square Table. Same as 3610, but 46" square, 25-1/2" h.

3620 Round Table. Same as 3610, but in 36" and 42" diameters, and 15-1/2", 25-1/2", and 28-1/2" heights.

3622 Round Table. Same as 3620, but 48" diameter.

Achille and Piero Castiglioni

51-319 Milano Table designed by Achille and Pier Giacomo Castiglioni. Base: solid wood. Top: wood veneer over solid wood core, 78-3/4" w, 34-1/4" d, 29-1/8" h. Available in a variety of finishes.

194

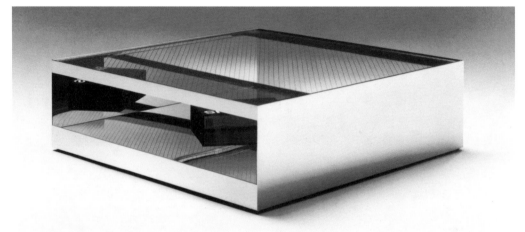

Robert De Fuccio

3951 Table designed by Robert DeFuccio in 1972. Base: curved laminated wood. Top: solid wood with hardwood edge. 30″ w, 30″ d, 19″ h.

3952 Table. Same as 3951, but 60″ w, 24″ d.

3954 Table. Same as 3951, but 66″ w, 36″ d, 28-1/4″ h.

3955 Table. Same as 3951, but 76″ w, 36″ d, 28-1/4″ h.

3957 Extension Table. Same as 3951, but with two 19″ leaves, 76″ to 114″ w, 40″ d, 28-1/2″ h.

3962 Table designed by Robert DeFuccio in 1972. Base: turned solid hardwood. Top: wood with matching hardwood edge. 40″ w, 40″ d, 16-1/2″ h.

3966 Table. Same as 3962, but 28-1/2″ h.

4200 Table. Same as 3966, but 66″ w.

4210 Table with pencil drawer on left. Same as 4200, but with pencil drawer.

4211 Table with pencil drawer on right. Same as 4210, but drawer on right.

4206 Table. Same as 4200, but 76″ w.

4216 Table with pencil drawer on left. Same as 4210, but 76″ w.

4217 Table with pencil drawer on right. Same as 4211, but 76″ w.

Joseph Paul D'Urso

6022 Low Rolling Table designed by Joseph Paul D'Urso, in 1980. Welded polished stainless steel with concealed castors, one-inch grid wire-reinforced tempered glass top. 22″ square, 14-1/2″ h.

6027 Low Rolling Table. Same as 6022, but 27″ square, 16-1/2″ h.

6048 Low Rolling Table. Same as 6022, but 48″ square, 14-1/2″ h.

6242 Round Table designed by Joseph Paul D'Urso in 1981, manufactured 1982. Base: polished chrome or metal in a variety of colors, on castors or glides. Top: laminate or veneer in a variety of colors, Italian cremo marble, or black granite. 42" diameter, 27-1/2" h. *Photo courtesy SOLLO:RAGO Modern Auctions, Lambertville, NJ*

6248 Round Table. Same as 6242, but 48" diameter.

6254 Round Table. Same as 6242, but 54" diameter.

6260 Round Table. Same as 6242, but 60" diameter.

6272 Round Table. Same as 6242, but 72" diameter.

6348 Square Table designed by Joseph Paul D'Urso in 1980, manufactured 1982. Received the 1983 Design Center Stuttgart Award in West Germany, and the 1983 Federal Award for Industrial Design in West Germany. Base: polished chrome or metal in a variety of colors, on castors or glides. Top: laminate or veneer in a variety of colors, Italian cremo marble, or black granite. 48" square, 27-1/2" h.

6354 Square Table. Same as 6348, but 54" square.

6360 Square Table. Same as 6348, but 60" square.

6472 Racetrack Table. Designed by Joseph Paul D'Urso in 1981, manufactured 1982. Base: polished chrome or metal in a variety of colors, on castors or glides. Oval top: laminate or veneer in a variety of colors, Italian cremo marble, or black granite. 72" w, 36" d, 27-1/2" h.

6484 Racetrack Table. Same as 6472, but 84" w, 42" d.

6496 Racetrack Table. Same as 6472, but 96" w, 48" d.

197

Jim Eldon

3411 Square Coffee Table designed by Jim Eldon in 1972. Base: solid wood in a variety of finishes. Top: vinyl fabric, leather, or marble. 30" w, 30" d, 15-1/2" h.

3412 Square End Table. Same as 3411, but 20-1/2" h.

3413 Rectangular Coffee Table. Same as 3411, but 54" w, 26" d.

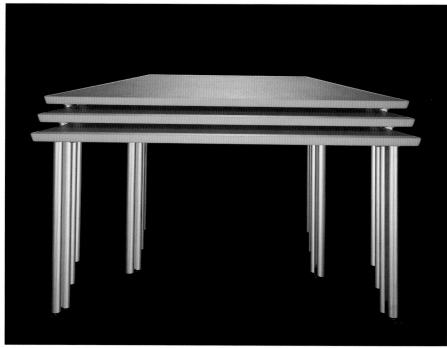

Neil Frankel

S20T20 Frankel Side Table designed by Neil Frankel in 1999. Laminated round top with black urethane edge on two 1" diameter powder-coated steel tube legs and one castor.

S20T30 Frankel Coffee Table designed by Neil Frankel in 1999. Laminated round top with black urethane edge on four 1" diameter powder-coated steel tubing legs. 29-1/2" diameter, 16" h.

S30T20 Frankel Round Side Table designed by Neil Frankel in 1999, manufactured 2000. Legs (3): 1" diameter steel tubing with powder coated finish, two with 5" black rubber wheels that do not swivel and one with a plastic glide. Shelf: stainless steel. Top: laminate with black urethane edge and cast aluminum pull with powder coated finish. 19-1/2" diameter, 20-1/2" h.

S30T30-G Frankel Round Coffee Table. Same as S30T20, but 29-1/2" diameter, 16" h.

Emanuela Frattini

P2 Training Table designed by Emanuela Frattini in 1994, manufactured 1995. Legs: aluminum with clear satin anodized or powder-coat finish. Top: Plastic laminate on 1-1/4" thick, 5-ply, hollow-core with honeycomb interior, within particleboard frame. Tables: 28-1/2" h.

Top shapes available:
trapezoid, 30" to 60" w, 26" d.
trapezoid, 36" to 72" w, 31" d.
pie-segment, 30 degrees, 30" d.
pie-segment, 30 degrees, 36" d.
rectangular, 48" to 72" w, 24" to 36" d.
bullet end, 72" w, 30" d.
bullet end, 72" w, 36" d.
folding, 60" to 72" w, 24" to 36" d.
3-leg semi-circular, 48", 60", and 72" w by 24", 30", and 36" d.
square, 36", 42", and 48" square
standing height, 48" to 72" w, 24" to 36" d, 38" h.

P2-F Propeller® Rectangular Folding Training Table, Same as P2, but with wood grain laminate top and 4 legs folding inward. 60", 66", or 72" w; 24", 30", or 36" d; 28-1/2" h.

P2-H Propeller® Standing Height Table, Same as P2, but 48", 60", or 72" w; 24", 30", or 36" d; 38" h.

P3 Conference Table Series designed by Emanuela Frattini in 1994 and thereafter, manufactured 1995 and variations until 2005. Legs: standard aluminum C-shape, T-shape, or S-shape, also drum and peanut-shaped, with clear satin anodized or powder-coat finish. Some tables have wood legs available. Top: plastic laminate on 1-1/4" thick, 5-ply, hollow-core with honeycomb interior, within particleboard frame. 28-1/2" h.

Top shapes available:
round, 42" to 60" diameter.
rounded square, 42" to 60" square.
rounded rectangle, 60" to 96" w, 42" to 60" d.
rounded rectangle in 2, 3, or 4 segments, 108" to
324" w, 42" to 60" d.
bullet shape, 54" to 96" w, 42" to 60" d.
square, 42" to 60" square.

P4 TR Rolling Cart designed by Emanuela Frattini in
1994, manufactured 1995. Legs: aluminum with clear
satin anodized or powder-coat finish. Top: Plastic
laminate on 1-1/4" thick, 5-ply, hollow-core with
honeycomb interior, within particleboard frame. 36"
or 44" w, 30" or 24" d, 27" or 28-1/2" h.

P6-C Propeller® Rectangular Flip-top Training Table
designed by Emanuela Frattini in 2002, manufactured
2004. Base: two C-legs or two T-legs of anodized
aluminum joined by a crossing bar at their tops and
flip mechanism. Top: wood veneer in a variety of
finishes. 48", 60", or 72" w; 18", 24", 30", or 36" d;
28-1/2" h.

P6-X Propeller Square Flip-top Training Table. Same
as P6-C, but square top, 30", or 36", or 42" w, on a 4-
star extruded aluminum base.

P6-Y Propeller Round Flip-top Training Table. Same
as P6-X, but 36" or 42" diameter round top.

Gianfranco Frattini

Kyoto Table and Etagers designed by Gianfranco
Frattini. Hand crafted from wooden crossmembers,
creating a concise geometric latticework pattern.

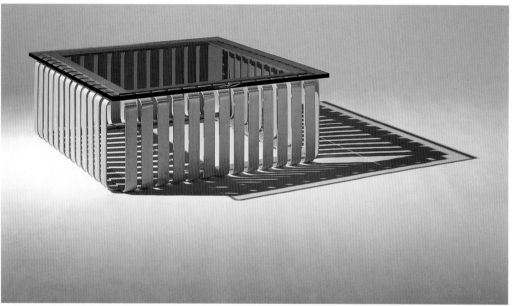

Frank Gehry

95T-36 Face Off Café Table designed by Frank Gehry in 1992, manufactured 1993. White maple veneer strips, 2″ wide by 1/24″ thick, laminated to 8-ply thickness and solid maple center column with arched supports. Top: 1/2″ thick tempered glass or 5/8″ thick textured laminate with 2-piece clear veneer edge band. 36″ diameter, 28-3/4″ h.

95T-40 Face Off Café Table. Same as 95T-36, but 40″ diameter

96T-G2 Icing Coffee Table. Designed by Frank Gehry in 1992, manufactured 1993. White maple veneer strips, 2″ wide by 1/32″ thick, laminated to 8-ply thickness. 40″ square, 14-7/8″ h.

Alexander Girard

107 Sofa Table designed by Alexander Girard c. 1948, manufactured c. 1948. Base: black metal legs. Top: birch wood in natural finish. 59" w, 17" d, 16" h.

Charles Gwathmey

GT101 Oval Table designed by Charles Gwathmey, manufactured in 1983. Tops and bases are always the same finish. Base: hardwood legs and stretchers veneered. Top: Veneers, 2" thick. 101" w, 39" d, 28" h.

GT399 Square Table. Same as GT101, but 39" square.

GT629 Rectangular Table. Same as GT101, but 62" w.

GT749 Table. Same as GT101, but 74" w.

Paul Haigh

6521 Coffee Table designed by Paul Haigh in 1978, manufactured 1982. Frame and legs: black or gray anodized aluminum. Top: textured laminate or gray glass. 82" w, 47" d, 15-3/4" h.

6522 Coffee Table. Same as 6521, but 47" w.

6525 Coffee Table. Same as 6521, but 59" w.

6528 Coffee Table. Same as 6521, but 71" w.

6551 Coffee Table designed by Paul Haigh in 1978, manufactured 1982. Frame and legs: black or gray anodized aluminum. Top: textured laminate or gray glass. 82" w, 59" d, 15-3/4" h.

6555 Table. Same as 6551, but 59" w.

6558 Table. Same as 6551, but 71" w.

6591 Coffee Table designed by Paul Haigh in 1978, manufactured 1982. Frame and legs: black or gray anodized aluminum. Top: textured laminate or gray glass. 82" w, 36" d, 15-3/4" h.

6592 Coffee Table. Same as 6591, but 47" w.

6595 Coffee Table. Same as 6591, but 59" w.

6598 Coffee Table. Same as 6591, but 71" w.

6621 Table designed by Paul Haigh in 1978, manufactured 1982. Frame and legs: black or gray anodized aluminum. Top: textured laminate or gray glass. 82" w, 47" d, 28-1/2" h.

6622 Table. Same as 6621, but 47" w.

6625 Table. Same as 6621, but 59" w.

6628 Table. Same as 6621, but 71" w.

6651 Table designed by Paul Haigh in 1978, manufactured 1982. Frame and legs: black or gray anodized aluminum. Top: textured laminate or gray glass. 82" w, 59" d, 28-1/2" h.

6655 Table. Same as 6651, but 59" w.

6658 Table. Same as 6651, but 71" w.

6691 Table designed by Paul Haigh in 1978, manufactured 1982. Frame and legs: black or gray anodized aluminum. Top: textured laminate or gray glass. 82" w, 36" d, 28-1/2" h.

6692 Table. Same as 6691, but 47" w.

6695 Table. Same as 6691, but 59" w.

6698 Table. Same as 6691, but 71" w.

6699 Table. Same as 6691, but 36" w.

Piet Hein and Bruno Mathsson

FHB40x Hein Super-circular Table designed by Piet Hein and Bruno Mathsson for the Fritz Hansen Collection in 1968, manufactured 2000. Legs (4): steel with mirror or satin chrome finish. Top to fit 4 to 8 chairs: 7/8" chip board with laminate or wood veneer and beveled edge. Optional higher span leg increases table height by 1". 39-1/2" or 45-1/4" or 57" w, 27-1/2" h.

FHB41x Hein Super-ellipse Table. Same as FHB40x, but top to fit 4 to 16 people. Largest top has 8 legs. 53-1/4 to 165-1/2" w, 35-1/2" to 55" d.

FHB41x Hein Extension Table. Same as FHB40x, but top extends to fit 6 to 12 chairs. Two models: 59" to 98-1/2" w, 39-1/4" d. or 71" to 118" w, 47-1/4" d.

FHB42x Piet Hein Round Table. Same as FHB40x, but round, 47-1/4" or 57" diameter.

FHB43x Piet Hein Square Table. Same as FHB40x, but square, 31-1/2" w or 55" w.

FHB43/4x Piet Hein Rectangular Table. Same as FHB40x, but 47-1/4" to 71" w, 23-1/2" to 31-1/2" d.

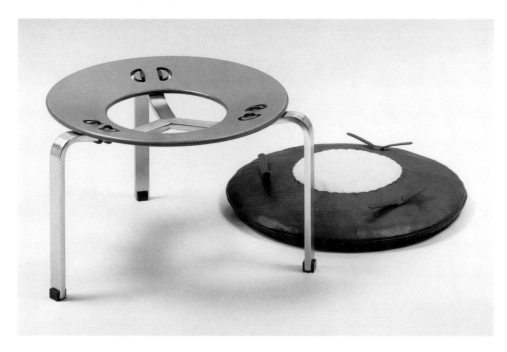

Poul Kjaerholm

FHPK33 Stool designed by Poul Kjaerholm in 1959 for Fritz Hansen, manufactured 1999. Frame: matte polished stainless steel. Round seat with leather seat cushion. 21" diameter, 13-1/2" h.

FHPK61 Coffee Table designed by Poul Kjaerholm in 1955 for Fritz Hansen, manufactured 2000. Frame: matte polished stainless steel. Top rests off center on the base: 3/4" thick clear glass, white marble, or honed slate, 31-1/2" square, 12-1/2" h.

FHPK62 Low Table. Designed by Poul Kjaerholm in 1955 for Fritz Hansen, manufactured 2000. Frame: matte polished stainless steel. Top rests with the legs at the corners: 3/4" thick clear glass, white marble, or honed slate. 31-1/2" w, 10-1/2" d, 6-3/4" h.

FHPK63 Low Table. Same as FHPK62, but 71" w, 23-1/2" d, 12-1/4" h.

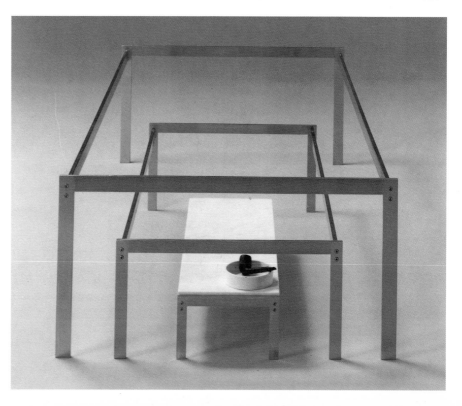

207

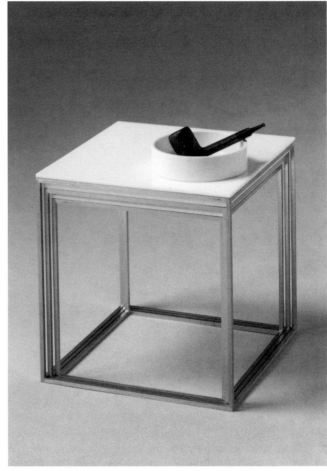

FHPK65 Coffee Table designed by Poul Kjaerholm in 1979 for Fritz Hansen, manufactured 2000. Same as FHPK61, but the top rests with the legs at the center of each side. 39-1/4" square, 15" h.

FHPK71 Nesting Set of 3 Cube Tables designed by Poul Kjaerholm in 1957 for Fritz Hansen, manufactured 2000. Base: matte polished stainless steel. Top: black or white solid acrylic. 10-1/2" to 11-1/2" square and h.

Florence Knoll

T-1 Boat-shaped Table designed by Florence Knoll
c. 1954. Bulging rectangular top on four raking wooden legs. 96" w, 40" d, 28-1/2" h.

106 Stacking Table designed by Florence Knoll
c. 1948, square top: birch wood edge around Formica, in a variety of colors, base: four tapering wooden legs. 32" square, 29" h.

108 Card or Dining Table designed by Florence Knoll in 1963. Manufactured 1964. Top: white, black, or walnut plastic laminate. Base: cast iron pedestal with fused plastic finish in white or beige, four feet. 36" square, 29" h.

109 Pedestal Table designed by Florence Knoll ca. 1948, square top: Formica in a choice of colors, base: iron tube pedestal with cast iron feet in baked-on gray enamel with crackle finish, 32" square, 29" h.

300 T-angle Conference or Dining Table designed by Florence Knoll c. 1951.

303 Extension Dining Table designed by Florence Knoll in 1967. Base and top: walnut, available in a variety of finishes. Single 28" leaf stores under the top. 56" to 84" w, 38" d, 28" h.

304 End Table designed by Florence Knoll c. 1952, manufactured 1953-1967. Top: White plastic laminate or solid redwood slats. Base: T-angle steel, black or white epoxy finish. 24" square, 16" h.

305 Corner Table designed by Florence Knoll c. 1952, manufactured 1953-1967. Top: Black or white plastic laminate or solid redwood slats. Base: T-angle steel, black or white epoxy finish. 30" square, 19" h.

306 Coffee Table designed by Florence Knoll c. 1952, manufactured 1953-1967. Top: black or white plastic laminate. Base: T-angle steel, black or white epoxy finish. 23" w, 45" d, 16" h.

307 Coffee Table designed by Florence Knoll c. 1952, manufactured 1953-1967. Top: black or white plastic laminate or solid redwood slats. Base: black or white epoxy finish. 23" w, 45" d, 16" h.

308 End Table designed by Florence Knoll c. 1952, manufactured 1953-1967 Top: black or while plastic laminate or solid redwood slats. Base: T-angle steel, black or white epoxy finish. 30" square, 16" h.

309 Card Table designed by Florence Knoll c. 1952, manufactured 1953-1967. Top: black or white plastic laminate or solid redwood slats. Base: T-angle steel, black or white epoxy finish. 34" square, 26-1/2" h.

310 Extension Table designed by Florence Knoll ca. 1950, manufactured 1955 to 1965. Top: white plastic laminate. Base: T-angle steel with black epoxy finish. Extends from 34-1/2" to 48" w, 34" d, 28" h.

404 Round Parallel Bar System Coffee Table designed by Florence Knoll in 1955, manufactured 1955-1965. Parallel bar steel base in brushed chrome and black. Round top in teak or walnut, available in a variety of finishes. 42" diameter, 15" h.

405 Rectangular Parallel Bar System Coffee Table designed by Florence Knoll in 1954. Crossed steel bar base of brushed chrome. Polished 7/16"-thick plate glass top. 42" w, 24" d, 16-1/2" h.

560 Coffee Table designed c. 1954. Square wooden top on four straight wooden legs joined by an h-shaped stretcher. 30" square, 19" h.

561 Coffee Table designed c. 1954. Rectangular wooden top on four straight wooden legs joined by an h-shaped stretcher. 42" w, 24" d, 16" h.

562 Coffee table designed c. 1954. Round top on three straight wooden legs joined by a triangular stretcher. 24" diameter, 19" h.

580 Boat-shaped Conference Table designed by Florence Knoll c. 1957. Top: natural or walnut finished wood, cherry, teak, and other woods by special order. 40" w tapering to 30" w at the ends, 8' long, 28-1/2" h. Also available as 9' 9" long, 12' 6" long, 15' 3" long, 18' long, 20' 9" long, 23' 6" long, and 26' 3" long.

1570 Rectangular Conference Table designed by Florence Knoll before 1964. Base: steel with brushed chrome finish, other finishes available. Top: walnut or plastic available in a variety of finishes. 76" w, 36" d, 28-1/2" h.

1571 Rectangular Conference Table. Same as 1570, but 96" w, 48" d.

1580 Boat-shaped Conference Table designed by Florence Knoll about 1957. Top: walnut veneer or walnut plastic laminate. Base: steel with brushed chrome or black finish. 8' long, center 40" tapers to 30" ends d, 28-1/2" h.

1581 Boat-shaped Conference Table. Same as 1580, but 9'9" long, 45" to 38" d.

1583 Boat-shaped Conference Table. Same as 1580, but 9'9" long, 45" to 32" d.

1584 Boat-shaped Conference Table. Same as 1580, but 18'0" long, 67" to 45" d.

1585 Boat-shaped Conference Table. Same as 1580, but 20'9" long, 73" to 48" d.

1586 Boat-shaped Conference Table. Same as 1580, but 23'6" long, 78" to 50" d.

1587 Boat-shaped Conference Table. Same as 1580, but 26'3" w, 82" to 53" d.

2480 Oval Table/Desk designed by Florence Knoll in 1961. Base: steel, polished chrome finish. Top: available in a choice of materials and finishes with beveled edge. Glides: nylon. 78" w, 48" d, 28" h.

2481 Oval Table/Desk. Same as 2480, but 96" w, 54" d.

2482 Round Table/Desk. Same as 2480, but 54" d.

2485 Executive Table/Desk designed by Florence Knoll. Same as 2480, but top: rectangular, wood veneer in a choice of finishes; 4 drawers with removable partitions, 1 pencil tray, and 2 plastic laminate writing shelves. 72" w, 38" d, 28-1/2" h. This design

won the Design Center Stuttgart Award in Germany, 1969-1970.

2510 Knoll Square End Table designed by Florence Knoll in 1954. Base: steel, polished chrome finish. Top: variety of materials and finishes, 24" square, 17" h.

2511 Knoll Rectangular End Table. Same as 2510, but 45" w, 23" d.

2514 Knoll Square End Table. Same as 2510, but 27" square.

2515 Knoll Square Coffee Table. Same as 2510, but 29-1/2" square, 19" h.

2517 Knoll Square Coffee Table. Same as 2515, but 35-1/2" square.

2518 Knoll Square End Table. Same as 2510, but 36" square.

2520 Knoll Square End Table. Same as 2510, but 42" square.

2562 Knoll Side Table. Same as 2510, but round top, 24" diameter, 19" h.

2583 Conference Table designed by Florence Knoll.

3570 Rectangular Conference Table designed by Florence Knoll, Base: walnut, available in a variety of finishes. Top: walnut, available in a variety of finishes.

3580 Boat-shaped Conference Table designed by Florence Knoll. Same as 1580, but solid wood base.

3581 Boat-shaped Conference Table. Same as 1581, but solid wood base.

3582 Boat-shaped Conference Table. Same as 1582, but solid wood base.

3583 Boat-shaped Conference Table. Same as 1583, but solid wood base.

3584 Boat-shaped Conference Table. Same as 1584, but solid wood base.

3585 Boat-shaped Conference Table. Same as 1585, but solid wood base.

3586 Boat-shaped Conference Table. Same as 1586, but solid wood base.

3587 Boat-shaped Conference Table. Same as 1587, but solid wood base.

Knoll International

3804 Table. Designed by Knoll International in 1973. Base: T-angle steel in white or black epoxy finish. Top: black, white, or walnut plastic laminate or walnut veneer. 24" w, 24-1/2" d, 16" h.

3805 Table. Same as 3804, but 27" w, 27-1/2" d.

3806 Table. Same as 3804, but 30" w, 30-1/2" d.

3807 Table. Same as 3804, but 45" w, 23-1/2" d.

3808 Table. Same as 3804, but 36" w, 36-1/2" d.

3809 Table. Same as 3804, but 42" w, 42-1/2" d.

3810 Table. Same as 3804, but 36" w, 36-1/2" d.

490T Contract Table designed by Knoll International in 1986. Base: rectangular and tubular steel bars in black epoxy finish and black finish with black nylon and steel glides. Top: natural and stained Techgrain with veneer edge. Round, square, rectangular, and trapezoid top shapes. 31-1/2" w, 29-1/2" h.

Lawrence Laske

80TR-20 Saguaro Cactus® Side Table designed by Lawrence Laske in 1993, manufactured 1995. Base: 4 legs of laminated hard maple or polished aluminum. Top: 1/2" thick black Italian slate or wood with veneer, and bullnose and beveled edge. 20" diameter, 20" h.

80TR-26 Saguaro Cactus® Side Table. Same as 80TR-20, but 26" diameter.

81TR-20 Toothpick Cactus Side Table designed by Lawrence Laske in 1993, manufactured 1995. Base: a cluster of 6 maple legs that taper from 7/8" to 1/2" at bottom. Top: 1/2" thick black Italian slate or wood with veneer, and bullnose and beveled edge. 20" diameter, 20" h.

81TR-26 Toothpick Cactus Side Table. Same as 81TR-20, but with 8 legs and 26" diameter.

81TR-35 Toothpick Cactus Round Coffee Table. Same as 81TR-20, but with 10 legs and 35-3/4" w, 16" h.

81TR-42 Toothpick Cactus Oval Coffee Table. Same as 81TR-20, but with 16 legs and 42" w, 24" d, 16" h.

81TR-54 Toothpick Cactus Oval Coffee Table. Same as 81TR-20, but with 16 legs and 54" w, 27" d, 16" h.

Opposite: Cactus tables designed by Lawrence Laske

Maya Lin

87TR Round Equator® Dining Table designed by Maya Lin in 1998, manufactured 1999. Base: maple plywood tube stretched to elliptical shape and twisted 90 degrees on top. Inside base has centered steel column to hold cast iron counter weights. Top: molded maple plywood with slightly convex curve, 12 degree incline from table edge to center, with lacquer and wax coating. 48" or 54" diameter, 28-1/2" h.

87TO Oval Equator® Dining Table. Same as 87TR, but oval, either 72" w and 48" d, or 84" w and 56" d.

85T Stones® Coffee Table designed by Maya Lin in 1998, manufactured 1999. Fiberglass reinforced concrete with integral color. Weight 155 pounds. 42" w, 29-1/2" d, 11" h.

221

Vico Magistretti

54-325 Caori Coffee Table designed by Vico Magistretti for the Fritz Hansen Collection in 1969, manufactured 1988. Base: hardwood in painted finish of various colors. Top: stainless steel with recessed center compartment and lift-up panel, and two pull-out drawers. 50-1/2" w, 37-3/4" d, 15-3/4" h.

FHVM65 Vico Pedestal Table designed by Vico Magistretti for Fritz Hansen in 1994, manufactured 2000. Pedestal base: 2-1/2" diameter steel tube column with satin chrome finish mounted to round steel top plate and round foot plate of 3/4" thick porcelain, both plates 25-1/4" diameter. Top: maple or cherry veneer with beveled edge. 65" w, 45-1/4" d, 28-1/4" h.

FHVM66 Vico 2-pedestal Table. Same as FHVM65, but 88-1/2" w, 49-1/4" d.

FHVM67 Vico 2-pedestal, 2-segment Table. Same as FHVM65, but 118" w, 59" d.

FHVM69 Vico 3-pedestal, 3-segment Table. Same as FHVM65, but 177-1/4" w, 59" d.

FHVM152 Round VicoDuo Table with 3-star column base designed by Vico Magistretti for Fritz Hansen in 1997, manufactured 1999. Top: 1" thick chipboard core with veneer and plastic surface and with a shaped edge. Base: Steel tubes with satin chrome finish. 31-1/2" diameter, 28-1.4" h.

FHVM16x Round VicoDuo Table with 4-star column base. Same as FHVM152, but 41-1/4" or 51-1/4" diameter.

FHVM173 Square VicoDuo Table. Same as FHVM16x, but top 31-1/2" square.

FHVM 18x Rectangular VicoDuo Table. Same as FHVM173, but two-column shaker-base and 63" or 94-1/2" w, 31-1/2" or 39-1/4" d.

FHVM 19x Rectangular VicoDuo Table. Same as FHVM 18x, but casters on one side of the base.

Richard Meier

840 Telephone Stand designed by Richard Meier, manufactured in 1983. Laminated hard maple veneer and hard maple with mortise and tenon construction. Richard Meier's personal mark is imprinted on each piece. 18-1/4" diameter, 27-1/2" h.

860 Square Table designed by Richard Meier, manufactured in 1983. Top: laminated hard maple veneer and hard maple with mortise and tenon construction.

Top: fiberboard and hard maple veneers in natural, black, or white finishes. Richard Meier's personal mark is imprinted on each piece. 40" square, 15-1/4" h.

865 Square Table. Same as 860, but 60" square, 27-1/2" h.

866 Rectangular Table. Same as 865, but 40" w, 80" d.

867 Rectangular Table. Same as 865, but 96" d.

Lucia Mercer

701 Stump Table designed by Lucia Mercer in 1982, manufactured 1984 to present. Nero Marquina Black or Calcutta White granite with polished finish. 14-3/8" w, 13" d, 15" h.

705 Elliptical Table designed by Lucia Mercer in 1982, manufactured 1983 to present. Solid polished black granite with onyx finish flat top on granite columnar base that is 13" diameter. 62" w, 50" d, 12" h.

Ludwig Mies van der Rohe

252 Barcelona Table designed by Mies van der Rohe in 1929. Base: welded stainless steel. Top: polished plate glass 3/4" thick. 36" to 40" square, 17" h.

259 Coffee Table designed by Ludwig Mies van der Rohe in 1927, Mies Archive Replica. Base: crossing tubular stainless steel legs, polished finish. Top: smoky gray glass 1/2" thick. 28-1/2" diameter, 19-1/2" h.

759 Krefeld® Square Side Table designed by Ludwig Mies van der Rohe in 1930, manufactured 2005. Oak with stained and clear finish, seamless connection between the top and base on black plastic glides. 27-1/2" square, 17-3/4" h.

760 Krefeld® Rectangular Coffee Table Same as 759, but 54" w.

225

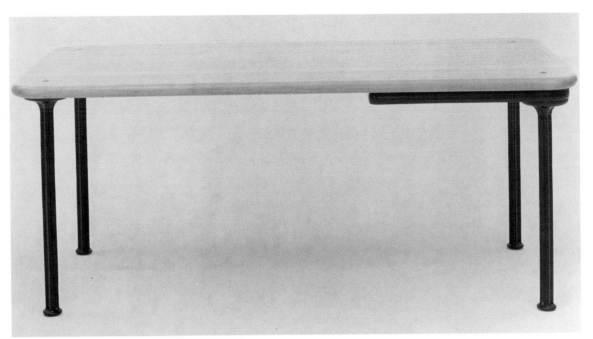

Andrew Ivar Morrison and Bruce R. Hannah

Baseball Bat Table designed by Andrew Ivar Morrison and Bruce R. Hannah. Cast aluminum base with beige powder-coat finish and butcher block wood top, 60" square, 23-1/2" d, 28 3/8" h.

3101 Square Table designed by Andrew Ivar Morrison and Bruce R. Hannah in 1972. Base: cast aluminum in a variety of finishes. Top: white plastic laminate or natural wood with a natural hardwood ply edge. 26" w, 26" d, 16" h.

3102 Table. Same as 3101, but 48" w.

3103 Table. Same as 3101, but 72" w.

3104 Round Table. Same as 3101, but 36" diameter.

3111 Square Table. Same as 3101, but with a differently shaped base.

3112 Table. Same as 3111, but 48" w.

3113 Table. Same as 3111, but 72" w.

3114 Round Table. Same as 3111, but 36" diameter.

Pascal Mourgue

47 Pascal Table System designed by Pascal Mourgue in 1985, manufactured 1987. Legs: 4 to 12 extruded aluminum sections in black epoxy finish. Top: wood or granite; in square, rectangular, round, or racetrack shapes. 48-1/2" to 108" w, 42-3/4" to 97" d, 28-3/4" h.

George Nakashima

N12 Table designed by George Nakashima c. 1944, manufactured 1952-1955. Birch wood with tapered, turned legs and solid top. 37 pounds weight, 24" or 54" w, 20" or 32" d, 28-1/2" h.

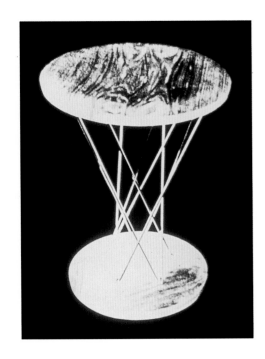

Isamu Noguchi

87 Child's Table designed by Isamu Noguchi in 1955, manufactured 1955-1974. Maple base and plastic laminated top joined by chrome plated steel wires. 23-3/4" diameter, 20" h.

311 Round Cyclone Dining Table designed by Isamu Noguchi in 1955, manufactured 1955-1974. Base:

black porcelain-finished cast iron and polished chrome steel rods. Top: white plastic. 36" diameter, 28-1/2" h.

312 Round Cyclone Dining Table. Same as 311, but 48" diameter.

Opposite: Table and chairs designed by Jorge Pensi.

228

Jorge Pensi

29TR-23 Pensi Café Table designed by Jorge Pensi in 1988, manufactured 1990. Base: 4 anodized polished cast aluminum feet and single column. Top: graphite or stainless steel finish, with etched pattern of concentric circles or disks, and edge band or wrapped edge. 23-3/5″ diameter, 28-1/4″ h.

29TR-27. Same as 29TR-23, but 27-1/2″ diameter.

29TR-H-23 Pensi Bar-height Café Table. Same as 29TR-23, but 43-1/4″ h.

29TR-35 Pensi Round Bistro Table. Same as 29TR-23, but 35-3/8″ diameter.

29TR-39 Pensi Round Bistro Table. Same as 29TR-23, but 39-3/8″ diameter.

29TR-43 Pensi Round Dining Table. Same as 29TR-23, but 43-1/4″ diameter.

29TR-47 Pensi Round Dining Table. Same as 29TR-23, but 47-1/4″ diameter.

29TS-27 Pensi Square Café Table. Same as 29TR-23, but 27-1/2″ square.

29TS-35 Pensi Square Bistro Table. Same as 29TR-23, but 35-3/8″ square.

Charles Pfister

3001 Coffee Table designed by Charles Pfister in 1977. Base: solid wood in a variety of finishes or steel with polished chrome or fused finish. Top: wood veneer in a variety of finishes. 22-1/2" w, 22-1/2" d, 15-3/4" h. Also available in other dimensions.

3002 Coffee Table. Same as 3001, but 27-1/2" w, 27-1/2" d, 15-3/4" h.

3003 Coffee Table. Same as 3001, but 39-3/8" w, 39-3/8" d, 15-3/4" h.

3004 Coffee Table. Same as 3001, but 47-1/4" w, 47-1/4" d, 15-3/4" h.

3013 Dining Table. Same as 3001, but 39-3/8" w, 39-3/8" d, 28-3/4" h.

3014 Dining Table. Same as 3001, but 47-1/2" w, 47-1/2" d, 28-3/4" h.

3015 Dining Table. Same as 3001, but 78-3/4" w, 39-3/4" d, 28-3/4" h.

3017 Dining or Conference Table. Same as 3001, but 94-1/2" w, 59" d, 28-3/4" h.

3055 Table designed by Charles Pfister in 1984, manufactured in 1988. Legs: Tubular steel in high gloss or polished chrome finish. Top: Leather on two wood sections sandwiched together with polished chrome profile. 39-3/8" w, 79" d, 28-3/4" h.

3065 Table. Same as 3055, but with pencil drawer on left. Can have pedestal or storage compartment on right side.

3066 Table. Same as 3055, but with pencil drawer on right. Can have pedestal or storage compartment on left side.

3067 Table. Same as 3055, but plain drawer at left and pencil drawer at right.

Warren Platner

3710 Side Table designed by Warren Platner in 1966, manufactured 1966-1996. Base: steel wire in a variety of finishes. Top: available in a choice of materials and finishes. Glides: plastic or felt ring. 16" diameter, 18-3/4" h.

3711 Side Table. Same as 3710, but 24" diameter, 18-3/4" h.

3712 Coffee Table. Same as 3710, but 36" diameter, 15" h.

3714 Coffee Table. Same as 3710, but 42" diameter, 15" h.

3716 Dining Table. Same as 3710, but 54" diameter, 28-1/2" h.

Piroinen

23TR Round Arena Café Table designed by Piroinen in 2003, manufactured 2005. Base: Steel column with 19-3/4" diameter round base plate in a powder-coat finish. Top: round 3/4" thick laminate. 24", 27", 36", or 42" diameter, 27-1/2" h.

23TRH Bar-height Round Café Table. Same as 23TR, but 24" or 27" diameter, 41-1/2" h.

23TS Square Arena Café Table. Same as 23TR, but 24" or 30" square.

23TSH Bar-height Square Café Table. Same as 23TR, but 24" or 27" square.

4312 Conference Table designed by Warren Platner in 1973, manufactured 1988. Legs: steel, polished chrome finish. Top: oak, lacquer finish with inset leather panel. Glides: steel, polished chrome finish. 78" w, 43" d, 29-1/4" h.

4314 Conference Table. Same as 4312, but 90-1/4" d.

4316 Conference Table. Same as 4312, but 107-3/4" d.

4317 Round Conference Table. Same as 4312, but 57" diameter.

Telephone Table designed by Warren Platner in 1973.

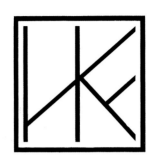

Ralph Rapson

55 Two-tier Table designed by Ralph Rapson in 1946. Wood frame with two molded plywood tops. 24-1/2" w, 21-1/2" d, 25" h.

56 Nesting Tables designed by Ralph Rapson in 1946.

Jens Risom

NK5 Side Table designed by Jens Risom for Nordisk Kompaniert (NDK) in 1941, manufactured 1944 to 1946. 17" w, 26" d, 20-1/2" h.

608 Dining Table designed by Jens Risom in 1941, cherry wood, 60" w extending with two 18" leaves, 36" d, 29" h.

608A Rectangular Dining Table designed by Jens Risom in 1941, cherry wood, 60" w, 36" d, 29" h.
Photo: From the 1942 Premier Knoll catalog. Design: Jens Risom, independent designer, 1941-1946.

237

611 Low Island-shaped Table designed by Jens Risom in 1941, cherry wood, 44" w, 36" d, 16" h. *Photo: From the 1942 Premier Knoll catalog. Design: Jens Risom, independent designer, 1941-1946.*

612 Island-shaped Table designed by Jens Risom in 1941, cherry wood, three legs, 16" w, 18" d, 24" h. *Photo: From the 1942 Premier Knoll catalog. Design: Jens Risom, independent designer, 1941-1946.*

613 Rectangular Side Table designed by Jens Risom in 1941, cherry wood, four legs, 24" w, 16" d, 24" h.

614 Low Table designed by Jens Risom in 1941. Cherry wood, 36" w, 21" d, 16" h. *Photo: From the 1942 Premier Knoll catalog. Design: Jens Risom, independent designer, 1941-1946.*

614 Square Side Table designed by Jens Risom.
Maple. 14" square, 18" h.

618 Round Side Table. Same as 614, but round top,
18" diameter, 20" h.

624 Side Table designed by Jens Risom in 1941.
Birch, four raking square legs and round or square
top.

642 *Round Dining Table* designed by Jens Risom.
Maple. 42" diameter, 28" h.

643 *Amoeba Coffee Table* designed by Jens Risom in
1941. Birch. 42" w, 32" d, 16" h.

John Rizzi

Round Table with Interaction Round Top and 4-star Base designed by John Rizzi in 1990. Fixed and adjustable heights available. 28-7/8" h.

Teardrop Table with Interaction Teardrop Top and 4-star Base designed by John Rizzi in 1990. Fixed and adjustable heights available. 28-7/8" h.

Blunted Round Table with Interaction Blunted Round Top and 4-star Base designed by John Rizzi in 1990. Fixed and adjustable heights available. 28-7/8" h.

Rounded Square Table with Interaction Rounded Square Top and 4-star Base designed by John Rizzi in 1990. Fixed and adjustable heights available. 28-7/8" h.

Rotary Table with Interaction Rotary Top and 4-star Base designed by John Rizzi in 1990. Fixed and adjustable heights available. 28-7/8" h.

Hotdog Table with Interaction Hotdog Top and C-leg Base designed by John Rizzi in 1990. Fixed and adjustable heights available. 28-7/8" h.

Counterforce® Interaction Table Top in Boomerang Shape and C-leg Base designed by John Rizzi c. 1993, shown fixed and in motion.

***Table with Interaction Racetrack Top and C-leg
Base*** designed by John Rizzi in 1990. 28" h.

***Table with Interaction Amoeba Top and Column
Base*** designed by John Rizzi in 1990. 28" h.

***Table with Interaction Rectangular Top and C-leg
Base*** designed by John Rizzi in 1990. Fixed and
adjustable heights available. 29-1/2" h.

243

Straight Table with Interaction Split-top and C-leg Base designed by John Rizzi in 1990. Fixed and adjustable heights available. 29-1/2" h.

Counterforce® Table with Interaction Rectangular Top and C-leg Base designed by John Rizzi and H. Peter Greene in 1990. Fixed and adjustable heights available. 28-7/8" h.

Corner Table with Interaction Split-top and C-leg Base designed by John Rizzi in 1990. Fixed and adjustable heights available. 26" to 41" h.

Equity Curved Corner Table Top designed by John Rizzi c. 1993.

Equity Table Top designed by John Rizzi c. 1993.

245

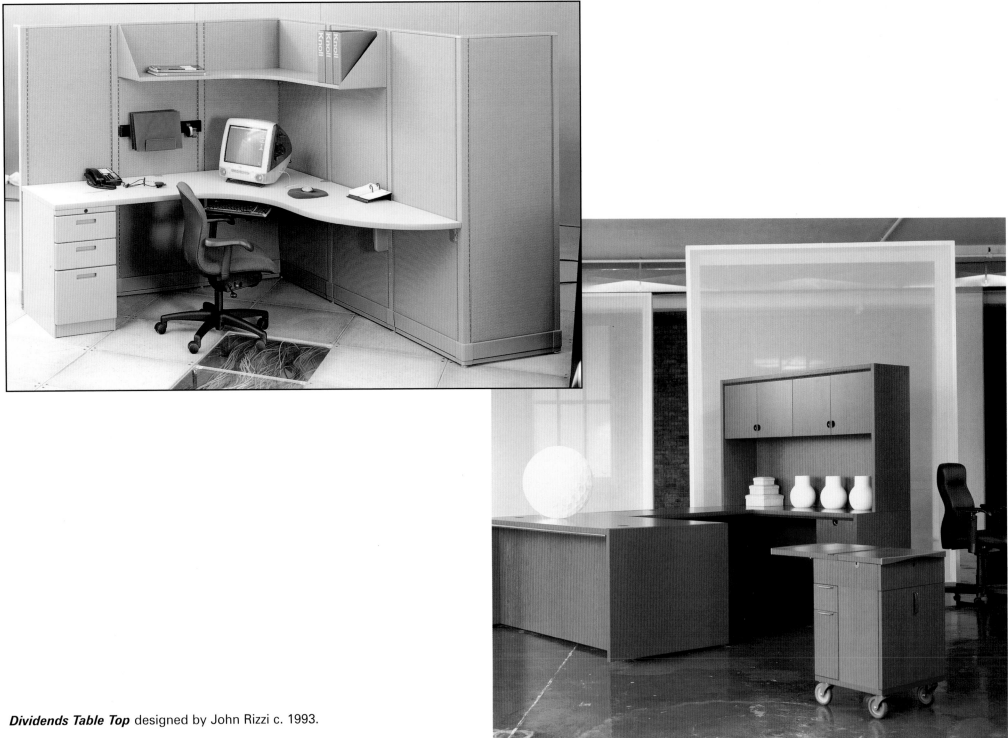

Dividends Table Top designed by John Rizzi c. 1993.

Derby Table Top designed by John Rizzi c. 1993.

Charles Rozier

Upstart Table designed by Charles Rozier in 2004.

Eero Saarinen

160 Pedestal Round Side Table designed by Eero Saarinen in 1956. Base: cast metal pedestal with white fused finish. Top: in a variety of materials and finishes with beveled edge. 16" diameter, 20-1/2" h.

161 Pedestal Oval Side Table. Same as 160, but 22-1/2" w, 15" d.

162 Pedestal Round Coffee Table. Same as 160, but 36" or 42" diameter, 15" h.

163 Pedestal Round Side Table. Same as 160, but 20" diameter.

164 Large Round Dining Table. Same as 160, but base with plastic finish available in a choice of colors, 54" diameter, 28-1/2" h.

165 Large Round Dining or Conference Table. Same as 164, but 54" diameter, 26" h.

166 Large Coffee Table. Same as 164, but 42" diameter, 15-1/4" h.

167 Oval Coffee Table. Same as 162, but 54" w, 36" d, 15-1/4" h.

172 Small Round Dining Table. Same as 164, but 36" diameter.

173 Medium Round Dining Table. Same as 164, but 42" diameter, 29" h.

174 Oval Dining Table. Same as 164, but 78" w, 48" diameter.

175 Large Oval Dining Table. Same as 164, but 96" w, 54" diameter.

Tobia Scarpa

53 Nibai Extension Table designed by Tobia Scarpa, manufactured 1982. Wood top and legs. 59" w, 40" to 80" d, 28" h.

53T1 Bastiano Square End or Coffee Table designed by Tobia Scarpa, manufactured 1982. Solid wood top on laminated wood base. 30" w, 30" d, 13-1/2" h.

53T2 Bastiano Rectangular Coffee Table. Same as 53T1, but 48" w, 24" d.

54 Coffee Table, c. 1948, with concave rectangular rosewood top on four tapering legs.

56-319 Cavaletto Table designed by Tobia Scarpa, Ufficio Technico in 1970. Base: 2 wooden sawhorse-style supports; top: rectangular plank.

56-332 Andre Coffee Table designed by Tobia Scarpa, Ufficio Tecnico in 1973. Base: steel, polished chrome finish. Top: polished plate glass 1/2" thick, clear or smoked gray. 45" w, 45" d, 15-1/4" h.

56-336 Andre Table. Same as 56-332, but 54" w, 54" d, 26-1/2" h.

56-337 Andre Table. Same as 56-336, but 29" h.

56-338 Andre Table. Same as 56-336, but 80" w, 40" d.

56-339 Andre Table. Same as 56-337, but 80" w, 40" d.

Richard Schultz

320 Petal End Table designed by Richard Schultz in 1960, manufactured 1960-1974. Base: cast iron with white plastic finish. Top: wood, available in a variety of finishes. 16" diameter, 19" h. Winner of the 1961 Design Award from *Industrial Design* magazine.

321 Petal Coffee Table. Same as 320, but 42" diameter, 15" h.

322 Petal Dining Table. Same as 320, but 48" diameter, 28" h.

3421 Square Coffee Table designed by Richard Schultz in 1966, manufactured 1967. Base: cast and extruded aluminum, available in a variety of finishes. Top: porcelain enameled steel in a choice of colors. Glides: nylon plastic. 28" w, 28" d, 15-1/2" h. Richard Schultz's Leisure Collection designs (with Lounge Chair 1421 and Dining Chair 1441) won the A.I.D. Award in 1967.

3425 Rectangular Coffee Table. Same as 3421, but 48" w, 24" d.

3426 Square Dining Table. Same as 3421, but 38" w, 38" d, 26-1/2" h.

3428 Rectangular Dining Table. Same as 3421, but 60" w, 28" d, 26-1/4" h.

Abel Sorenson

50 Tray Table designed by Abel Sorenson about 1946, manufactured c. 1946-1950. Wooden frame with ribbed top and detachable plywood serving tray. 24-3/4" w, 19" d, 17-3/4" h.

56abc Nesting Tables designed by Abel Sorenson in 1946 or 1947. Three rectangular, molded, graduated, plywood tops on steel legs, 19" w, 25" d, 16-1/2" h.

100 Coffee Table designed by Abel Sorensen c. 1948, rectangular wood top with doughboard ends , base: four flat wooden tapering legs

101 Coffee Table designed by Abel Sorensen c. 1948, base: four flat tapering wooden legs, top: square wood.

110 Coffee Table designed by Abel Sorensen c. 1948, base: birch legs, bulging top: natural mahogany, 59-3/4" w, 19-3/4" to 23-3/4" d, 17" h.

112 Extension Table designed by Abel Sorensen c. 1948, rectangular top over four tapering and raking wood legs.

Ettore Sottsass

32TR1 Spyder Table designed by Sottsass Associati in 1985, manufactured 1988. Base: Four painted steel tubes with transparent glides. Top: 1/2" thick tempered glass. 47-1/4" diameter, 28-1/3" h.

32TR2 Spyder Table. Same as 32TR1, but 53-1/4" diameter.

33 Shift Table designed by Sottsass Associati in 1986, manufactured 1988. Solid marble or wood with a variety of color finishes. 59" w, 59" d, 28-1/3" h.

34T1 Central Park Square Table designed by Ettore Sottsass in 1983, manufactured 1988. Base: red or white marble block with black or white marble columns and plastic glides. Top: 1/2" thick plate glass. 29-1/2" square, 15-3/4" h.

34T2 Central Park Rectangular Table. Same as 34T1, but 46-1/2" w.

34T3 Central Park Square Table. Same as 34T1, but 45" square.

3471 Central Park Table designed by Ettore Sottsass in 1984. Marble box base with molded plastic glides and four marble columns with plastic hemispheres supporting 1/2" plate glass top.

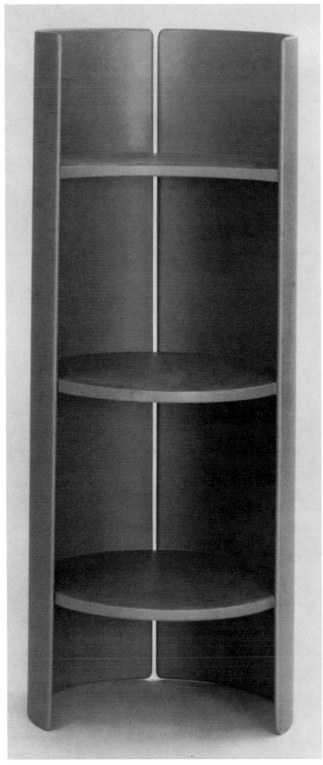

Kazuhide Takahama

55-821 Gea Table designed by Kazuhide Takahama in 1973. Base, case, and shelves of plywood with black or white lacquer finish. 21-1/4" w, 16-7/8" d, 20-1/2" h.

55-822 Gea Table. Same as 55-821, but 14-7/8" w, 14-3/4" d, 38-1/2" h.

55-823 Rotating Gea Table. Same as 55-822, but rotates on base and 27-7/8" h.

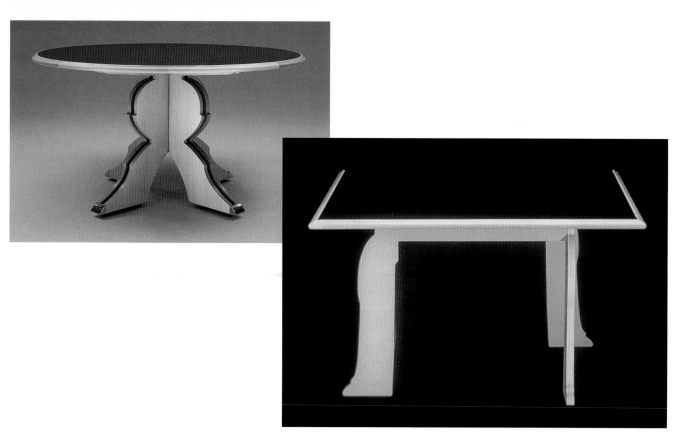

Robert Venturi

64R54T Urn Base Round Table designed by Robert Venturi in 1984, manufactured 1984-1988. Base: laminate and veneer natural or bird's eye maple. Top: natural or bird's eye maple. 54" diameter, 28-1/2" h.

64R60T Urn Base Round Table. Same as 64R54T, but 60" diameter.

64S120T Double Urn Base Rectangular Table. Same as 64R54T, but 120" w, 60" d.

65 Cabriole Leg Square Table designed by Robert Venturi in 1984, manufactured 1984-1988. Laser-cut wood plywood legs with plastic laminate face material and natural edges, plastic top with wood edges. 48" square, 28" h.

690 Low Table designed by Robert Venturi in 1984, manufactured 1984-1988. Molded fiberglass base and wood top with laminate inset. 41" diameter, 11" h.

Massimo and Lella Vignelli

49TR-36 PaperClip® Café Table designed by Vignelli Design in 1994, manufactured 1995. Base: 7/16″ steel rod with polyester and chrome-plated finish. Top: 3 options— 1″ thick laminate; 3/4″ slate; 1/2″ tempered clear glass. 36″ round, 28-1/8″ h.

49TR-42. Same as 49TR-36, but 42″ round.

49TR-48. Same as 49TR-36, but 48″ round.

49TS-30*. Same as 49TR-36, but 30″ square.

49TS-36. Same as 49TR-36, but 36″ square.

49TS-42. Same as 49TR-42, but 42″ square.

254

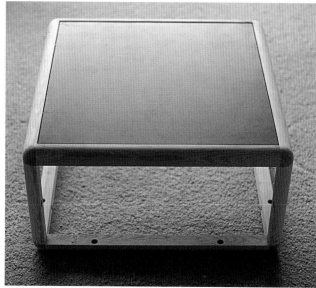

Hans Wegner

60-930 Table designed by Hans Wegner. Base: flat sled-style legs of stainless steel with chrome finish. Top: rectangular wood with 2 pencil drawers in the skirt flanking the center.

Otto Zapf

62TA Follow Me Low Square Table designed by Otto Zapf, manufactured in 1982. Frame and border: oak with black lacquer finish. Top: white or black laminate with oak. 50" w, 50" d, 16" h.

62TB Follow Me Rectangular Table. Same as 62TA, but 66" w, 34" d.

DESKS

Franco Albini

80 Albini Mini-desk with "Floating" Pedestal designed by Franco Albini in 1958, manufactured earlier and again in 1987. Frame: square steel tube in polished chrome. "Floating" wood drawer has rear recess. Top: 1/2" clear polished plate glass. 26" w, 48" d, 27-1/4" h.

Marcel Breuer

Canaan desk designed by Marcel Breuer. Base: beech wood, both solid and plywood. Designed for Gavina, it was also available with aluminum or solid wood frame. 78" w, 26" d, 28" h.

Vincent Cafiero

5802 Desk designed by Vincent Cafiero. Base: solid wood or square tubular steel in a variety of finishes. Top and pedestals: wood veneer or plastic laminate in a variety of finishes. 2- or 3-drawer pedestals are available, 64-1/4″ w, 33-5/8″ d, 29″ h. Glides: adjustable.

5806 Desk. Same as 5802, but 72″ w.

5808 Desk. Same as 5802, but 76″ w, 36″ d.

5812 Secretarial Desk. Same as 5802, but with lower typewriter platform.

5816 Secretarial Desk. Same as 5812, but 72″ w.

Gianfranco Frattini

7D16 Executive Desk designed by Gianfranco Frattini in 1988, manufactured 1990. Legs: mahogany veneer or polyester. Top: 5/8″ mahogany veneer or saddle leather. 65-3/4″ w, 32″ d, 28-1/8″ h.

7D18 Executive Desk. Same as 7D16, but 72″ w, 36-1/2″ d.

7D19 Executive Desk. Same as 7D16, but top leather insert available at the writing area, 76-3/4″ w, 41-3/8″ d, 29-1/8″ h.

7D22 Executive Desk. Same as 7D19, but 86-5/8″ w, 36-1/2″ d, 29-1/8″ h.

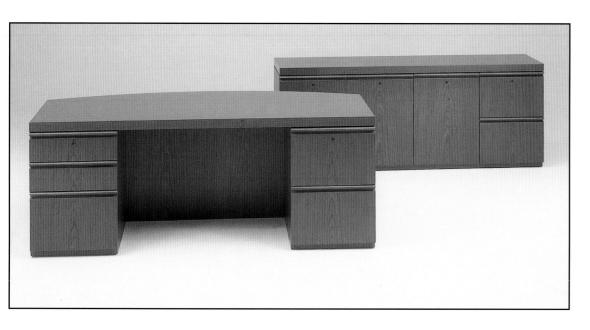

Charles Gwathmey and Robert Siegel

64 Rounded End Desk designed by Charles Gwathmey and Robert Siegel in 1981, manufactured 1988. Base and top: natural wood veneer or Figured Techgran® over hardwood frame. Available with 55", 47", and 42" machine extensions and a variety of drawer and cabinet combinations. 82-3/8" w, 39-1/16" d, 28" h.

72 Overhang Desk. Same as 64, but top overhangs front of base. 74-13/16" w.

73 Rounded Front Desk. Same as 64, but bowed top overhangs front of base. 74-13/16" w.

G6220 Cabinet with Pedestals designed by Charles Gwathmey and Robert Siegel. Pedestals: inside surface lined with black vinyl. Drawers and compartment shelves: vinyl covered fibreboard, solid wood pulls. Top: hinged to kneehole panel, available in a variety of wood veneers and laminates. 62" w, 20" d, 28" h.

G6230 Desk with Pedestals. Same as G6220, but without center cabinet.

Derby Desk designed by Charles Gwathmey and Robert Siegel in 1990.

Florence Knoll

13 Executive Desk designed by Florence Knoll.

14 Secretarial Desk designed by Florence Knoll.

15 Single Pedestal Desk designed by Florence Knoll c. 1948, manufactured 1950-1960. Maple plywood with walnut-finished, round tapering legs. 50" w, 28" d, 29" h.

16 Double Pedestal Desk designed by Florence Knoll. Wood.

17 Single Pedestal Desk designed by Florence Knoll c. 1954. Wood with square tapering legs. 48" w, 24" d, 29" h

18 Secretarial Return designed by Florence Knoll.

500 Small Secretarial Desk designed by Florence Knoll c. 1957. Similar to 503 but with side typing stand with a pencil tray drawer and two stationery drawers. 28" d, 54" long, 29" h.

501 Executive Secretarial Desk similar to 500 but 60" long.

502 Executive Desk designed by Florence Knoll c. 1957. Available as a table with single drawer, with one pedestal of one drawer and one file drawer, or with two pedestals with four drawers and one file drawer. Top: burn and stain resistant plastic laminate in birch and walnut. Frame: metal with nonabrasive, oxidized, satin black finish. Additional front panel available. 32" d x 66" long.

503 Executive Desk. Same as 502, but 36" d x 76" long.

1503 Double Pedestal Executive Desk designed by Florence Knoll c. 1956. Three drawers on the left pedestal and a drawer and a file drawer on the right pedestal. Top: available in various wood and plastic finished. Base: steel with black oxide or chrome finish or wood, with optional can kneehole panel. 36" d, 76" long, 29" h.

1504 Single Pedestal Desk designed by Florence Knoll. Base: square tubular steel or wood, in a variety of finishes. Top: wood veneer or plastic laminate, available in a variety of finishes. Pedestal and op-

tional kneehole panel: wood veneer in same finish as top; with right-hand two- or three-drawer pedestal. Glides: nylon. Choice of top sizes: 60" or 66" w, 30" d; or 72" w, 32" d; or 76" w, 36" d; 29" h.

1505 Single Pedestal Desk. Same as 1503, but two drawers on the left.

1506 Metal Base, Single Pedestal Desk designed by Florence Knoll in 1956. Base: square tubular steel, brushed chrome finish, available in a variety of finishes. Case and drawers: ebonized finish, available in a variety of finishes; also available with wood base. Top: walnut, available in a variety of finishes. Available with right-hand, two- or three-drawer pedestal. 76" w, 36" d, 29" h.

1507 Single Pedestal Desk. Same as 1506, but pedestal on left.

1508 Metal Base Table/Desk designed by Florence Knoll. Base: tubular steel, brushed chrome finish, available in a variety of finishes. Top: walnut, available in a variety of finishes. 76" w, 36" d, 29" h.

1509 Metal Base Table/Desk. Same as 1508, but with a pencil drawer on left.

1510 Metal Base Table/Desk. Same as 1508, but with a pencil drawer on right.

1513 Small Executive, Metal Base, Double Pedestal Desk designed by Florence Knoll. Base: square tubular steel, polished chrome finish, available in a variety of finishes. Top and pedestal: walnut, available in a variety of finishes. Also available with walnut plastic top or wood base. 32" d, 66" long, 29" h.

1514 Small Executive, Metal Base, Single Pedestal Desk. Same as 1513, but two drawers on right.

1515 Small Executive Single Pedestal Desk. Same as 1513, but two drawers on left.

1516 Small Executive Single Pedestal Desk. Same as 1513, but three drawers on right.

1517 Small Executive Single Pedestal Desk. Same as 1513, but three drawers on left.

1518 Metal Base Table/Desk. Same as 1508, but top 66" w, 32" d.

1519 Metal Base Table Desk. Same as 3509, but with square tubular steel base in a variety of finishes and with pencil drawer on left. 66" w, 32" d, 29" h.

1520 Metal Base Table/Desk. Same as 1518, but with pencil drawer on right.

1523 Secretarial Desk designed by Florence Knoll c. 1956. Same as 1543, but with disappearing typewriter mechanism on the left and three drawers on the right. 30" d, 60" long, 29" h.

1524 Secretarial Desk. Same as 1523, but with disappearing typewriter mechanism on the right and three drawers on the left.

1525 Secretarial Desk. Same as 1523, but with disappearing typewriter mechanism on the left and two drawers on the right.

1526 Secretarial Desk. Same as 1523, but with disappearing typewriter mechanism on the right and two drawers on the left.

1533 Metal Base Desk. Same as 1503 with top 60" w, 30" d.

1534 Metal Base, Single Pedestal Desk. Same as 1504, but top 60" w, 30" d.

1535 Metal Base, Single Pedestal Desk. Same as 1505, but top 60" w, 30" d.

1536 Metal Base, Single Pedestal Desk. Same as 1506, but top 60" w, 30" d.

1537 Metal Base, Single Pedestal Desk. Same as 1507, but top 60" w, 30" d.

1543 Metal Base, Double Pedestal, L-shaped Secretarial Desk designed by Florence Knoll c. 1956. Base: square tubular steel legs with brushed chrome finish, other finishes available. Walnut case and pedestal with 3 drawers, available in a variety of finishes. Walnut plastic tops, available in a variety of finishes and with right-hand typewriter platform. Desk 66" w, 32" d, 29" h. Typewriter platform 44-1/2" w, 19-1/4" d, 26-1/4" h.

1544 Metal Base, Double Pedestal, L-shaped Secretarial Desk designed by Florence Knoll. Same as 1543, but with typewriter platform on the left.

1545 Metal Base, Double Pedestal, L-shaped Secretarial Desk. Same as 1543, but with typewriter platform on the right and 2-drawer pedestal.

1546 Metal Base, Double Pedestal, L-shaped Secretarial Desk. Same as 1543, but with typewriter platform on the left and 2-drawer pedestal.

1547 Metal Base Desk. Same as 1501 with three-drawer pedestal and right-hand cabinet. Cabinet 56" w, 19" d, 27-1/2" h.

1548 Desk. Same as 1501 with two-drawer pedestal and right-hand cabinet. Cabinet 56" w, 19" d, 27-1/2" h.

1549 Desk. Same as 1501 with three-drawer pedestal and right-hand cabinet. Cabinet 56" w, 19" d, 27-1/2" h.

1550 Desk. Same as 1501 with three-drawer pedestal and right-hand cabinet. Cabinet 56" w, 19" d, 27-1/2" h.

1553 Metal Base Desk. Same as 1503 with top 72" w, 32" d.

1554 Metal Base, Single Pedestal Desk. Same as 1504, but top 72" w, 32" d.

1555 Metal Base, Single Pedestal Desk. Same as 1505, but top 72" w, 32" d.

1556 Metal Base, Single Pedestal Desk. Same as 1506, but top 72" w, 32" d.

1557 Metal Base, Single Pedestal Desk. Same as 1507, but top 72" w, 32" d.

1563 Metal Base, Single Pedestal, L-shaped Secretarial Desk designed by Florence Knoll. Base: square tubular steel, brushed chrome finish, available in a variety of finishes. Case: 3-drawer pedestal on right. Panels: walnut, in a variety of finishes. Top: beige plastic. Right typewriter platform. 60" w, 30" d, 29" h.

1564 Metal Base, Single Pedestal, L-shaped Secretarial Desk. Same as 1563, but 3-drawer pedestal on left.

1565 Metal Base, Single Pedestal, L-shaped Secretarial Desk. Same as 1563, but 2-drawer pedestal on right.

1566 Metal Base, Single Pedestal, L-shaped Secretarial Desk. Same as 1563, but 2-drawer pedestal on left.

2485 Desk/Table designed by Florence Knoll in 1961. Base: polished chrome steel four-star pedestal. Top: rosewood veneer. Meant to be accessed from both sides, the design has four drawers on each side. Each drawer has removable partitions, one pencil tray, and two plastic laminate writing shelves. 50" w, 28" d, 29" h. Winner of the prestigious Design Center Stuttgart Award, Germany, 1969-1970. Larger version manufactured in 1988, 37-3/4" w, 72" d, 28-1/2" h.

3503 Wood Base, Double Pedestal Desk. Base: walnut, available in a variety of finishes; also available with metal base. Top: walnut, available in a variety of finishes. 76" w x 36" d, 29" h.

3504 Wood Base, Single Pedestal Desk designed by Florence Knoll. Base and pedestal, available in a variety of finishes; also available with metal base. Top: walnut, available in a variety of finishes. 2-drawer pedestal on right. 76" w, 36" d, 29" h.

3505 Wood Base, Single Pedestal Desk. Same as 3504, but 2-drawer pedestal on left.

3506 Wood Base, Single Pedestal Desk. Same as 3504, but 3-drawer pedestal on right.

3507 Wood Base, Single Pedestal Desk. Same as 3504, but 3-drawer pedestal on left.

3508 Wood Base Table/Desk. Same as 1508, but wood base.

3509 Wood Base Table/Desk designed by Florence Knoll. Same as 1508, but with wood base and pencil drawer on left.

3510 Wood Base Table/Desk designed by Florence Knoll. Same as 1508, but with wood base and pencil drawer on right

3513 Wood Base, Double Pedestal Desk designed by Florence Knoll. Base: ebonized pedestal, available in a variety of finishes; walnut case, available in a variety of finishes; also available with metal base. Top: walnut, available in a variety of finishes. 66" w, 32" d, 29" h.

3514 Wood Base, Single Pedestal Desk. Same as 3504, but top 66" w, 32" d.

3515 Wood Base, Single Pedestal Desk. Same as 3505, but top 66" w, 32" d.

3516 Wood Base, Single Pedestal Desk. Same as 3506, but top 66" w, 32" d.

3517 Wood Base, Single Pedestal Desk. Same as 3507, but top 66" w, 32" d.

3518 Wood Base Table/Desk. Same as 3508, but top 66" w, 32" d.

3519 Wood Base Table/Desk. Same as 3509, but top 66" w, 32" d.

3520 Wood Base Table/Desk. Same as 3510, but top 66" w, 32" d.

3523 Wood Base, Double Pedestal Desk. Same as 1523, but wood base.

3524 Wood Base, Double Pedestal Desk. Same as 1524, but wood base.

3525 Wood Base, Double Pedestal Desk. Same as 1525, but wood base.

3526 Wood Base, Double Pedestal Desk. Same as 1526, but wood base.

3533 Wood Base, Double Pedestal Desk. Same as 3503, but top 60" w, 30" d.

3534 Wood Base, Single Pedestal Desk designed by Florence Knoll. Same as 1504, but wood base. Base and pedestal: walnut, available in a variety of finishes; also available with metal base. 2-drawer pedestal on right. Top: walnut plastic. 60" w, 30" d, 29" h.

3535 Wood Base, Single Pedestal Desk, Same as 3534, but 2-drawer pedestal on left.

3536 Wood Base, Single Pedestal Desk. Same as 3534, but 3-drawer pedestal on right.

3537. Wood Base, Single Pedestal Desk. Same as 3534, but 3-drawer pedestal on left.

3543 Wood Base, Double Pedestal, L-shaped Secretarial Desk designed by Florence Knoll. Same as 1543, but with solid wood base.

3544 Wood Base, Double Pedestal, L-shaped Secretarial Desk designed by Florence Knoll. Same as 1544, but with solid wood base.

3545 Wood Base, Double Pedestal, L-shaped Secretarial Desk. Base: walnut, available in a variety of finishes; walnut case and 3 drawers, available in a variety of finishes. Top: walnut, available in a variety of finishes. Right-hand typewriter platform. Desk 66" w, 32" d, 29" h. Typewriter platform 44-1/2" w, 29-1/4" d, 26-1/4" h.

3546 Wood Base, Double Pedestal, L-shaped Secretarial Desk designed by Florence Knoll. Same as 1546, but with solid wood base.

3553 Wood Base, Double Pedestal Desk. Same as 3503, but top 72" w, 32" d.

3554 Wood Base, Single Pedestal Desk. Same as 3504, but top 72" w, 32" d.

3555 Wood Base, Single Pedestal Desk. Same as 3505, but top 72" w, 32" d.

3556 Wood Base, Single Pedestal Desk. Same as 3506, but top 72" w, 32" d.

3557 Wood Base, Single Pedestal Desk. Same as 3507, but top 72" w, 32" d.

3563 Wood Base, Single Pedestal, L-shaped Secretarial Desk. Base: walnut, available in a variety of finishes. Case: 3-drawer pedestal, available in a variety of finishes. Top: available in a variety of finishes. Right-hand typewriter platform. Desk: 60" w, 30" d, 29" h. Typewriter platform: 24" w, 17-3/4" d, 26-1/4" h.

3564 Wood Base, Single Pedestal, L-shaped Secretarial Desk. Same as 1564, but wood base.

3565 Wood Base, Single Pedestal, L-shaped Secretarial Desk. Same as 1565, but wood base.

3566 Wood Base, Single Pedestal, L-shaped Secretarial Desk. Same as 1566, but wood base.

3602 Rectangular Table Desk. Base: cast aluminum. Top: white or beige plastic laminate. 60" w, 30" d, 28-1/2" h.

3603 Rectangular Table Desk. Same as 3602, but 25-1/2" h.

3605 Rectangular Table Desk. Same as 3602, but 72" w, 32" d.

3606 Rectangular Table Desk. Same as 3602, but 72" w, 32" d, 25-1/2" h.

Carl Magnusson

NT Magnusson Midtown Desk designed by Carl Magnusson in 1993. Single and doulble pedestals available in a variety of woods and colors. Drawer pull grommets of stainless steel finish. 60" or 66" or 72" w, 30" or 36" d, 28-1/2" h.

NT Magnusson Uptown Desk designed by Carl Magnusson in 1993. Same as Midtown Desk, but leather drawer pulls in brown or black pointing up.

NT Magnusson Downtown Desk designed by Carl Magnusson in 1993. Same as Midtown Desk, but leather drawer pulls in brown or black pointing down and top edge is sculptured.

Charles Pfister

Desk designed by Charles Pfister, matching credenza 1050.

Warren Platner

4302 Table/Desk designed by Warren Platner in 1973, manufactured 1988. Base: steel, polished chrome finish. Top: oak, lacquer finish with inset leather panel. Glides: steel, polished chrome finish. 43" w, 78" d, 29-1/4" h.

4304 Table/Desk. Same as 4302, but 90-1/4" w.

4306 Table/Desk. Same as 4302, but 107-3/4" w.

4321 File Box Drawer. Coordinates with Platner desks.

4322 Double Box Drawer. Case: wood, upholstered in leather. 18" w, 20" d, 14-1/4" h.

4323 Pencil Drawer. 18" w, 20" d, 4-1/2" h.

Robert Reuter

Desk and Work Station designed by Robert Reuter c. 1990-95, manufactured 1995.

Desk-Cubicle designed by Robert Reuter c. 1990-95, manufactured 1995.

Currents Reality Office System designed by Robert Reuter and Charles Rozier in 1997, manufactured 1998.

Upstart Office System designed by Robert Reuter and Charles Rozier in 2001.

Jens Risom

609 Desk designed by Jens Risom c. 1942, cherry wood, with one pedestal, two single drawers, and one double drawer for files, 50" w, 30" d, 29" h. *Photo: From the 1942 Premier Knoll catalog. Design: Jens Risom, independent designer, 1941-1946.*

610 Desk designed by Jens Risom c. 1942, cherry wood, with four drawers, 40" w, 24" d, 29" h. *Photo: From the 1942 Premier Knoll catalog. Design: Jens Risom, independent designer, 1941-1946.*

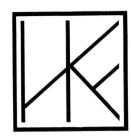

Charles Rozier

Currents Reality Office System designed by Charles Rozier and Robert Reuter in 1997, manufactured 1998.

Upstart Office System designed by Robert Reuter and Charles Rozier in 2001.

AutoStrada Office System designed by Charles Rozier in 2004.

609A Desk designed by Jens Risom c. 1942, cherry wood, with two pedestals, two single drawers, and one double drawer for files in each pedestal, 62" w, 30" d, 29" h. This desk and credenza were exhibited at the "Design for Today" exhibition in 1944.

269

Richard Schultz

4106 Table Desk designed by Richard Schultz in 1963. Base and top inlay: steel in a variety of finishes. Top: wood veneer in a choice of finishes. Glides: nylon. 76" w, 36" d, 26" h.

4108 Table Desk with Pencil Drawer. Same as 4106, but with drawer, 32" d.

4144 Executive Desk. Same as 4106, but 2 short pedestals, kneehole panel, and 2 pullout shelves with removable glass. Same finish as top. 72" w, 32" d, 29" h.

4164 Executive Desk. Same as 4144, but with 2 full pedestals.

William Stephens

5202 Desk designed by William Stephens in 1972. Oak veneer top, end, and front panels with polished chrome glides. Top filing box and short front panel. Machine extension available. 64" w, 32" d, 28-3/4" h.

5207 Desk. Same as 5202, but 72" w, 36" d.

5212 Desk. Same as 5202, but with machine extension 42" w, 22-1/4" d, 26-3/4" h.

5252 Desk With Top Filing Box and Full Front Panel designed by William Stephens. Top, end, and front panels: oak veneer, simulated oil finish. Glides: polished chrome. 64" w, 32" d, 28-3/4" h.

5257 Desk With Top Filing Box and Full Front Panel.
Same as 5352, but 72" w, 36" d.

5262 Desk With Top Filing, Full Front Panel, and Machine Extension. Same as 5252, but with machine extension 42" w, 22-1/4" d, 26-3/4" h

5267 Desk With Top Filing, Front Panel, and Machine Extension. Same as 5262, but desk larger, 72" w, 36" d, 28-3/4" h.

5302 Desk With Full Top and Short Front Panel
designed by William Stephens. Top, end, and front panels: oak veneer, simulated oil finish. Glides: polished chrome. 64" w, 32" d, 28-3/4" h.

5307 Desk With Full Top and Short Front Panel.
Same as 5302, but larger, 72" w, 36" d.

5312 Desk With Full Top, Short Front Panel, and Machine Extension. Same as 5302, but with machine extension.

5317 Desk With Full Top, Short Front Panel, and Machine Extension. Same as 5307, but with machine extension.

5401 Desk designed by William Stephens. Top and end panels: oak veneer, lacquer finish. Front panel: plastic laminate. Glides: polished chrome. 60" w, 30" d, 28-3/4" h.

5405 Desk. Same as 5401, but 66" w, 32" d.

5407 Desk. Same as 5401, but with 5321 File Drawer Pedestal, 72" w, 36" d.

5410 Work Surface Extension. Same as 5401, but 48" w, 24" d, 28-3/4" h, also available in other sizes.

5413 Work Surface Extension. Same as 5401, but with plastic laminate kneehole panel, 60" w, 24" d, 27" h; also available in other sizes.

5420 Single Box Drawer. Case: steel with baked finish and front plastic laminate. 18" w, 15-1/2" d, 6" h.

5421 File Drawer With File Box. 18" w, 15-1/2" d, 12" h.

5423 Pencil Drawer With Plastic Insert. Molded plastic. 18" w, 15-1/2" d, 1-3/4" h.

5425 Mobile File. Oak veneer end panels and white plastic laminate recessed sides. 29-1/2" w, 20" d, 24-3/4" h.

5426 Mobile File with Top. Same as 5425, but with oak veneer top.

5504 Machine Station designed by William Stephens. Panels and work surface: wood veneer. Pedestal storage, steel case, wood veneer or plastic laminate front, stackable. Top cap: aluminum, polished chrome or baked finish. Glides: polished chrome or baked finish. Wood veneers: Techgrain, Aniere, Mahogany with polymer oil finish. 76" w, 27" d, 58-1/2" h, available in other sizes.

5531 Hanging Sound Panels designed by William Stephens. Wood frame with glass fiber and foam, fabric covered. 36" w, 1-7/8" d, 56-3/4" h.

5534 Freestanding Screens designed by William Stephens. Wood frame with expanded metal reinforced glass fiber covered with foam and fabric. 30", 36", 60", or 72" w, 18" d, 58-1/2" h.

5338 Curved 2-section Screen. Same as 5534, but 70" radius and 74-3/4" overall width.

5539 Curved 3-section Screen. Same as 5534, but 70" radius and 104-1/4" overall width.

5546 Overhead Storage Unit with Top and Door Assembly. Same as 5504, but back, bottom, top, and door: steel, in a variety of finishes. 30" w, 15" d, 14" h.

5547 Overhead Storage Unit with Top and Door Assembly. Same as 5546, but 36" w.

CHESTS, CABINETS AND CREDENZAS

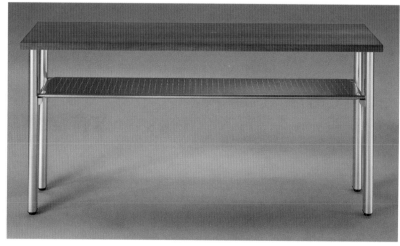

Vincent Cafiero

5840 Cabinet designed by Vincent Cafiero. Base: solid wood or square tubular steel in a variety of finishes. Top and case: solid wood or plastic laminate in a variety of finishes. Glides: adjustable. 33-5/8" w, 19-1/8" d, 27-1/4" h.

5841 Cabinet. Same as 5840, but 45" w.

5842 Cabinet. Same as 5840, but 48-15/16" w.

5843 Cabinet. Same as 5840, but 64-1/4" w.

5844 Cabinet. Same as 5840, but 64-1/4" w.

5845 Cabinet. Same as 5840, but 64-1/4" w, 19-1/8" d, 27-1/4" h.

Emanuela Frattini

P5-1 Propeller 4-position Credenza designed by Emanuela Frattini in 1994, manufactured 1995. Legs: aluminum with clear satin anodized or powder-coat finish. Case: cabinets and drawers in various combinations with aluminum pulls. Top: Plastic laminate on 1-1/8" thick, 3-ply fiberboard. 67-3/8" w, 20" d, 28-1/2" h.

P5-2 Propeller 6-position Credenza. Same as P5-1, but 98-1/2" w.

P5-C Small Sideboard designed by Emanuela Frattini in 1994, manufactured 1995. Legs: aluminum with clear satin anodized or powder-coat finish. Top: Plastic laminate on 1-1/8" thick, 3-ply fiberboard. 67-3/8" w, 20" d, 28-1/2" h.

P5-D Large Sideboard. Same as P5-C, but 98-1/2" w.

Gianfranco Frattini

7X16 Credenza designed by Gianfranco Frattini in 1988, manufactured 1990. Base: Mahogany or colored polyester. Top: Saddle leather in a variety of colors. Case of six units can contain drawers, shelves, and cabinets in a variety of arrangements. 125-5/8" w, 20-1/2" d, 25-7/8" h.

7X36 Storage Unit. Same as 7X16, but 65-7/8" h.

Bruce Hannah

CH2-11 Cabinet designed by Bruce Hannah. Two Pedestals: formed steel frame with black fused finish. Pedestal back panels are vacuum-formed ABS plastic; baraboard pedestal slides. Metal brackets connect pedestals. Drawers: black vinyl-covered fibreboard. Drawer pulls are extruded aluminum, painted finish. Top: finished in a variety of wood veneers and plastic laminates. All other surfaces available in six painted finishes. 32" w, 23" d, 26-5/8" h.

CH3-121 Cabinet. Same as CH2-11, but Three Pedestals, different drawer arrangement, 48" w.

CH4-1221 Cabinet. Same as CH2-11, but Four Pedestals, different drawer arrangement, 64" w.

CH5-12421 Cabinet. Same as CH2-11, but Five Pedestals, 80" w.

Florence Knoll

116 Sideboard or Cabinet designed by Florence Knoll c. 1948. Case: birch wood in natural finish with sliding doors covered in Pandanus, saddle leather pulls, and white enamel interior. Base: 9" h black or chrome finished tubular steel legs. 72" w, 18" d, 31" h.

118 Cabinet designed by Florence Knoll c. 1957.

119 Sideboard/Cabinet designed by Florence Knoll. Base: walnut, available in a variety of finishes. Case: walnut, available in a variety of finishes, with white lacquered doors, two felt-lined silver drawers, and four adjustable shelves. 75-3/8" w, 18" d, 29" h.

121 Hanging Cabinet designed by Florence Knoll c. 1948. Case: walnut, available in a variety of finishes, white lacquered interior with three adjustable wood shelves and two adjustable glass shelves. Hinged drop doors: white lacquered, available in a variety of finishes. 72" w, 15-1/4" d, 17-3/4" h.

123 Hanging Cabinet. Same as 121, but white lacquered sliding doors available in a variety of finishes.

125 Three-drawer Chest designed by Florence Knoll in 1948, manufactured 1948-1956. Birch wood and plywood, resting on four round, tapering wooden legs. 36" w, 18" d, 28" h.

126 Four Drawer Chest designed by Florence Knoll in 1948, manufactured 1948-1956. Birch wood and plywood, 34-3/4" w, 18" d, 28" h.

127 Three Drawer Chest designed by Florence Knoll in 1948, manufactured 1948-1956. Birch wood and plywood, 18" w, 18" d, 28" h.

128 Three Drawer Chest with Luggage Rack designed by Florence Knoll in 1948, manufactured 1948-1956. Birch wood and plywood, 108" w, 18" d, 33-1/4" h.

129 Three Drawer Chest with Luggage Rack and Dressing Table Compartment designed by Florence Knoll in 1948, manufactured 1948-1956. Birch wood and plywood, 108" w, 18" d, 33-1/4" h.

130 Three Drawer Chest with Luggage Rack and Desk Compartment designed by Florence Knoll in 1948, manufactured 1948-1956. Birch wood and plywood, 108" w, 18" d, 33-1/4" h.

134 Chairside Radio Phonograph designed by Florence Knoll c. 1954. Wooden case on straight legs with radio and phonograph in sliding single drawer. 31" w, 24-1/2" d, 21" h.

135 Three Drawer Chest designed by Florence Knoll c. 1954. Wooden case resting on four straight tubular metal legs. 36" w, 18" d, 28" h.

136 Four Drawer Chest designed by Florence Knoll c. 1954. Wooden case resting on four straight tubular metal legs. 36" w, 18" d, 34-3/4" h.

137 Three Drawer Chest designed by Florence Knoll c. 1954. Wooden case resting on four straight tubular metal legs. 18" w, 18" d, 28" h.

155 Double Chest designed by Florence Knoll c. 1954. Wooden case with two section of three drawers. 72-1/2" w, 18" d, 28" h.

323 Three Drawer Chest designed by Florence Knoll in 1957. Walnut or white plastic laminate top, white plastic back, walnut front, sides and legs, satin aluminum pulls, oak drawer sides with metal slides and nylon wheels. 36" w, 19-1/2" d, 29-1/4" h.

324 Four Drawer Chest. Same as 323, but four drawers.

325 Four Drawer Chest. Same as 324, but 36-5/8" h.

326 Five Drawer Chest. Same as 325, but five drawers.

327 Bed Table designed by Florence Knoll in 1957. Walnut or white plastic laminate top, walnut front, sides, back, and legs. Finger grip under drawer, with optional shelf at bottom. 19-1/2" square, 18" h.

329 Suspended Vanity to be used between two 323s and 324s. Walnut or white plastic top and one drawer. 28" w, 19-1/2" d, 4-1/2" h.

523 Three Drawer Chest designed by Florence Knoll about 1964. Top: white plastic or wood. Case: Teak or rosewood veneer. Base: rosewood or steel with brushed or polished chrome finish. 36" w, 19-1/4" d, 29" h. Sold in multiple units with spacer between 2, 3, or 4 chests.

527 Bed Table designed by Florence Knoll about 1964. Top: white plastic laminate or wood veneer. Case and base: teak or rosewood with drawer and matching shelf. 19-1/2" w, 19-1/2" d, 18" h.

530 File Drawer Unit designed by Florence Knoll. File drawer: solid wood with lacquer finish, for use with cabinets 540, 541, 542, 543, 544, and 545. Adjustable metal bar for hanging letter- or legal-size folders.

531 File Drawer Unit. Same as 530, but 4 tray drawers.

532 File Drawer Unit. Same as 530, but sliding tray for standard dictating equipment.

540 Cabinet designed by Florence Knoll about 1957. Base: tubular steel legs, black finish, other finishes available. Case and 20" sliding or hanging doors: available in a variety of finishes, and with 8 adjustable shelves. Optional file and tray drawers and sliding dictating machine shelf available. 36" w, 17-3/4" d, 27-1/2" h.

541 Cabinet. Same as 540, but with 4 shelves and 72" long.

542 Cabinet. Same as 540, but 48" w.

543 Hanging Cabinet. Same as 540, with four adjustable shelves.

544 Hanging Cabinet. Same as 540. 71-1/2" w, 17-3/4" d, 20" h

545 Hanging Cabinet. Same as 543 with 4 adjustable shelves.

2540 Cabinet designed by Florence Knoll. Base: steel available in a variety of finishes. Case: wood veneer, available in a variety of finishes, with shallow and deep drawers and aluminum pulls. Top: available in a variety of materials and finishes. 37-1/4" w, 17-3/4" d, 25-1/2" h.

2541 Cabinet. Same as 2540, but with one door.

2542 Cabinet. Same as 2540, but with a different arrangement of drawers.

2543 Cabinet. Same as 2540, but with a different arrangement of drawers, 74-1/2″ w.

2544 Cabinet. Same as 2540, but with hinged doors, no exterior drawers, 74-1/2″ w.

2545 Cabinet. Same as 2540, but with hinged doors.

2546 Cabinet. Same as 2540, but 74-1/2″ w.

2549 Storage Module for use with cabinets 2545 and 2546, designed by Florence Knoll, manufactured 1982. One to three drawers on the left and/or right side, can be used in combination with an open cabinet. 37-1/4″ w.

3540 Cabinet designed by Florence Knoll. Same as 540 but with solid wood legs in same finish as case.

3541 Cabinet. Same as 3540, but 71-1/4″ w.

Enzo Mari

59-911 'Glifo' foot for panel system designed by Enzo Mari in 1972. White antistatic plastic.

59-912 'Glifo' top and bottom for panel system designed by Enzo Mari in 1972. White antistataic plastic.

59-913 'Glifo' back for panel system designed by Enzo Mari in 1972. White antistataic plastic.

59-914 'Glifo' side for panel system designed by Enzo Mari in 1972. White antistataic plastic.

59-915 'Glifo' cube for panel system designed by Enzo Mari in 1972. White antistataic plastic.

Charles Pfister

1050 Credenza designed by Charles Pfister.

3046 Credenza designed by Charles Pfister. Black polyester finish. 56-3/4″ w, 21″ d, 23″ h.

3075 Credenza Extension designed by Charles Pfister in 1984, manufactured 1988. Used with two pedestals and/or storage compartments, center shelf covered with leather. 20-1/2″ w, 81-1/2″ d, 25-1/5″ h

3076 Credenza Extension. Same as 3075, but used with four pedestals and/or storage compartments.

3077 Credenza Extension. Same as 3075, but used with four pedestals and/or storage compartments and center shelf covered with leather. 119-2/3″ d.

3078 Credenza Extension. Same as 3075, but used with six pedestals and/or storage compartments, 119-2/3″ d.

Warren Platner

4344 Credenza designed by Warren Platner in 1973, manufactured 1988. Base: steel, polished chrome

finish. Top: oak, lacquer finish with inset leather panel. Glides: steel, polished chrome finish. Used alone or with 2 or 4 pedestals or storage compartments. 23-1/2″ w, 76-3/4″ d, 29-1/4″ h.

4345 Credenza. Same as 4344, but used alone or with 2, 4, or 5 pedestals or storage compartments. 95″ w.

4346 Credenza. Same as 4344, but used alone or with 2, 4, or 6 pedestals or storage compartments. 112-1/2″ w.

4356 Credenza with Overhead Storage. Same as 4346, but with overhead storage: wood, upholstered in leather.

Robert Reuter

Opposite page:
Overhead Cabinet designed by Robert Reuter c. 1990-95, manufactured 1995.

Jens Risom

601 Chest of four drawers designed by Jens Risom c. 1942, cherry wood, 36″ w, 16″ d, 32-1/2″ h. *Photo: From the 1942 Premier Knoll catalog. Design: Jens Risom, independent designer, 1941-1946.*

602 Cabinet with two sliding doors and two adjustable shelves inside, designed by Jens Risom c. 1942, cherry wood, 36″ w, 16″ d, 32-1/2″ h. *Photo: From the 1942 Premier Knoll catalog. Design: Jens Risom, independent designer, 1941-1946.*

603 Cabinet with two hinged doors and two adjustable shelves inside, designed by Jens Risom c. 1942, cherry wood, 36″ w, 16″ d, 32-1/2″ h.

604A Bookcase with four shelves designed by Jens Risom c. 1942, cherry wood, 36" w 16" d tapering to 11", 32-1/2" h. *Photo: From the 1942 Premier Knoll catalog. Design: Jens Risom, independent designer, 1941-1946.*

604B Bookcase with four shelves designed by Jens Risom c. 1942, cherry wood, 36" w, 16" d tapering to 11" on the opposite side as no. 604A, 32-1/2" h.

605 Bookcase with four shelves, two adjustable, designed by Jens Risom c. 1942, cherry wood, 36" w, 11" d, 32-1/2" h.

606 Bar Cabinet designed by Jens Risom c. 1942, cherry wood, deep central compartment for standing bottles and two hinged doors with three trays on each door for glasses, 36" w, 16" d, 32-1/2" h. *Photo: From the 1942 Premier Knoll catalog. Design: Jens Risom, independent designer, 1941-1946.*

607 Sideboard designed by Jens Risom c. 1942, cherry wood, two drawers for flat silver lined with felt, two deep drawers for linen, and two cabinets

with sliding doors and adjustable shelves, 66" long, 21" d, 32-1/2" h. *Photo: From the 1942 Premier Knoll catalog. Design: Jens Risom, independent designer, 1941-1946.*

William Stephens

5243 Cabinet. Same as 5244, but 50-3/4" w.

5244 Cabinet designed by William Stephens. Top, end, and front panels: a variety of veneers, polymer oil finish. Glides: polished chrome. 68-1/2" w, 22-1/2" d, 27" h.

5245 Cabinet. Same as 5244, but 84-1/4" w.

Hans Wegner

Opposite page:
60-920 Cabinet designed by Hans Wegner. Case: wood veneer with solid hardwood edges available in a variety of finishes. Shelf: oak with one-inch vertical adjustments. Door: drop tambour finished to match

case. 32-1/4" w, 18-3/4" d, 25-1/2" h.

60-921 Cabinet. Same as 60-920, but with 6 oak tray drawers with white metal dividers.

60-922 Cabinet. Same as 60-920, but with one large oak tray drawer with white metal dividers.

60-923 Cabinet. Same as 60-920, but with 2 oak tray drawers with white metal divider; and one double file drawer, oak with metal rod hangers.

60-924 Cabinet. Same description was 60-920, but with five large oak tray drawers with white metal dividers and one oak divider.

60-925 Cabinet. Same as 60-920, but with 2 small oak tray drawers with white metal dividers; one single file drawer; and one oak divider with two adjustable shelves.

60-926 Cabinet. Same as 60-920, but with one oak shelf and one double file drawer.

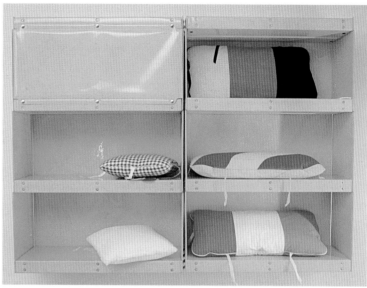

ACCESSORIES

Ashtrays

Sergio Asti

Asti Umbrella Stand and Kamal Ashtray designed by Sergio Asti.

89-20 Ashtray designed by Sergio Asti, of ceramic colored white or black, 8" w, 8" d, 2-1/8" h.

89-21 Ashtray. Same as 89-20, with different design including corner blocks.

89-40 Ashtray designed by Sergio Asti in polished black Italian marble, 10" diameter, 2-1/4" h.

89-41 Ashtray designed by Sergio Asti in 1974, polished grey Italian marble, 11-1/8" diameter, 3-1/4" h.

Florence Knoll

8515 Pedestal Ashtray. Bowl: stainless steel, polished finish with black sand and black wire screen. Base: cast iron in a choice of colors. 12-3/4" diameter, 21-5/16" h.

Eero Saarinen

8915 Ashstand designed by Eero Saarinen in 1956, manufactured 1962-1976. Cast aluminum base with black fused epoxy finish, bowl of spun stainless steel. 12-3/4" diameter, 21-1/4" h.

Vases and Bowls

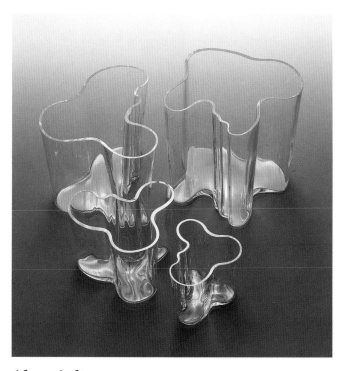

Alvar Aalto

Three Aalto Vases and a Savoy Vase designed by Alvar Aalto in 1937 for Ittala of Finland. Fluted glass.

Sergio Asti

89-01 Vase designed by Sergio Asti, manufactured 1974, of Venetian glass colored white, black, or amber, 12" diameter, 5" h.

89-02 Vase. Same as 89-01, 8-1/8" h.

89-03 Vase. Same as 89-01, 12" h.

89-13 Vase designed by Sergio Asti ca. 1972, manufactured 1972-75, of Venetian glass in filigrana nera, blanca irise, or nero irise, 9-3/4" diameter, 10-1/4" h.

89-14 Vase. Same as 89-13, but 10-1/4" diameter and 11-3/4" h.

89-23 Vase designed by Sergio Asti in 1972, of ceramic colored white or black, 11-7/8" w, 9-3/4" d, 11-3/4" h.

89-24 Vase. Same as 89-23, but different design, 9-3/4" h and square.

89-25 Vase. Same as 89-23, but different design, 13-1/2" w, 14" d, 9-5/8" h.

89-26 Vase designed by Sergio Asti, ceramic colored white, black, or platinum, 15-5/8" w, 4-3/4" d, 15" h.

89-27 Vase. Same as 89-26, but different design, 14-3/8" w, 15-3/4" d, 9-5/8" h.

89-28 Vase. Same as 89-26, but different design, 9-7/8" w, 15-1/8" d, 9-5/8" h.

89-29 Vase. Same as 89-26, but different design, 8-1/4" w, 7-5/8" d, 9-1/2" h.

89-42 Bowl designed by Sergio Asti in polished white Italian marble, 7-1/4" diameter, 4-1/2" h.

89-43 Bud Vase designed by Sergio Asti with polished grey or black marble base and polished chrome shaft, 7-3/4" diameter, 11-3/4" h.

89-45 Marble bowl, same as 89-42, 17-1/4" diameter, 6-1/4" h.

8710 Flower Bowl. Spun aluminum with black or white enamel finish. 5" w, 2" diameter, 3-1/2" h.

8720 Flower Bowl. Same as 8710, but 3" diameter.

Florence Knoll

8730 Flower Vase designed by Florence Knoll c. 1950, manufactured 1962-1974. Solid spun brass, polished finish. 4-3/8" diameter, 5-3/4" h.

Angelo Mangiarotti

85-36 Bowl designed by Angelo Mangiarotti in 1970, manufactured 1970-1974. Polished Italian marble. 10-1/2" diameter, 6" h.

85-46 Cilindro vase designed by Angelo Mangiarotti in 1970, manufactured 1970-1974. Polished Italian rosa marble, 4-3/4" diameter, 11" h.

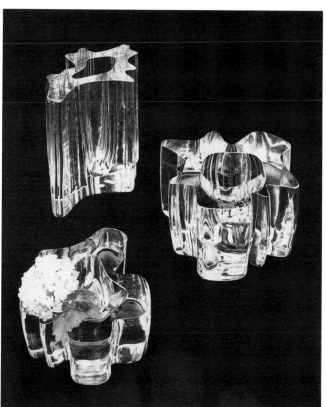

Left: 85-51 Vase designed by Angelo Mangiarotti in 1970, manufactured 1970-1974. Crystal in free-form shapes.

Charles Pfister

Above and right: 74-01 Glass Bowl designed by Charles Pfister. Clear Venetian glass, 5-3/4"d., 3-1/8"h.

74-02 Glass Bowl. Same as 74-01, but 11-1/8" diameter, 5" h.

74-03 Glass Bowl. Same as 74-01, but 11-1/2" diameter, 7-1/8" h.

74-04 Glass Bowl. Same as 74-01, but 18" diameter, 2-5/8" h.

74-05 Glass Bowl. Same as 74-01, but 10" diameter, 2-5/8" h.

Desk Accessories

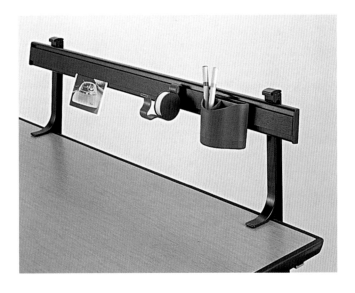

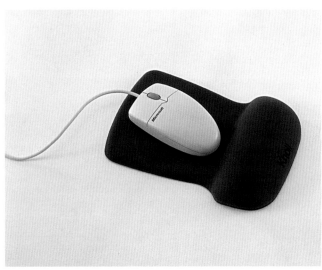

Ayse Birsel

Shelf with Clips Desk Accessory designed by Ayse Birsel.

Mouse Pad Desk Accessory designed by Ayse Birsel.

Ross Lovegrove

Surf Collection desk pads designed by Ross Lovegrove.

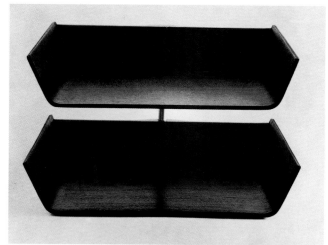

Florence Knoll

1 Single Letter Tray designed by Florence Knoll c. 1950, manufactured 1950-1976. Laminated walnut plywood available in a variety of finishes. 11-1/2" w, 14" d, 2-1/2" h.

2 Double Letter Tray. Same as 1, but with aluminum support rod and 7" h.

6 Small Desk Pad. Fiberboard padding covered in a choice of black or tan cowhide or Naugahyde. 30" w, 21" d.

7 Large Desk Pad. Same as 6, but 33" w.

8220 Pencil or Cigarette Cup, designed by Florence Knoll c. 1960, manufactured 1962-1970. Solid rosewood. 3-1/8" diameter, 4-1/4" h.

8230 Lighter, designed by Florence Knoll, manufactured 1962-1970. Solid rosewood.

8240 Pencil Cup, designed by Florence Knoll, manufactured 1962-1970. Solid rosewood. 2-1/2" diameter, 2-1/2" h.

Erik Magnussen

International Collection Accessories, including crystal pitcher and glasses, designed by Erik Magnussen.

Lucia Mercer

711 Granite Tray designed by Lucia Mercer in 1984.

Bruce Tippett

58-811 Renna Hat Stand designed by Bruce Tippett.

Lighting

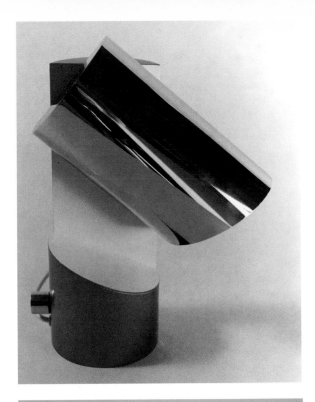

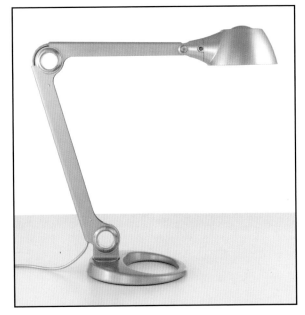

Donald Copeland

Copeland Light designed by Donald Copeland in 2005.

Peter Hamberger

78-001 Crylicord Table Lamp designed by Peter Hamberger c. 1972, manufactured 1974. Clear one-inch diameter extruded bent acrylic tubing with concealed wiring and metal shade with polished chrome finish. 13-1/2" w, 7-1/2" d, 11" h.

78-002 Crylicord Table Lamp designed by Peter Hamberger c. 1972, manufactured 1974. Clear one-inch diameter extruded bent acrylic tubing with concealed wiring and metal shade with polished chrome finish. 28-1/3" w, 22-1/2" d, 38-3/4" h.

78-003 Crylicord Floor Lamp designed by Peter Hamberger c. 1972, manufactured 1974. Clear one-inch diameter extruded straight acrylic tubing with concealed wiring and metal shade. 13-3/4" w, 14-1/2" d, 60" h.

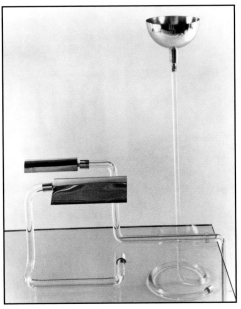

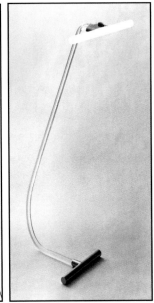

78-004 Crylicord Floor Lamp designed by Peter Hamberger c. 1972, manufactured 1974. Clear one-inch diameter extruded acrylic tubing with concealed wiring and metal shade. 7-1/4" diameter, 60-1/4" h.

78-005 Crylicord Floor Lamp designed by Peter Hamberger c. 1972, manufactured 1974. Clear one-inch diameter bent extruded acrylic tubing with concealed wiring and metal shade for a fluorescent tube lighting element. 19-2/3" w, 18-1/2" d, 43-2/3" h.

78-006 Crylicord Lighting for Wall Mounting designed by Peter Hamberger c. 1972, manufactured 1974. Clear one-inch diameter straight extruded acrylic tubing with concealed wiring. Wall Mount brackets included. 4-3/4" w, 6" d, 25" h.

78-007 Crylicord Lighting. Same as 78-006, but 37" h.

78-008 Crylicord Lighting. Same as 78-006, but 49" h.

Angelo Lelii

Altalena Table Light designed by Angelo Lelii.
Iceberg Table Lamp designed by Angelo Lelii.

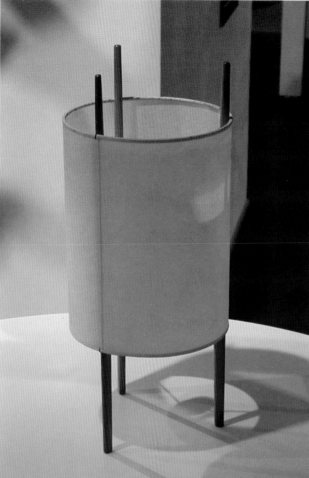

Marc Lepage

75-001 Parachute Lamp designed by Marc Lepage in 1972. Steel base with blower and two lights, nylon parachute cloth shade. Base 12" h, inflated 32" h.

Clay Michie

8 Desk Lamp designed by Clay Michie c. 1950, manufactured 1950-1960. Brass plated base and metal shade with swivel adjustment and brushed finish. 9 pounds weight, 12" diameter, 18" h.

Isamu Noguchi

9 Small Table Lamp designed by Isamu Noguchi in 1944, manufactured 1947-1967. Translucent paper shade with straight cherry wood supports. 7-1/4" diameter, 16" h.

John Rizzi

Rizzi Desktop Lamp designed by John Rizzi.

Richard Sapper

Halley Light designed by Richard Sapper in 2005.

Nanda Vigo

73-003 Utopia Lamp designed by Nanda Vigo.

292

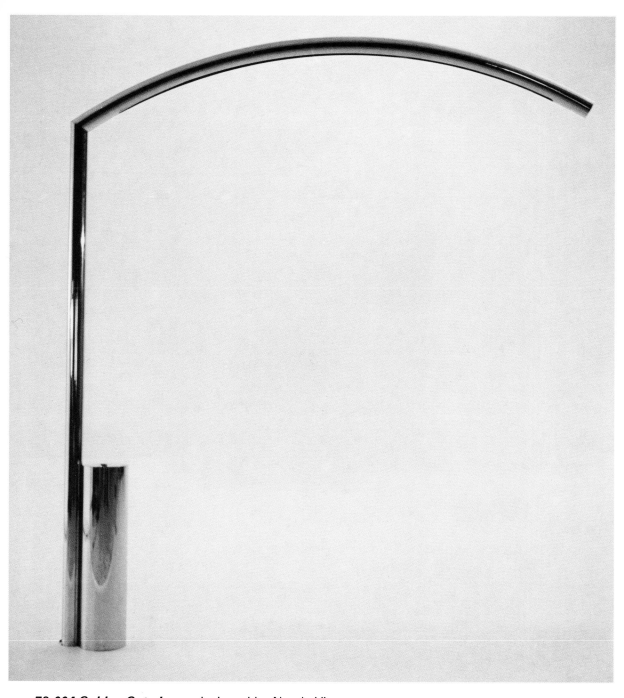

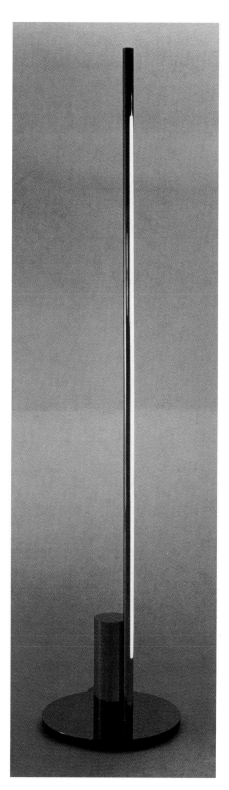

73-004 Golden Gate Lamp designed by Nanda Vigo.

73-005 Linea Lamp designed by Nanda Vigo.

73-006 Manhattan Lamp designed by Nanda Vigo.

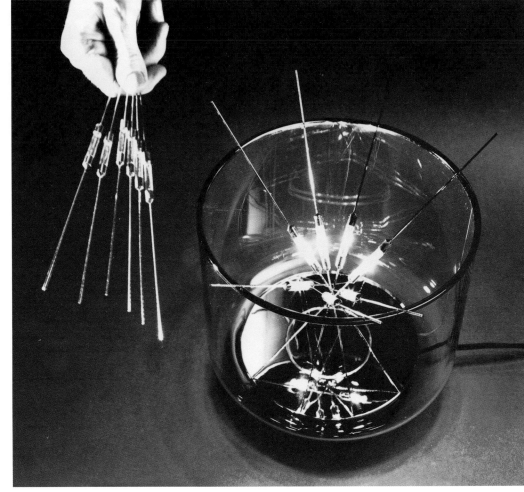

Ted Waddell

76-001 Light Sticks designed by Ted Waddell in
1972. Black plastic box with two steel rods and seven
"light sticks" containing 3-watt lamps. 23" w, 4" d,
3-3/4" h.

Easel, Screens and Panels

Emanuela Frattini

P4 Easel designed by Emanuela Frattini in 1994, manufactured 1995. Legs: aluminum with clear satin anodized or powder-coat finish. Top: erasable magnetic porcelain enamel writing board. 30" w, 76" h.

Hans Sandgren Jakobsen

FHVA300 Viper® Screen designed by Hans Sandgren Jakobsen in 1996, manufactured 1998. Screen is composed of oval tubes of (1) laminated cardboard, aluminum foil, and polyester foil; or (2) natural or black hollow and closed anodized aluminum; or (3) natural or black perforated aluminum filled with sound-absorbing foam. The individual tubes have stainless steel hinges on top and bottom to form variations in the screen's shape, from coiled to crescent to s-shape. 118" w, 63" h.

Lars Mathiesen and Niels Gammelgaard

FHLA Labyrint® Curved Wood Screen designed by Pelikan Design, Lars Mathiesen and Niels

Gammelgaard for Fritz Hansen in 1993, manufactured 2000. Screen is composed of curved panel of maple, beech, or cherry wood slats on plate feet or double casters, that can be used alone or as two or more hinged together. 29-1/2" w, 65" h.

FHLC Labyrint® Curved Linoleum Screen. Same as FHLA, but curved wood frame and black linoleum panel.

FHLL Labyrint® Straight Wood Screen. Same as FHLA, but straight panel of maple, beech, or cherry wood slats.

FHLN Labyrint® Straight Linoleum Screen. Same as FHLA, but straight wood frame and black linoleum panel.

FHWA94 Wing® Screen designed by Pelikan Design, Lars Mathiesen and Niels Gammelgaard for Fritz Hansen, in 1996, manufactured 2000. This room divider is made of individual curved panels on casters, linked together in two or more units to be used in straight or curved configurations. Two solid

panels of aluminum or wood veneer joined at the edges. 37" w, 5-1/4" to 8-1/4" d, 71" h.

FHWB94 Wing® Screen. Same as FHWA94, but panels are perforated to see through.

FHWC94 Wing® Screen. Same as FHWA94, but panels are perforated and filled with sound-absorbent foam.

William Stephens

SP-527 Side Panel designed by William Stephens. Oak veneer, in simulated oil finish or covered in acoustic fabric. 27" w, 1-3/4" d, 58-1/2" h, also available in other sizes.

BP or CP-536 Back Straight or Curved Panel . Same as SP-527, but 36" w or radius.

SP-727 H Side Panel. Same as SP-527, but 74-1/2" h.

BP or CP-736 H Back Straight or Curved Panel. Same as CP-536, but 74-1/2" h.

DESIGNERS FOR KNOLL

Aalto, Alvar (1898-1976) Birthplace: Kuortane, Finland

Knoll Products: Savoy vase

Alvar Aalto studied art, design and form through his extensive European travels, architecture studies in Helsinki, and lengthy experimental career. After testing the potentials of wood - especially bentwood - with his first wife, architect Aino Mariso, he designed furniture and several buildings, including a sanitorium in Paimo and much of the Sunila Cellulose Factory. In 1935 he co-established the first modern furniture shop in Helsinki. Two years later he designed glass pieces for Ittala, including the Savoy vase, later produced by Knoll. Aalto enjoyed a well-recognized career, celebrated with many honors, teaching and guest lecture positions, as well as several exhibitions.

Abramovitz, Gerald (1928-) Birthplace: South Africa

Knoll Products: Armchair

Gerald Abramovitz first studied architecture at the University of Pretoria, South Africa, and then design at the Royal College of Art in London. He briefly opened his own office in Johannesburg and received second prize for his cantilevered armchair by the British Furniture Manufacturers Association. He later worked for Knoll, designing his armchair, which in 1963 won an international furniture competition. He also developed a cantilever desk lamp for Best and Lloyd, now a part of Museum of Modern Art's permanent collection.

Aferiat, Paul (1952-) Birthplace: USA

Knoll Products: Salsa lounge seating

Paul Aferiat attended Carnegie Mellon University, where he received his Bachelor of Architecture in 1975. He began his architectural training in the offices of Hardy Holzman Pfeiffer and Giorgio Cavalieri. He later worked in the offices of Richard Meier and Partners Architects, on projects that included the Suarez Apartment, the Aye Simon Reading Room in the Guggenheim Museum and the Hartford Seminary Foundation. In the office of Gwathmey Siegel and Associates he was the associate in charge of the American Museum of the Moving Image in Astoria, New York, Westover School in Middlebury, Connecticut, and other commercial and residential projects.

Albini, Franco (1905-1977) Birthplace: Italy

Knoll Products: Albini desk

After graduating in architecture at Milan Politecnico, Franco Albini worked simultaneously in fields of furniture, product design, architecture, urban planning and interior design. His sentiments as a rationalist architect translated into remarkably transparent furniture designs, which display a knowledgeable use of materials while presenting their internal structure and processes of production.

Albinson, Don (1915-) Birthplace: USA

Knoll Products: stacking chair

Educated at the Cranbrook Academy of Art in Bloomfield Hills, Michigan, Don Albinson worked in the offices of mid-century modernists Eero Saarinen and Charles Eames prior to opening his Los Angeles-based industrial design firm in 1959. From 1964-1971 he served as the Knoll director of design. Subsequently, he consulted on the design of office seating and furniture systems for Westinghouse and taught industrial design at the University of California, Los Angeles.

Alessandri, Marc (1932-) Birthplace: France

Knoll Products: Alessandri System

Since earning his architecture degree at Beaux-Arts, Marc Alessandri has spent much of his career designing commercial buildings in and near his native France. His winning design for the French Ministry of Culture competition was manufactured by Knoll as the Alessandri System, an interchangeable office system that has endured since its introduction in 1986.

Allen, Davis (1916-1999) Birthplace: USA

Knoll Products: Exeter chair

Davis Allen was one of the talented few responsible for the emergence of interior design as a real profession in post-World War II America. Educated at Brown University, the Kungliga Tekniska in Sweden and Yale University, Allen worked at the Knoll Planning Unit. He also worked in the offices of industrial designer Raymond Loewy and the architecture firm of Harrison and Abramowitz, which served as master planners for the United Nations and Lincoln Center, among other sites. Subsequently, Allen was longtime director of interiors for Skidmore, Owings & Merrill. He designed furniture for Steelcase, GF, Stow Davis, Bernhardt, Stendig and Hickory Business Furniture and was elected to the Interior Design Hall of Fame.

Ambasz, Emilio (1943-) Birthplace: Argentina

Knoll Products: Visor stacking chair, office accessories collection

Emilio Ambasz's successful career began with his legendary studies at Princeton University, where he earned an undergraduate and master's degree in architecture in just two years. Since then, he has helped pioneer green architecture as an economical, sensible and attractive mode of design and living. With his Visor stacking chair for Knoll or any of his genre-crossing architectural works, Ambasz consistently constructs his works as extensions of nature and the human form. Ambasz was the MoMA curator for the famous exhibitions "Italy: The New Domestic Landscape" and "The Taxi Project." He has many credits to his name, as the director of design for Cummins Diesel, designer of several lamps, pens, suitcases, author, critic, and member of the Museum of Modern Art board of design for architecture and design.

Asti, Sergio (1926-) Birthplace: Italy

Knoll Products: desktop accessories

An Italian architect and designer and graduate of the Politecnico di Milano, Sergio Asti established a studio in Milan in 1953. He became a founding member of ADI (Associazione per il Disegno Industriale). He has designed furniture, lighting, glassware, wood products, ceramics, electrical appliances, interiors, stores and exhibitions, and has lectured widely. Asti has received numerous prizes, including the 1962 Compasso d'Oro. His work has been exhibited widely, including at the Museum of Modern Art, New York.

Aulenti, Gae (1927-) Birthplace: Italy

Knoll Products: Jumbo coffee table, dining tables, side chair and lounge seating

Architect and designer Gae Aulenti studied architecture at the Politecnico di Milano. A member of ADI (Associazione per il Disegno Industriale), she has taught at the Politecnico di Milano. She has designed furniture, lighting, textiles, showrooms, stage sets for opera and the interior of the Musée D'Orsay, Paris. She has participated in numerous Triennale di Milano, winning many awards. She is an honorary member of the American Society of Interior Designers.

Baleri, Enrico (1942-) Birthplace: Italy

Knoll Products: Mega tables, Coloforte table system

Enrico Baleri studied, although never graduated from, the University of Milan and soon afterwards formed the design company Pluri. In 1979 he designed the Coloforte table system for Knoll. That same year he founded the design company Alias, which he would direct artistically until 1983, and produced works by Philippe Starck, Alessandro Mendini and Hans Hollein, among others. In 1982 he designed the Mega tables for Knoll, and then founded his studio, Baleri and Associati.

Bellman, Hans (1911-1990) Birthplace: Switzerland

Knoll Products: Tripod side table, dining table

After 1943, Hans Bellman was attracted to Knoll because of the policy of paying royalties on furniture designs, and the reputation Knoll began to enjoy for well-designed products.

Berthier, Marc (1935-) Birthplace: France

Knoll Products: easy chair

Marc Berthier's industrial design career began in 1973 with the introduction of "Twentytube" children's furniture. After his first museum exhibit in Paris and his work with Japanese and Italian manufacturers, Berthier began designing for Knoll in 1979. In that year he designed his easy chair for Knoll, and went on to win several awards and continue to design innovative furniture products.

Bertoia, Harry (1915-1978) Birthplace: Italy

Knoll Products: Bertoia side chair, Bertoia Large Diamond lounge, Bertoia Bird lounge chair and ottoman, Bertoia bench, Bertoia Asymmetric Chaise.

Italian-born sculptor, teacher, lecturer, and furniture designer Harry Bertoia displayed a unique stroke of genius with his patented Diamond Chair for Knoll International in 1952. Bertoia was an inventor of form and enriched furniture design with his introduction of a new material: he turned industrial wire rods into a design icon. Educated at Detroit Technical High School, the Detroit School of Arts and Crafts, and Cranbrook Academy of Art in Bloomfield Hills, Michigan, Bertoia taught metal crafts at Cranbrook. He worked with Charles Eames to develop his signature molded plywood chairs. Eero Saarinen commissioned him to design a metal sculptured screen for the General Motors Technical Center in Detroit. His awards include the craftsmanship medal from the American Institute of Architects, as well as AIA's Gold Medal.

Birsel, Ayse (1938-) Birthplace: Turkey

Knoll Products: Orchestra universal accessories

Ayse Birsel's career began in the capital of her native Turkey at the Middle Eastern Technical University in Ankara. A Fulbright Scholarship brought her to New York, where she earned her master's at Pratt Institute. A self-admitted eternal student, Birsel flourishes in collaborations with the office accessory system designed under Bruce Hannah's direction in the late 1980s. This collection epitomizes the simplicity and practicality that govern their work.

Boeri, Cini (1924-) Birthplace: Italy

Knoll Products: Lunario tables, Brigadier lounge, gradual lounge

A graduate of Milan Politecnico, Cini Boeri has incorporated her ideas of expandability and pliability into many mediums. Her furniture and lighting designs use varied materials such as formless foam pieces, bent glass and polyurethane pieces. Her architecture studio continues in Milan, Italy.

Bonet, Antonio (1913-1989) Birthplace: Spain

Knoll Products: Hardoy sling chair

Shortly after graduating from Barcelona's School of Architecture, Antonio Bonet was exiled in the midst of the Spanish Civil War. In 1938 he moved to Argentina, where he assembled the Grupo Austral. This collaborative group designed the Bonet, Kurchan, and Ferrari-Hardoy chair, or "Hardoy Sling," which was produced by Knoll a decade later in 1948, and has since become an established and often imitated icon. Bonet enjoyed a long architecture and urban planning career, with many projects in Latin America, California, and his native Spain.

Breuer, Marcel (1902-1981) Birthplace: Pecs, Hungary

Knoll Products: Reclining Chair, MB lounge chair, Wassily chair, Cesca chair, Laccio tables

Protégé of Bauhaus founder Walter Gropius, Marcel Breuer embodied many of the school's distinctive concepts and was one of the Bauhaus's most famous students. He returned shortly thereafter to teach carpentry from 1925 to 1928, and during this time designed his tubular-steel furniture collection: functional, simple and distinctly modern. His attention drifted towards architecture, and after practicing privately, he worked as a professor at Harvard's School of Design under Gropius. Breuer was also honored as the first architect to be the sole artist of an exhibit at the Metropolitan Museum of Art. The Wassily chair was named after his Bauhaus roommate Wassily Kandinsky, the Cesca after his daughter Francesca.

Butler, Lewis (1924-) Birthplace: USA

Knoll Products: lounge chair, settee, sofa and table collection

A graduate of Pratt Institute with a degree in interior design, Lewis Butler, in 1950, became a senior designer and assistant to Florence Knoll. He then became associated with Russel Wright in 1954. Named design director of the Knoll Planning Unit in 1965, he worked on all major Planning Unit projects.

Cafiero, Vincent (1930-) Birthplace: New York City, USA

Knoll Products: table

Upon completing his design studies at Pratt Institute, and business administration, ceramics and sculpture at Pace University and Texas Western University, Vincent Cafiero found applications for his diverse talents at Knoll. After joining Knoll in 1956, he led many interior design projects as Senior Designer of the Knoll Planning Unit from 1956 to 1967. During this time he coordinated Knoll work in residences, universities, executive offices and showrooms, including the Knoll showrooms in Philadelphia, Boston and Saint Louis. In addition to designing the massive CBS building project, Cafiero was a believer and outspoken proponent of the "Knoll approach" to business and design. From 1965 to 1969, Cafiero also designed Knoll library furniture and equipment, and in 1974, the Cafiero 5800 series desk line, among many other related products.

Castiglioni, Achille (1918-2002) Birthplace: Italy

Knoll Products: Sanluca chair

After graduating from Milan Politecnico, Achille Castiglioni began working with brother Pier Giacomo, simultaneously igniting their industrial design careers. From furniture to lighting, Achille constantly reinvented himself with his designs, choices of projects and adaptation of emerging technologies. At once ironic, logical and exquisite, the Castiglioni brothers' work dramatically changed - and in some ways defines - modern Italian design.

Castiglioni, Pier Giacomo (1913-1968) Birthplace: Italy

Knoll Products: Sanluca chair

Pier Giacomo Castiglioni studied architecture at Milan Politecnico, as did his two brothers, Achille and Livio. Pier worked with the former for much of his career, collaborating on innovative designs of lighting, furniture, architecture and domestic products. The trio is widely acknowledged as major catalysts of twentieth century Italian design. They originally designed the Sancluca chair for Gavina. Gavina was later acquired by Knoll.

Chadwick, Don (1936-) Birthplace: Los Angeles, California

Knoll Products: Chadwick Chair

Don Chadwick has pioneered the use of modern materials, molding processes, and mechanisms leading to cutting-edge products that have raised the standard for their market. A native of Southern California, Don Chadwick received his principal training in design at the University of California, Los Angeles. He then worked for architect Victor Gruen before establishing his own practice in 1964. In 1974, Chadwick designed Chadwick Modular Seating. In collaboration with William Stumpf, he designed the Equa 1 flexing-plastic chair (1984). Then in 1994, the landmark Aeron chair catapulted Chadwick to national attention; the Industrial Designers Society of America and *Business Week Magazine* awarded Design of the Decade to the Aeron chair in 1999. Chadwick has received numerous awards over the past three and a half decades. Chadwick's relationship with Knoll marks a milestone in the career of an inventive designer. "I am gratified to be part of the Knoll legacy; I consider Knoll to be at the highest level of contemporary design, and our collaboration is a notable one for me." With the Chadwick chair, he has proven himself as effective at bringing a product to market as he has been at creating the market itself.

Christen, Andreas (1936-) Birthplace: near Basel, Switzerland

Knoll Products: Christen office system and accessories, Christen library, Christen tables

Andreas Christen studied design at the Kunstgewerbe Schule at Zurich, and subsequently worked as a freelancer. He also worked as an artist, and was intrigued by the theme of the square. His career featured many exhibitions. His designs with Knoll include not only works bearing his name, as he collaborated with the Stephens office system and desks and cabinets.

Colebrook Bosson Saunders 1981 Birthplace: England

Knoll Products: Wishbone flat panel monitor arm system, Zorro flat panel monitor system, and Jellyfish laptop stand

A commitment to the highest quality in design, production, and service has established Colebrook Bosson Saunders as one of the market leaders in this field, and a list of recent awards and an impressive and well-established client list is testament to their continuing development and success. Technological progress and a universal aim for a healthier workplace provide CBS with an ongoing range of design opportunities, and recent successes have been born out of developments within flat screen environments and flexible workspacing. The firm is led by Martyn Colebrook, Peter Bosson, and Brenda Saunders.

Cortès, Pepe (1945-) Birthplace: Barcelona, Spain

Knoll Products: Jamaica barstool

A native of Barcelona, Pepe Cortès established the design group Grupo Abierto de Diseno, designed stores and offices, furnished resturaunts with Oscar Tusquets, collaborated with Javier Mariscal to design furniture and took part in countless other collaborations. From 1984 to 1988 he was part of the committee for the FAD Awards, or Fomento de las Artes Decorativas, and won the first prize FAD public opinion award from 1983 to 1990.

Couture, Lise-Anne (1959-) Birthplace: Canada

Knoll Products: A3 office system

Lise-Ann Couture, a graduate of Carleton University in Ottawa and Yale University's architecture program, and her partner Hani Rashid are members of a young generation of designers who incorporate information technology with modern designs. As co-princi-pals of Asymptote, an architecture and design firm, the pair recently designed the Knoll A3 Office System. See also Hani Rashid.

Crinion, Jonathan (1953-) Birthplace: England

Knoll Products: contributed to the Reff system and New Generation System 6 office furniture system, Crinion Collection, Crinion side chair, Crinion Open Table

Jonathan Crinion was educated in Canada, where he studied architecture and industrial design at Carleton University and the University of Toronto, and product and systems design at the Ontario College of Art and Design. He founded Crinion Associates, an industrial design consulting firm, and has developed for Knoll since 1995. His work with Knoll began with his design and development of the Reff system and the New Generation System 6. His Crinion chair was introduced in 1999, and in 2001 Knoll introduced the Crinion Collection, a contemporary version of the traditional wooden executive office.

de Armas, Raul (1941-) Birthplace: Cuba

Knoll Products: Palio office accessories, de Armas chair, Vertical de Armas chair

As a strong proponent of modernist philosophy, award-winning Cuban-born designer Raul de Armas applied fundamental architectural principles to his furniture design. After graduating from Cornell University with a degree in architecture, he joined prominent architecture firm Skidmore, Owings and Merrill in 1967, with whom he is now a partner. Since joining the firm more than thirty years ago, de Armas has won international fame and prestige for his work in the architectural industry. In the late 1980s, Knoll began production of the Palio collection of office accessories designed with Carolyn Iu and acquired with Smokador, and the classic de Armas chair. In all his work, he strikes a deft balance between architectural art and science from which emerges a synergy of structure, interior space and function. In 1984, *Interiors* magazine named him Designer of the Year.

DeFuccio, Robert (1936-) Birthplace: USA

Knoll Products: DeFuccio tables, laminated leg conference tables, turned leg tables, children's chairs and tables

An industrial arts education major at the State University of New York in Oswego, Robert DeFuccio was a student at the School for American Craftsmen in the furniture design and woodworking departments and holds a master's degree in English from Syracuse University. DeFuccio combines such diverse skills in his furniture production. After teaching briefly, he joined the Knoll design and development group in 1960, with whom he developed many projects, including the Petitt chair with Bill Stephens, and the DeFuccio tables, a series of wooden, extendable Shaker-like tables that utilized wood technology of the time in a stealthy, unobtrusive manner.

Diffrient, Neils (1928-) Birthplace: USA

Knoll Products: Sled based chair, office and multiple seating collection

After high school studies in aeronautical engineering in Detroit, Niels Diffrient completed his academic training at Cranbrook Academy of Art in Bloomfield Hills, Michigan. He subsequently worked in Marco Zanuso's Milan office, with Eero Saarinen, and with Henry Dreyfuss, with whom he began a partnership in 1986. He has since established his own studio in Connecticut. Diffrient, who is married to textile artist Helena Hernmarck, has also designed furniture for Sunar-Hauserman. The winner of countless design awards, he has also served as chair of the International Design Conference in Aspen, Colorado.

D'Urso, Joseph (1943-) Birthplace: Newark, New Jersey USA

Knoll Products: work and conference tables

As a former interior design and architecture student at Pratt Institute, Royal College of Art in London, and Manchester College of Art and Design, Joseph D'Urso used his schooling at his practice, D'Urso Design, which focuses on the design of private residences and showrooms. D'Urso then worked for Knoll, developing his collection of high rolling tables, low tables, and low, horizontal sofa seating in 1980. Once a designer for Esprit, D'Urso straddles different mediums but maintains his minimalist principles and continues to create three-dimensional spaces on a human scale.

Eldon, Jim (1943-)
Birthplace: USA

Knoll Products: Eldon seating, Eldon benches, Eldon tables

An industrial design graduate of Kent State University, Jim Eldon joined the Knoll design team in 1966. With Knoll, he developed the Eldon benches in 1972, Eldon table and Eldon seating, a chair, settee and sofa set in 1971. The latter met Knoll's need for a seating system with modular, interchangeable, easily replaced parts.

Fahnstrom, Dale (1940-) Birthplace: USA

Knoll Products: Bulldog chair

Dale Fahnstrom received a B.A. and M.F.A. from the University of Illinois at Urbana-Champaign. Fahnstrom has been highly praised for his years of instruction at the Illinois Institute of Technology, where he is former head and professor of the Institute of Design since 1966. He has been Managing Partner of Design Planning Group Inc., and designed packages and products for brands such as Unimark, Phillips, and Nec. He and his long-time collaborator, Michael McCoy, designed the Bulldog chair for Knoll.

Ferrari-Hardoy, Jorge (1914-1977) Birthplace: Argentina

Knoll Products: Hardoy Chair

Jorge Ferrari Hardoy was born in Buenos Aires in 1914. He received his degree in architecture from the Universidad de Buenos Aires in 1939. He had lived the previous year in Paris, where he worked with le Corbusier in the development of the "Plan Director para Buenos Aires." On his return to Buenos Aires he became an active participant in the creation of CIAM Argentina and Grupo Austral. He is probably best known internationally for the Hardoy chair, designed together with Juan Kurchan and Antonio Bonet in 1939. Ferrari-Hardoy remained active as a designer, architect, and city planner until his death.

Formway Design (1956-) Birthplace: New Zealand

Knoll Products: Life chair

Baptized as Petone Engineering Company in 1956, Formway Design initially produced typical steel chairs for the islands' needs. In 1979 a design focus was added to the company, and soon after it changed its name and identity. Formway's reputation grew into an environmentally conscious, youthful furniture design group keenly aware of its surroundings. Formway designed the highly successful Life task seating for Knoll in 2002, praised for its simplicity, minimalist, ergonomic design, environmentally friendly production and use of bold fabrics.

Frankel, Neil (1938-) Birthplace: New York, USA

Knoll Products: Frankel chair and table

A graduate of the University of Illinois architecture program, award-winning Chicago architect and furniture designer Neil Frankel is known as a true master of clean design. Frankel works in partnership with his wife in the Chicago-based firm Frankel + Coleman. His remarkable versatility is evidenced in his designs for numerous corporate, performing arts, exhibition, education and residential spaces.

Franzolini, Enrico (1952-) Birthplace: Udine, Italy

Knoll Products: Franzolini chair

Enrico Franzolini graduated with an architectural degree from his studies in Florence and Venice. In 1972 he participated in the decorative arts division of the Venice Biennale. He established his own atelier, restoring architecture and practicing as an industrial designer. His products, among others, are in the Alias and Cappellini collections.

Frattini, Emanuela (1959-) Birthplace: Milan, Italy

Knoll Products: Propeller system, umbrella stand, Cecilia side chair

The daughter of prominent architect and designer Gianfrano Frattini, Emanuela has built her career upon her own accomplishments. After receiving her master's in architecture at Milan Politecnico, she worked for Charles Pfister's London office and Tibor Kalman in New York before she opened her self-titled design and architecture firm, EFM, in New York City. With accomplishments in fields as varied as architecture, industrial, interior and graphic design, Frattini designed the award winning Knoll Propeller table system.

Frattini, Gianfranco (1926-) Birthplace: Padua, Italy

Knoll Products: Frattini Executive Office Collection, Kyoto table

An architecture graduate of Milan Politecnico, Gianfranco Frattini became an industrial designer by default when he lacked appropriate lighting and furniture for his interiors. In 1956 he co-founded the ADI, Associazone per il Disegno Industriale. During his distinguished career, he collaborated with Gio Ponti, worked for Cassina and Acerbis, designed lamps for Artemide, was a board member of the Triennale di Milano, designed for Knoll and won many gold medals and other prizes. He is a member of the generation that made up the Italian design movement in the late 1950s through the 1960s. His work for Artemide resulted in the Boa lamp together with Livio Castiglioni, and the Megaron lamp as well as several furniture collections for Cassina and exhibits for Ferrari.

Gavina, Dino (1932-) Birthplace: Italy

Dino Gavina is best known for founding the Gavina Group in Bologna in 1949, an Italian furniture production company established to manufacture and sell experimental works by local unknown designers. Over 19 years, Gavina worked with Pier Giacomo Castiglioni, Carlo and Tobia Scarpa, Cini Boeri, Roberto Sebastian Matta, Vico Magistretti and Mario Bellini, among others. In 1968 Knoll bought the rights to Gavina's holdings, including rights to produce Marcel Breuer's Cesca, Wassily and Laccio chairs and tables, and works by many of the above designers. Gavina also established Flos lighting company in the early 1960s.

Gehry, Frank O. (1929-) Birthplace: Canada

Knoll Products: FOG chair and table, Bentwood collection of tables and chairs

This Pritzker Prize-winning architect turned the Basque backwater of Bilbao into a household name with his miraculous, titanium-wrapped structure for the Guggenheim Museum's most ambitious outpost. The confidence with which he has expanded the vocabulary of architecture is clearly demonstrated in his furniture designs. Frank Gehry studied architecture at UCLA and pursued graduate studies at Harvard's Graduate School of Design. He later worked as a designer with Victor Gruen Associates, Robert and Co. Architects in Atlanta, Pereira and Luckman in Los Angeles and André Remondet in Paris. For Knoll, he created the bentwood furniture collection (1989) and the FOG* table and chair (2000). He has also collaborated on projects with sculptors Richard Serra and Claes Oldenburg. His collection of cardboard furniture, Easy Edges, set a new precedent for the use of materials. He has been on the faculty at Harvard and Yale, and is a Fellow of the American Institute of Architects. Frank Gehry has been the subject of several exhibitions, including a retrospective at New York's Guggenheim Museum.

Gwathmey, Charles (1938-) Birthplace: Charlotte, North Carolina USA

Knoll Products: Gwathmey Siegel desk and credenza

A Yale University graduate and Fulbright Scholar with a master's degree in architecture, Charles Gwathmey has become an icon of contemporary design. Since establishing Gwathmey Siegel & Associates Architects in 1968, he has physically changed the American landscape with countless designs over the past four decades. One of his collaborations with Siegel is the Knoll Boston building on fashionable Newbury Street. The pair also worked together to design the wooden desk and credenza for Knoll, which they consider a microcosm of their guiding architectural principles: function and simplicity, and, thus, attractive and modern.

Haigh, Paul (1949-) Birthplace: Yorkshire, England

Knoll Products: Haigh table

Paul Haigh studied furniture design at Leeds College and continued at the Royal College of Art in London. After working for an architectural group, he established a freelance practice. In 1978 he designed the

Haigh tables for Knoll, in both square and rectangular versions.

Hamburger, Peter

Knoll Products: Crylicord lighting collection

Peter Hamburger developed his Crylicord lighting collection for Knoll in 1974. Comprised of table, floor and wall-mounted lamps, he sought to create sparing, minimizing, visually non-jarring forms that produced similarly simple light.

Hannah, Bruce (1941-) Birthplace: USA

Knoll Products: modular desk system; office seating, lounge seating and table collection co-designed with Andrew Morrison; Orchestra office accessories co-designed with Ayse Birsel

Bruce Hannah received an industrial design degree from Pratt Institute, New York. He established his own design office in 1976 after collaborating with Andrew Morrison. He has served as chairman of Pratt's Graduate Department of Industrial Design.

Haussmann, Robert and Trix (Robert: 1931-) (Trix: 1933-) Birthplace: Zurich, Switzerland

Knoll Products: Haussmann Lounge Collection

Swiss architects Robert and Trix Haussmann have established an international reputation as arbiters of style and form. In their own words, architecture and design are "indissolubly linked." Furnishings exist "as an integral part of the artichtectonic concept, never an addition." Their 1988 lounge seating collection introduces clean, elegant lines and superlative comfort into a wide variety of residential and commercial interiors.

Held, Marc (1932-) Birthplace: France

Knoll Products: Rocking lounge chairs and ottoman

After studying kinesitherapy and the dramatic arts, Marc Held established his firm Archiform in 1960. He has designed interiors for the ocean liners *Wind Star* and *Mermoz*, the Grand Drawing Room at the Elysée Palace in Paris, and interiors for Lintas advertising agency. Held is the founder of the magazine *Echoppe*.

Hollien, Hans (1934-) Birthplace: Austria

Knoll Products: Conference table

A graduate of the University of California, Hans Hollien has come to embody postmodernism because of his experimentation against the modernist movement and use of historical references. Also very concerned about the interior appearance of his buildings, Hollien was a one-time designer for Knoll, producing his conference table for the company.

Ivièeviæ, Dragomir (1949-) Birthplace: Yugoslavia

Knoll Products: Parachute chair

Dragomir Ivièeviæ studied at the famous multidisciplinary program at the Academy of Applied Art in Belgrade, which involved studies in furniture design, architecture, art history, mathematics and philosophy. He later earned his master's degree in industrial design at Ohio State University. He founded the DI research and design group in 1982. Intrigued by the idea of product design as functional art, his work is consistently aesthetically pleasing, as evidenced in his Parachute chair for Knoll.

Jacobsen, Arne (1902-1971) Birthplace: Denmark

Knoll Products: Cylinda line of stainless boardroom accessories

As a multi-talented architect, Arne Jacobsen conceived a signature design language that merged modernism with his Scandinavian reverence for nature. He possessed a unique ability to balance the bold and feminine form against superior function and industrial capability. Jacobsen's relationship with Fritz Hansen, which began in 1932, furthered his name and influence in furniture history. His talents made him one of the outstanding designers of the 20th century.

Jeanneret, Pierre (1896-1967) Birthplace: Switzerland

Knoll Products: Scissor chair

Pierre Jeanneret collaborated with his cousin Le Corbusier, born Charles Edouard Jeanneret, on furni-

ture designs, grand urban plans and architectural projects over three decades. Their most famous furniture, designed with Charlotte Perriand circa 1928, incorporated modern simplicity and abandonment of conventional wisdom for economical and industrial furnishings. Other noteworthy accomplishments include the partnership's first place design of the League of Nations building in 1926, and the design of a massive complex for the capital center of Punjab, Chandigarh, India, for which he spent 14 years in India. Jeanneret's design for Knoll is the famous scissor chair, made of wooden frame and elastic straps to hold cushions.

Knoll Bassett, Florence (1917-) Birthplace: Saginaw, Michigan USA

Knoll Products: Office and residential furniture and accessories, including the Executive Collection, Lounge Collection, conference tables and low tables

While a student at the Kingswood School on the campus of the Cranbrook Academy of Art in Bloomfield Hills, Michigan, Florence Knoll Bassett (neé Schust) became a protegée of Eliel Saarinen. She studied architecture at Cranbrook, the Architectural Association in London and the Armour Institute (Illinois Institute of Technology in Chicago). She worked briefly for Walter Gropius, Marcel Breuer and Wallace K. Harrison. In 1946, she became a full business and design partner and married Hans Knoll, after which they formed Knoll Associates. She was at once a champion of world-class architects and designers and an exceptional architect in her own right. As a pioneer of the Knoll Planning Unit, she revolutionized interior space planning. Her belief in "total design" - embracing architecture, manufacturing, interior design, textiles, graphics, advertising and presentation - and her application of design principles in solving space problems were radical departures from the standard practice in the 1950s, but were quickly adopted and remain widely used today. For her extraordinary contributions to architecture and design, Florence Knoll was accorded the National Endowment for the Arts' prestigious 2002 National Medal of Arts. An exhibition of some of her designs, Florence Knoll Bassett at the Philadephia Museum, took place in 2004.

Knorr, Donald R. (1922-) Birthplace: USA

Knoll Products: Side chair

After studying at the University of Illinois and Cranbrook Academy of Art, Donald Knorr worked in Eero Saarinen's office and, later, for Skidmore, Owings & Merrill. He subsequently became a partner in Knorr-Elliot Associates.

Kotilainen, Antti (1966-) Birthplace: Helsinki, Finland

Knoll Products: CHIP chair, CHIP barstool

Young product designer Antti Kotilainen has created a variety of products for both residential and contract applications. Kotilainen was educated at Finland's esteemed Lahti Design Institute and was the recipient of the Chicago Athenaeum Museum of Architecture and Design's prestigious Good Design Award in 2002. A versatile designer who values practicality, experimentation and intuition, he says of his craft: "A writer writes on life, a designer designs on life."

Kulicke, Robert (1924-) Birthplace: USA

Knoll Products: Floating Frame

A graduate of Tyler University, Kulicke is perhaps most famous for co-founding the Kulicke-Stark Academy of Jewelry Art in 1972. The school intended to and largely succeeded in teaching ancient jewelry arts to modern jewelry-makers, and bringing a sense of history to the craft. Primarily a painter, Kulicke became engaged in the New York School of abstract expressionism-a style not served by traditional frames. In 1960, he developed the welded corner frame for the Museum of Modern Art, New York, and later the Plexi-box frame. In 1953, Kulicke designed and developed the Floating Frame for Knoll, employing smoothly welded, distinctively simple and modern polished metal. He continued to develop his frame concept, which was aesthetically based upon Mies van der Rohe's Barcelona chair.

Laske, Lawrence (1963-) Birthplace: Chicago, USA

Knoll Products: Saguaro and Toothpick Cactus tables

After completing his industrial design work at the

University of Illinois, Lawrence Laske went on to do post-graduate work in urban scenography design at the prestigious Domus Academy in Milan. He afterwards collaborated with Ettore Sottsass, whose group he joined for one year. He had the same relationship with Emilio Ambasz one year later. In 1989 he formed Laske Design, a product and interior design firm that has designed for Alessi, Copco, Dansk, Knoll and Maxray. For Knoll, Laske designed the Saguro Cactus tables and Toothpick Cactus tables, both of which became instant classics with their sleek lines, light weights, recognizable profiles, and shockingly stable balance.

Lee, Gary Birthplace: USA

Knoll Products: Lee Lounge Collection

A graduate of the University of Michigan School of Architecture and Design, Gary Lee has worked as National Director of Design at ISI, Officer-In-Charge at ISD Incorporated and Creative Director for Niedermaier. His approach to design is rooted in modern classicism. During his 25 years in the industry, he has cultivated an aesthetic that conveys a refined style of clean lines and well-proportioned forms, with projects that have included a multitude of corporate, professional and financial clients. Mr. Lee was named Designer of the Year by *Interiors* magazine and has been inducted into the Interior Design Hall of Fame.

Lelii, Angelo

Knoll Products: Altalena table light, Iceberg table lamp

Angelo Lelii designed for Knoll the Altalena chrome table light and the Iceberg table lamp, comprised of stainless steel, frosted glass and an encased florescent tube.

Lepage, Marc (1946-) Birthplace: Canada

Knoll Products: Parachute lamp

Marc Lepage's areas of discipline at the Rhode Island School of Design - fine arts, design and sculpture - reflect his diverse product designs. His inflatable products were a direct product of the 1960s counterculture movement and the mechanization of the modern world; Lepage's works were described as "soft, sensitive machines-to be touched." Whether they be inflatable lamps, such as the Parachute lamp he designed for Knoll, or his more interactive inflated appliances, Lepage created items meant to be touched so that individuals could interact with the work and respond personally.

Lin, Maya (1959-) Birthplace: USA

Knoll Products: Stones, Longitude chaise, side chair and Equator

Frequently cited as a benchmark of modern cross-national design, Lin draws influence from Japanese gardens, American Indian earthen mounds, her parents, and her architectural design training at Yale University. While studying there as a senior, Lin won a nationwide contest for her controversial design of the Vietnam Veteran's Memorial. Her career has been marked by her memorials, public spaces, and keen sense of simple, elegant beauty. These elements are gracefully displayed in her work for Knoll, which includes outdoor seating stones, a chaise lounge and side chair. In 2003, Maya Lin won the Finn Juhl award for good design.

Lissoni, Piero (1956-) Birthplace: Italy

Knoll Products: Divina lounge collection

After receiving his degree in architecture from the Milan Polytechnic, Piero Lissoni worked as a furniture designer before founding his own studio in 1986, specializing in architecture and interior and graphic design. He has collaborated with Boffi Cucine, Living Divani, Mateograssi and Kartell, and worked on a number of architecture projects in Japan, with design projects that have included a shopping center, an art gallery, a Cordon Bleu cooking school, logos and trademarks. His awards include the 1991 Esprit kitchen design and the Compasso d'Oro design prize.

Living Divani (1969) Birthplace: Italy

Knoll Products: Divina lounge collection

Living Divani is a specialist in the production of sofas and armchairs. Artisan tradition, coupled with an intrinsic blend of research, creativity and development, informs the company's development of clean, elegant, timeless furniture.

Lluscà, Josep (1948-) Birthplace: Barcelona, Spain

Knoll Products: Street stacking chair

One of Spain's most lauded industrial designers, Josep Lluscà is an artist and a teacher. A professor at the Escuela Eina of Barcelona, Lluscà's design innovations transcend the boundaries of science and art, with works that extend beyond furniture and into industrial applications such as lighting, applied electronics, toys and urban facilities. Very much an environmental designer, Lluscà has addressed the issue of practicality and art in public venues; his "Global Seating System" is known as one of the pioneering innovations in the area of public seating. He has received many prestigious accolades throughout his career, including the American Industrial Design Excellence Award and the National Design Award in Spain. His works are in the permanent collections of museums throughout the world.

Lovegrove, Ross (1959-) Birthplace: Wales

Knoll Products: Lovegrove table, Surf Collection, Decathalon Collection, Bebop mobile cart, Sprite chair

Ross Lovegrove studied design at Manchester Polytechnic and subsequently trained at the Royal College of Art, London. He then worked for the well-known design consultancy frogdesign, where he worked on projects that included the design of the Sony Walkman and computers for Apple. As an in-house designer for Knoll International in Paris, Lovegrove designed the successful Alessandri Office System, and as a co-member of the Atelier de Nimes, along with Philippe Starck and Jean Nouvel, he acted as design consultant to Luis Vuitton, Cacharel, Dupont, and Hermes. In 1990, he set up his own design office in London called Studio X. Lovegrove is inspired by forms of the natural world, the possibilities of new manufacturing techniques and the ability to evoke an emotional response in users. Lovegrove's humanistic approach and organic sensibility have set a direction for design in the next century.

Lucci, Roberto (1942-) Birthplace: Italy

Knoll Products: K chair collection, SoHo chairs, desks, VIP coat tree (for Velca/Knoll), seat system, Golf ad- justable stool (for Velca/Knoll), Eco office furniture (for Velca/Knoll), Solto desk system and chair

Roberto Lucci and Paolo Orlandini started their Milano-based partnership in 1968 and have since developed a vast and diverse array of industrial products. Lucci studied at the Chicago Institute of Design. Together they have participated in various editions of the Milan Triennial, have numerous international prizes to their credit and have works on exhibition in the design collections of New York's Museum of Modern Art, Chicago's Museum of Contemporary Art, Hamburg's Museum fur Kunst und Gewerbe and Paris' Centre National D'Art Contemporain of the Louvre. They have taught at the European Institute of Design, at the Polytechnic of Milan and in numerous universities in Belgium, the USA, Australia and South America. Their highly successful partnership has produced everything from televisions and kitchens to inflatable boats, including a significant number of classic and modern Knoll items designed from 1970 to 1994.

Magistretti, Vico (1920-) Birthplace: Milan, Italy

Knoll Products: Caori table, Silver stacking chair, Cirene side chair

Vico Magistretti is regarded as one of the most outstanding Italian designers of the post-war years. After studying at the Milan Polytechnic, he worked as an architect in his father's company. A firm believer that ideas arise from dialogue, his design process has involved executives in charge of design at distinguished companies, including Artemide, DePavoda, Rosenthal and Fritz Hansen. He is the recipient of numerous awards, including the German Design Innovation Award, the Italian "ADI Design Index" and, most recently, the prestigious Good Design Award from the Chicago Athenaeum: Museum of Architecture and Design. His creations are exhibited in museums worldwide.

Magnussen, Erik (1940-) Birthplace: Copenhagen, Denmark

Knoll Products: International accessories collection

Erik Magnussen was educated at the Danish School of Arts and Crafts. Working from his own design studio, he has become one of Denmark's most prominent and versatile designers. His works - ranging from tableware to furniture, lamps and high-tech products - are all characterized by simplicity and functional elegance. He has lectured at the Royal Danish Academy of Fine Arts and been awarded several design prizes. His products are exhibited in museums worldwide.

Magnusson, Carl Gustav (1940-) Birthplace: Sweden

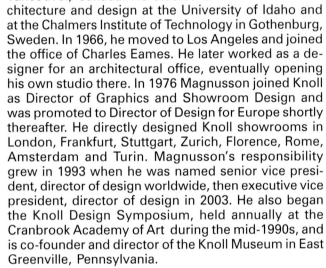

Knoll Products: Magnusson Uptown, Midtown, and Downtown desks, RPM chair, Spello Executive desk

Although born in Sweden, Carl Magnusson grew up in Toronto and Vancouver, Canada. He studied architecture and design at the University of Idaho and at the Chalmers Institute of Technology in Gothenburg, Sweden. In 1966, he moved to Los Angeles and joined the office of Charles Eames. He later worked as a designer for an architectural office, eventually opening his own studio there. In 1976 Magnusson joined Knoll as Director of Graphics and Showroom Design and was promoted to Director of Design for Europe shortly thereafter. He directly designed Knoll showrooms in London, Frankfurt, Stuttgart, Zurich, Florence, Rome, Amsterdam and Turin. Magnusson's responsibility grew in 1993 when he was named senior vice president, director of design worldwide, then executive vice president, director of design in 2003. He also began the Knoll Design Symposium, held annually at the Cranbrook Academy of Art during the mid-1990s, and is co-founder and director of the Knoll Museum in East Greenville, Pennsylvania.

Mangiorotti, Angelo (b. 1900) Birthplace: Italy

Knoll Products: Venetian Glass Vases, Marble Bowls and Ashtrays

After completing architectural studies at the Politecnico di Milani, Angelo Mangiarotti worked on a wide range of projects, including architecture, design, and town planning emphasizing industrial solutions. He has designed for Cassina, Cleto Munari, Zanotta, Danese, Skipper, Poltronova and Artemide. He has been a guest professor at the Illinois Institute of Technology in Chicago, the University of Hawaii and the Facolt de Architettura in Palermo and Florence. He is a member of the ADI (Associazione per il Disegno Industriale).

Maran, Marco (1963-) Birthplace: Siena, Italy

Knoll Products: Gigi stacking chair, Gigi swivel chair, Gigi barstool

Marco Maran is celebrated for designs that are light in spirit and flexible in application. Trained as an architect and industrial designer, he has already been the recipient of several design awards. He was voted Best Young Designer for the Sinue chair, which was introduced in 1996. In 1997, he won a Product Design Achievement Award from the IIDA for the Scoop chair, as well as an honorable mention from the same organization for the Bla-Bla-Bla chair. Among his notable completed interiors is the Press Room for the 1998 World Cup in Paris, France. The official introduction of his Maxdesign brand at the Orgatec International Furniture Fair in Cologne in October 2000 launched a company that has secured its place in both the contract and domestic furnishings arenas through a range of products that are at once original, recognizable and affordable.

Matta, Roberto Sebastian (1911-) Birthplace: Chile

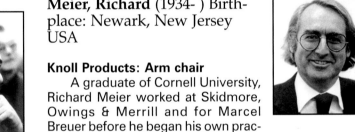

Knoll Products: Malitte polyurethane seating system

Roberto Sebastian Matta, who trained as an architect in his native Santiago, worked in Le Corbusier's Paris office. His designs have been produced by Gavina, and his work has been exhibited at the Philadelphia Museum of Art.

Matter, Herbert (1907-1984) Birthplace: Engelberg, Switzerland

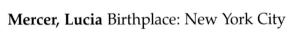

Knoll Products: Knoll logo, posters and advertisements

A painting student at Ecole des BeauxArts in Geneva and Academie Moderne in Paris, Matter established himself as an expert graphic designer. His famous advertisements for the Swiss tourism office used photography for an appealing, visually lasting and decisively modern look. From 1946 to 1966, when Matter was a design consultant for Knoll, he designed the Knoll logo, numerous advertisements, posters and the catalog format, each of which contributed greatly to the public image and reputation of Knoll.

McCoy, Michael (1944-) Birthplace: USA

Knoll Products: Bulldog chair

Michael McCoy is a senior lecturer at Chicago's Institute of Design of the Illinois Institute of Technology. He was co-chair of the Design Department at the Cranbrook Academy of Art for 23 years and Distinguished Visiting Professor at the Royal College of Art in London from 1994 to 1996. As an award-winning designer of products, furniture and interiors, he is also an innovator in design thinking. His design strategies for interpreting technology and information have been widely published and he lectures internationally on the subject. His work has been exhibited in museums worldwide and he is the author of many papers on design. He is also a partner in the design firm of McCoy & McCoy with his wife, Katherine.

Meier, Richard (1934-) Birthplace: Newark, New Jersey USA

Knoll Products: Arm chair

A graduate of Cornell University, Richard Meier worked at Skidmore, Owings & Merrill and for Marcel Breuer before he began his own practice in 1963. Meier's furniture has been described as combining different aspirations of the modern movement—from Wright's emphasis on materials, to Mackintosh's sense of proportion and scale, to the International Style's air of self-assurance.

Mercer, Lucia Birthplace: New York City

Knoll Products: stump tables

Lucia Mercer's knowledge of stone is first-hand and in-depth. After training in landscape architecture at Cornell University and subsequently studying in the Soviet Union, she returned in 1979 to form an apprenticeship with the Cold Spring Granite Quarry in Ausable Forks, New York. Mercer began working with Knoll in 1980, when she first presented her concept for her collection. Her desire for an industrial studio of her own led her recently to Granite Industries of Vermont, and she currently works on several commissions in conjunction with Judith Stockman & Associates.

Michie, Clay

Knoll Products: desk lamp

Mies van der Rohe, Ludwig
(1886-1969) Birthplace: Germany

Knoll Products: Barcelona Collection, MR series, Brno chair, Krefeld Collection, Tugendhat chair, Four Seasons barstool

Ludwig Mies van der Rohe began his career working in his father's stonemasonry business. After an apprenticeship with furniture designer Bruno Paul in Berlin, he joined the office of architect Peter Behrens, whose work presaged the modern movement. In 1912, Mies established his own office in Berlin, and later became a member of the Deutscher Werkbund and, in 1930, Director of the Dessau-Berlin Bauhaus. He immigrated to the United States in 1938, setting up a practice in Chicago. His buildings include the German Pavilion for the 1929 Barcelona Exposition; the Tugendhat Villa in Brno, Czechoslovakia; the Seagram Building, designed with Philip Johnson; a cluster of residential towers along Chicago's Lakeshore Drive in Chicago; the Farnsworth House in Plano, Illinois (1946-1951), and the Illinois Institute of Technology campus, where he was the Director of Architecture.

Morrison, Andrew Ivar
(1939-) Birthplace: USA

Knoll Products: Morrison System, Morrison Network; table and seating collection co-designed with Bruce Hannah

Andrew Morrison studied at Pratt Institute. He has collaborated with designer Bruce Hannah and taught at Pratt Institute. His work at Knoll International spans many years and many furniture products.

Mourgue, Pascal (1943-) Birthplace: France

Knoll Products: Pascal tables

Pascal Mourgue had been a wood sculpture student at L'Ecole Boulle and pursued his interest in design and interior architecture at L'Ecole Nationale des Artes Decoratifs in his native France. In 1985, he developed the Pascal table system of conference tables, designed to be easily and attractively combined and interchanged to suit new commercial needs, especially those of the emerging home office. Lauded for his modern yet timeless style, Pascal Mourgue's product designs for both home and office illustrate his belief that utility and fine art are not mutually exclusive. A consummate artist, Mourgue's designs extend well beyond the realm of furniture to include sailboats; crystal, glass and ceramic objects; showrooms and houses.

Nakashima, George (1905-1990) Birthplace: USA

Knoll Products: dining table, coffee table, and side chair

George Nakashima studied architecture at the University of Washington, Seattle, the Ecole Americaine des Beaux-Arts Fontainebleau in France, and Massachusetts Institute of Technology. He worked for Antonin Raymond. Nakashima received the gold medal for craftsmanship from the American Institute of Architects and the Hazlett Award. His furniture has been the subject of several one-man exhibitions in museums throughout the world.

Noguchi, Isamu (1904-1988) Birthplace: USA

Knoll Products: Noguchi Cylone tables and a table lamp

Isamu Noguchi studied at Columbia University and trained as a cabinetmaker in Japan. He assisted Constantin Brancusi in his Paris atelier. His visionary set and costume designs for the New York City Ballet and the Martha Graham Company transposed mythological elements into abstract form to great effect. Noguchi developed products for Zenith, Steuben Glassworks and Herman Miller. In the 1980s, a museum of his work was established at his studio in Long Island City, New York.

Nordstrom, Kurt Birthplace: Sweden

Knoll Products: side chair

Orlandini, Paolo (1941-) Birthplace: Italy

Knoll Products: K chair collection, SoHo chairs, desks, VIP coat tree (for Velca/Knoll), seat system, Golf adjustable stool (for Velca/Knoll), Eco office furniture (for Velca/Knoll), Solto desk system and chair.

Roberto Lucci and Paolo Orlandini started their Milano-based partnership in 1968, and have since developed a vast and diverse array of industrial products. Orlandini studied at the Milan Politecnico's architecture department. Together they have participated in various editions of the Milan Triennial, have numerous international prizes to their credit and have works on exhibition in the design collections of New York's Museum of Modern Art, Chicago's Museum of Contemporary Art, Hamburg's Museum fur Kunst und Gewerbe and Paris' Centre National D'Art Contemporain of the Louvre. They have taught at the European Institute of Design, at the Polytechnic of Milan and in numerous universities in Belgium, the USA, Australia and South America. Their highly successful partnership has produced a significant number of classic and modern Knoll items designed from 1970 to 1994.

Pearson, Max (1933-) Birthplace: Washington, DC, USA

Knoll Products: 46S Pearson secretarial chair, Pearson Executive office seating, swivel arm chair

Max Pearson was educated at the University of Michigan School of Design, and the School of American Crafts in Rochester, New York. He joined the Knoll design and development team in 1950, and designed the 46S in 1961 and executive seating in 1968. Pearson also developed many major Knoll products until he left in 1970. His attention to detail and strong sense of proportion lend a straightforward quality to his designs.

Pensi, Jorge (1946-) Birthplace: Argentina

Knoll Products: Pensi Collection, Toledo table and chair, Paris table

After completing architecture school in Buenos Aires, Jorge Pensi co-established a design practice with Alberto Lievore in Barcelona. Pensi has worked alone and in design groups in many varying fields, as furniture designer, lighting designer, product image designer and designer of special setting concepts. He designed the Paris table and Toledo Chair and Table for Amat, which were then adopted by Knoll. Pensi also collaborates with his wife, Carme Casares, on graphic design projects. He has lectured on design in Spain, the United States, and at the Royal College of Art, London.

Petitt, Don (1925-) Birthplace: Cleveland, Ohio USA

Knoll Products: Petitt chair, residential furniture, 181 high back arm chair, 3505 double pedestal desk

After studying at the Institute of Design and working in the office of George Nelson, Petitt joined the Knoll design development group in 1952. For his first two years, he worked with Harry Bertoia developing welding fixtures for his metal furniture collection. After assisting Eero Saarinen for three years, Petitt spent his time researching laminated and bent wood processes. In 1965, the 1105 Petitt chair was introduced. During his time with Knoll, he also maintained his own New York-based freelance design office.

Pfister, Charles (1939-1990) Birthplace: USA

Knoll Products: Pfister Lounge Collection

Charles Pfister was an associate partner and director of the interior design department at Skidmore, Owings & Merrill. He established his firm in 1981 with offices in San Francisco and London. Much-admired is the elegance of his interiors and furniture designs. Pfister studied architecture and design at the University of California, Berkeley.

Piiroinen (1949-) Birthplace: Finland

Knoll Products: CHIP side chair and barstool, Arena table

Founded in 1949 as a metal finishing company, Finland-based Piiroinen has evolved over the years to become an established and respected high-end contract furniture design and manufacturing company. Its metal and surface treatment skills, combined with the intuition and commitment of Finnish top designers, stand as a guarantee and requirement for the existence of its collection.

Platner, Warren (1919-) Birthplace: USA

Knoll Products: Platner dining and low tables, Platner lounge collection

Warren Platner studied architecture at Cornell University. Following his work with legendary designers

Raymond Loewy, Eero Saarinen and I. M. Pei, he immersed himself in the creation of steel wire furniture, devising the method and tooling to produce the lounge chair in the line as well. Notable among his residential and commercial projects are the Georg Jensen Design Center in New York City.

Pollock, Charles (1930-) Birthplace: USA

Knoll Products: Pollock Executive Chair

Charles Pollock worked in George Nelson's office after receiving a bachelor's degree in industrial design from Pratt Institute. As well as his work for Knoll, he designed chairs for Thonet and Castelli.

Rapson, Ralph (1914-) Birthplace: Michigan USA

Knoll Products: Sofa, side chair, lounge and rocking chairs

A graduate of Alma College, the University of Michigan, and Cranbrook Academy of Art in Bloomfield Hills, Michigan, Ralph Rapson practiced architecture with Eliel and Eero Saarinen. He headed the Dept. of Architecture at the Institute of Design, Chicago, and the University of Minnesota School of Architecture. He received the AIA Gold Medal and the Topaz Medallion for Excellence in Architecture Education.

Rashid, Hani (1958-) Birthplace: Egypt

Knoll Products: A3 office system

Hani Rashid combines his architectural background from Carleton University in Ottawa, Canada, and Cranbrook with an emphasis on emerging technologies. He and co-principal Lise-Anne Couture founded Asymptote, a New York-based design firm that designed the information center for the New York Stock Exchange. The pair co-designed the A3 office system for Knoll in 2002.

Rasmussen, Jorgen (1931-) Birthplace: Denmark

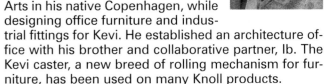

Knoll Products: Rasmussen swivel chair (side and arm versions), stool, Kevi caster

Jorgen Rasmussen studied architecture at the Royal Academy of Fine Arts in his native Copenhagen, while designing office furniture and industrial fittings for Kevi. He established an architecture office with his brother and collaborative partner, Ib. The Kevi caster, a new breed of rolling mechanism for furniture, has been used on many Knoll products.

Reuter, Robert (1950-) Birthplace: USA

Knoll Products: Reuter overhead storage, Morrison Access wire management system, BackPack storage, Calibre desk system, and Currents, Upstart and AutoStrada office systems, co-designed with Charles Rozier

After earning a degree in architecture from Virginia Polytechnic Institute, Robert Reuter spent three years developing the Morrison office system for Knoll with Andrew Morrison, from 1977 to 1980. Until 1987, Reuter was senior development manager at Knoll, and much of the time was dedicated to the design and engineering of the Morrison office system. Reuter has designed numerous office products for Knoll from 1989-2005. His currently heads his own design consultancy, Reuter Design, and is an adjunct faculty member of Virginia Tech College of Architecture and Urban Studies.

Riart, Carlos (1944-) Birthplace: Spain

Knoll Products: Rocking Chair

In addition to designing furniture for Tecno and Écart, Carlos Riart has collaborated with designers Santiago Roqueta, Oleguer Armengol and Victor Mesalles on the interiors of several bars in Barcelona. He studied industrial design at Barcelona's Escuela de Dise-o Eina.

Ricchio, Linda and Joseph (Linda: 1956-) (Joseph: 1955-) Birthplace: USA

Knoll Products: Ricchio side chair, Ricchio barstool, Joe side chair

Both California State University graduates, Linda and Joseph Ricchio have adhered firmly to their credo that "excellent design must be both contemporary and timeless." Joseph Ricchio studied on CSU international programs, including one focusing on art and design in Florence. After working as a designer at several private practices, he taught at the Art Center College of Design in Pasadena, California, in product and graphic design. Linda Ricchio is a member of the Industrial Designer Society of America. Their respective backgrounds in industrial design and education in interiors have produced successful collaborations in many furniture and graphic design ventures.

Risom, Jens (1916-) Birthplace: Denmark

Knoll Products: Risom dining and low tables, Risom lounge chair, Risom side chairs

Jens Risom, who designed the first Knoll manufactured chair 666 in 1941 as an independent freelance job, received his education in Denmark at the Krebs' School, St. Anne Vester School, University of Copenhagen, and Copenhagen's Kunståndvaerkerskolen. He worked as a designer of furniture and interiors in the Copenhagen office of architect Ernst Kuhn. After moving to the United States in 1939, he became the design director of Dan Cooper in New York and also designed for Georg Jensen. In 1946 he founded Jens Risom Design and later founded Design Control. He is responsible for designs dating to the mid-20th century. Risom is a trustee of the Rhode Island School of Design and was knighted by Queen Margrethe of Denmark in 1966.

Rozier, Charles (1951-) Birthplace: USA

Knoll Products: Zapf, Morrison, Currents and AutoStrada office systems

Charles Rozier and his firm, Rozier Studio, have received numerous awards for industrial design including the Braun Prize and the ID Best of Category award for consumer products. Holding graduate degrees in both engineering and art, Rozier also served as vice president for product development at Knoll. He directed the Knoll Morrison Office System design, and is co-designer of the Knoll Currents modular furniture system, introduced in 1998, and AutoStrada, introduced 2004. He has served on the adjunct industrial design faculty at the University of the Arts in Philadelphia, and has lectured at the Rhode Island School of Design and the Cranbrook Academy of Art. He holds a bachelor's and master's degree from Brown University, as well as a master's degree from Cranbrook.

Saarinen, Eero (1910-1961) Birthplace: Finland

Knoll Products: dining and low tables, executive chair, executive side chair, Tulip chairs, Womb chair and ottoman

The son of architect and Cranbrook Academy of Art director Eliel Saarinen and his wife, textile artist Loja, Eero Saarinen studied fine arts in Paris and architecture at Yale before working on furniture design with Norman Bel Geddes and practicing architecture with his father in Ann Arbor, Michigan. He collaborated on several projects, including a plywood leg splint for the U.S. Army, with his friend and Cranbrook alumnus Charles Eames. He opened his own practice in Ann Arbor in 1950. Among the many buildings for which he is known are Dulles Airport in Washington, D.C. and the TWA Terminal at Kennedy International Airport in New York. He designed the huge memorial arch in St Louis, Missouri. He recived numerous awards and was the subject of many exhibitions.

Sapper, Richard (1932-) Birthplace: Munich, Germany

Knoll Products: Sapper office chair, Lambda chair

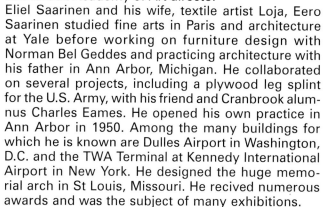

Richard Sapper's training in philosophy, anatomy, business, and engineering at the University of Munich have not been forgotten during his design career. He has designed a range of household products and experimental transportation products that encompass clever modern design. Clients include Artemide, Allessi, and IBM. He designed the Lambda chair in conjunction with Marro Zanusso. His main interest has always been the design of technically complex objects, with fifteen of his products on permanent display at the Museum of Modern Art, New York.

Among this distinguished group is the Knoll Sapper office chair, introduced in 1979. Sapper is the recipient of 10 Compasso d'Oro prizes.

Scarpa, Tobia (1935-) Birthplace: Venice, Italy

Knoll Products: Bastiano lounge chair, armchair, Andre table

With design training in Venice and his famous architect-father, Carlo Scarpa, Tobia Scarpa's career grew steadily as a designer of lamps and glass objects. Scarpa and his wife Afra later designed geometric, three-dimensional collages of steel, wood and leather. Scarpa was a member of the Gavina group, comprised of several international designers whose work was sold by Knoll.

Schultz, Richard (1926-) Birthplace: USA

Knoll Products: Outdoor furniture collection, single and double bed group, convertible sofa bed, stacking side chair, Petal Table Collection, chaise lounge, coffee table, modular sofa, desks and tables

Richard Schultz joined Knoll Associates in 1951 to work with Harry Bertoia, after studying at Iowa State University and the Illinois Institute of Technology in Chicago. In addition to his work for Knoll, he designed an office system for Stow/Davis. He also taught basic design at the Philadelphia College of Art and had a one-man show of his sculpture at the Museum of Modern Art, New York. He founded Richard Schultz Designs that has produced award-winning lines of outdoor furniture.

Seiler, Mathias (1963-) Birthplace: Munich, Germany

Knoll Products: Open Up family of office seating

Mathias Seiler studied industrial design at the Academy of Fine Arts in Hamburg, Germany. While still a student, he received an honorable mention for a 1992 Braun Prize for his "electric bicycle." Since graduating, he has served as product designer for a number of German firms, among them, Sedus Stoll AG in Waldshut, where he designed the Knoll Open Up family of chairs in 2001. Seiler has received numerous accolades for Open Up, including a 2001 Best of NeoCon Silver Award for Office Seating; a 2001 Chicago Athenaeum Good Design* Award; a 2001 Design Award from the International Forum Design; a 2001 Red Dot from Design Zentrum; and a 2002 Baden-Württemberg International Silver Design Award.

Siegel, Robert (ca. 1940-) Birthplace: New York City, USA

Knoll Products: Wooden desk and credenza

With a degree from Pratt Institute and a master's of architecture from Harvard University, Robert Siegel has established himself as one of America's most revered architects. During his long collaborative career with Charles Gwathmey, he has designed countless projects, notably the Newbury Street Knoll building in Boston. Gwathmey and Siegel also worked together in designing a wooden desk and credenza for Knoll, among numerous other projects in their collaboration.

Sottsass, Ettore (1917-) Birthplace: Austria

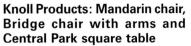

Knoll Products: Mandarin chair, Bridge chair with arms and Central Park square table

Ettore Sottsass studied architecture at the Politecnico di Torino and established a studio in Milan in 1947. In 1982, he organized Sottsass Associates-the group responsible for the Memphis Movement. Associates Aldo Cibic, Marco Zanini and Matteo Thun worked with Sottsass to develop a wide range of products for Clego Munari, Fusital, Zanotta, Artemide, Swid Powell, Olivetti and Poltranova. Sottsass has won numerous awards, including the Compasso d'Oro.

Stamberg, Peter Birthplace: USA

Knoll Products: Salsa lounge chair

Peter Stamberg attended Columbia University, Rhode Island School of Design and the Architectural Association of London Graduate School of Architecture. He began his architectural training in the offices of Davis Brody and Associates. He has written two books and has authored and been the subject of many magazine articles. His Cardinal Dotts chair is in the Contemporary Design Archive of the Cooper-Hewitt National Design Museum in New York.

Stephens, Bill (1932-) Birthplace: USA

Knoll Products: Arm Chair, Executive Chair, Lounge Chair, Stand-up Desk, Executive open office system

Bill Stephens started working at Knoll as an assistant prototype builder after his graduation from the Philadelphia Museum School of Art. He first tried to make a cane chair on a minimal frame without success. He then changed the seat to a plastic shell that, when connected to the frame, formed a total structure; with this design innovation, the 1305 chair was born. It was originally designed for installation at the Yale School of Architecture student center.

Takahama, Kazuhide (1930-) Birthplace: Japan

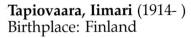

Knoll Products: Suzanne Lounge Collection

After graduating from the Tokyo Institute of Technology in 1953, Takahama went to Italy to work for the Gavina Group. While there in 1965, he introduced a knocked-down storage unit called "DaDa" to great acclaim. His simple but well-harmonized work exemplifies his internationally acclaimed talent for his balance of the Japanese aesthetic and Western culture.

Tapiovaara, Iimari (1914-) Birthplace: Finland

Knoll Products: Stacking chair

Ilmari Tapiovaara served as a department head at the Illinois Institute of Technology in Chicago and designed for Knoll, as well as Merva, Thonet, Schaman, Hackman and Olivetti. After studying industrial and interior design at the Taideteollisuuskeskuskoulu in Helsinki, he worked for Aalto, Le Corbusier, and Mies van der Rohe. In 1937, he established his own office with Annikki Tapiovaara.

Ufficio Tecnico, Birthplace: Foligno, Italy

Knoll Products: Spoleto chair

Based in Foligno, Italy, Knoll International's in-house technical team of engineers and designers adheres to the philosophy of quality and high design. They created the Spoleto chair, inspired by Mies Van der Rohe's classic design.

Venturi, Robert (1925-) Birthplace: USA

Knoll Products: Collection of chairs, sofa, high and low tables

"Less is bore." A maverick of 20th century modernism, Robert Venturi delights in design that is purely decorative. The collection of chairs, tables, and sofa created for Knoll in the 1980s by Venturi and his wife, architect Denise Scott-Brown, broke down barriers between traditional and modern design. The couple established their Philadelphia-based firm, Venturi, Rauch and Scott-Brown, in 1964. They have designed numerous residential and commercial buildings around the world. Venturi studied architecture at Princeton University. The recipient of a Prix de Rome, he continued his education at the American Academy in Rome. Subsequently, he worked in the offices of Eero Saarinen and Louis Kahn. He has taught architecture at the University of Pennsylvania and a graduate seminar with Denise Scott-Brown and Stephen Izenour.

Vignelli, Massimo and Lella (1931-) Birthplace: Italy

Knoll Products: Handkerchief chair, PaperClip table, Knoll graphic design

Massimo Vignelli and his wife, Lella, served as graphic and advertising design consultants to Knoll during the 1970s. They championed a graphic design for Knoll, which made them famous worldwide, and which continues to inform the company's work. Massimo Vignelli once described the Knoll assignment as "the most exciting, rewarding" of his professional career. The Vignelli work provided the foundation for all basic communication needs, including stationery, business cards, stickers, tags, boxes, brochures and four-color ads for trade and commercial magazines. The Vignellis have also collaborated on myriad projects incorporating their industrial, furniture, and graphic design talents. Their New York firm, Vignelli Associates, applies a Modernist aesthetic to each assignment. In 2003, the couple received the

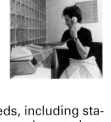

prestigious Lifetime Achievement Award from the Cooper-Hewitt National Design Museum.

Wegner, Hans (1914-) Birthplace: Tonder, Jutland, Denmark

Knoll Products: Peacock lounge chair, swivel arm chair, Verve, Valet chair, 60-155 arm chair, 60-171 side chair, Classic.

Hans Wegner's trade began shortly after his apprenticeship to a cabinetmaker at age 14, and it matured during and after his furniture design studies at the Copenhagen Technical College. His career as designer and maker of fine wooden furniture accelerated. The fine quality, simplicity, and tradition of Wegner's works placed him among the school of Danish modernists of the 1950s.

Zapf, Otto (1931-) Birthplace: Rossbach, CSSR

Knoll Products: Executive chair, Zapf System, Follow Me, Heli lounge chairs

Otto Zapf arrived at Knoll in 1973, having designed numerous products in the European market, but chose to work for Knoll because "they are still an island of humanitarianism." Seeking to design office products that improve the feel of workplaces, Zapf designed furniture that is user-friendly, comfortable, and welcoming. The Zapf System represented the major Knoll foray into the systems business.

BIBLIOGRAPHY

"A Portrait of Change," *KnollTalk.* New York: The Knoll Group, 1993.

Bauhaus 50 Years. Stuttgart: Württembergischer Kunstverein, 1969.

Blake, Peter. *No Place Like Utopia, Modern Architecture and the Company We Kept.* New York: W. W. Norton, 1993.

Bradley, Kass. "The National Medal of Arts, Celebrating Design Collaboration." New York: Knoll, 2003.

Clark, Robert Judson, et al. *Design In America, The Cranbrook Vision, 1925-1950.* New York: Harry N. Abrams, Inc. in association with the Detroit Institute of Arts and The Metropolitan Museum of Art, 1983.

Dempsey, Amy. *Art in the Modern Era, A Guide to Styles, Schools, & Movements.* New York: Harry N. Abrams, Inc., 2002.

Ellison, Michael and Leslie Piña. *Scandinavian Modern Furnishings 1930-1970, Designed for Life.* Atgen, Pennsylvania: Schiffer Publishing, Ltd., 2002.

Girard, A. H., and W. D. Laurie, Jr. ed. *An Exhibition for Modern Living.* Detriot: The Detroit Institute of Arts, 1949.

Hiesinger, Kathryn B. *Design Since 1945.* Philadelphia: Philadelphia Museum of Art, 1983.

Izutsu, Akio. *The Bauhaus: A Japanese Perspective and A Profile of Hans and Florence Schust Knoll.* Tokyo: Knoll International Japan and Kajima Institute Publishing Co. Ltd., 1992.

Jackson, Lesley. *'Contemporary' Architecture and Interiors of the 1950s.* London: Phaidon Press Ltd., 1994.

Knoll company archives, including brochures, catalogs, correspondence, furniture guides, indexes, and price lists, 1942 to 2005.

"Knoll, 50 Years of Design." New York: Knoll International, 1987.

Larabee, Eric and Massimo Vignelli. *Knoll Design.* New York: Harry N. Abrams, Inc., Publishers, 1981.

Piña, Leslie. *Fifties Furniture.* Atgen, Pennsylvania: Schiffer Publishing, Ltd., 2000.

Rouland, Steven and Linda. *Knoll# Furniture 1938-1960.* Atglen, Pennsylvania: Schiffer Publishing Ltd., 1999.

Sembach, Klaus-Jürgen, editor. *Modern Furniture Designs 1950-1980s, An International Review of Modern Furniture.* Atgen, Pennsylvania: Schiffer Publishing, Ltd., 1997.

Smith, Tobi, editor. *Modern Design, The Fabulous 50s.* Atgen, Pennsylvania: Schiffer Publishing, Ltd., 2002.

"The Knoll Interior," *Architectural Forum, the Magazine of Building*, March 1957, p.137-140.

Weber, Nicholas Fox. *Joseph and Anni Albers: designs for living.* London: Merrell Publishers and Cooper-Hewitt, National Design Museum, 2004.

INDEX